Three Revenge Tragedies

EDITED WITH AN INTRODUCTION AND NOTES
BY GĀMINI SALGĀDO

●

Tourneur
THE REVENGER'S TRAGEDY

Webster
THE WHITE DEVIL

Middleton/Rowley
THE CHANGELING

PENGUIN BOOKS

PENGUIN BOOKS

Published by the Penguin Group
Penguin Books Ltd, 80 Strand, London WC2R 0RL, England
Penguin Group (USA), Inc., 375 Hudson Street, New York, New York 10014, USA
Penguin Books Australia Ltd, 250 Camberwell Road, Camberwell, Victoria 3124, Australia
Penguin Books Canada Ltd, 10 Alcorn Avenue, Toronto, Ontario, Canada M4V 3B2
Penguin Books India (P) Ltd, 11 Community Centre, Panchsheel Park, New Delhi – 110 017, India
Penguin Group (NZ), cnr Airborne and Rosedale Roads, Albany, Auckland 1310, New Zealand
Penguin Books (South Africa) (Pty) Ltd, 24 Sturdee Avenue, Rosebank 2196, South Africa

Penguin Books Ltd, Registered Offices: 80 Strand, London WC2R 0RL, England

www.penguin.com

First published as *Three Jacobean Tragedies* in Penguin Books 1965
Reprinted with revisions 1969
Reprinted under the present title 2004

7

Introduction and notes copyright © Gāmini Salgādo, 1965
All rights reserved

Set in Garamond Monotype
Printed in England by Antony Rowe Ltd, Chippenham, Wiltshire

ISBN 13: 978-0-14-144124-5

TO MY FATHER

CONTENTS

*

ACKNOWLEDGEMENTS

*

My grateful thanks to : Laurence Lerner and Tony Inglis for reading through and commenting on the Introduction, Brenda Magurran, Gay Massey, and Judith Everitt for typing the manuscript, and my wife and Peppy Barlow for helping with the proofs.

In revising this book for the 1969 reprint, I have been greatly helped by the 'Revels' Revenger's Tragedy, *edited by* R. A. Foakes.   G. S.

INTRODUCTION

I

IN the closing moments of *Hamlet*, Horatio looks back on the trail of intrigue and violence which has reached its tragic climax in the death of the prince and addresses the following words both to the company assembled on the stage and beyond it to us, the audience:

> ... So shall you hear
> Of carnal, bloody, and unnatural acts,
> Of accidental judgements, casual slaughters,
> Of deaths put on by cunning and forced cause,
> And, in this upshot, purposes mistook
> Fall'n on the inventors' heads.

Horatio here sums up more than the action of a single play. His comment gives us an accurate description of a whole genre of plays, sometimes called Revenge Tragedy (itself a subdivision of a wider group, 'the tragedy of blood') which appeared during the last few years of the sixteenth century and the first decade or so of the seventeenth. The earliest notable example of the form is Thomas Kyd's *The Spanish Tragedy* (*c.*1589) and the greatest is *Hamlet* itself (1600). Each of the three plays in this volume is an outstanding example of this kind of play. Together they give some idea of the range, richness, and intensity of English tragic drama in its greatest period.

A brief account of the origin and development of this form will help the reader to understand the individual plays and appreciate their distinctive qualities. But before beginning such an account, I want to clear up a possible source of misunderstanding. The last thing I wish to suggest is that each of the dramatists represented here is striving to attain the Ideal Type of the Revenge Play. Literary categories are always arbitrary and creative artists have always shown a healthy disrespect for them (if, indeed, they have been aware of their existence). Everyone knows that there is a class of fiction called the thriller; it is perhaps the most popular form of fiction in our day. It has certain broad characteristics, detection, mystery, suspense, and so on, and its practitioners range from Mr Mickey Spillane to Mr Graham Greene. In reading a work which falls within this class, it may be useful to understand the conventions of the form, if only so that we may not read with the wrong kind of expectation. But it would never occur to the ordinary reader to think that there is some Ideal Thriller which could be abstractly defined in terms of history, development, and convention and to which the works of M. Georges Simenon, Edgar Allan Poe, and Mr Erle Stanley Gardner are more or less successful approximations. Categories exist for the better appreciation of works of art, not vice versa, whatever pedants may suggest to the contrary. The works themselves come first, both in time and in importance. So that what I have to say about revenge tragedy is in no sense intended as an inclusive definition or a yardstick by which to measure the success or failure of individual plays. Such a definition would be impossible to give and useless if it could be given, for no play with any life in it could be forced into a categorical straitjacket, and no sensitive reader would want to constrict a live play in this way. What is offered here is a broad general outline, a point of vantage from which the individuality of the separate plays may be better seen. First and last 'the play's the thing'.

My reference to the thriller was not entirely for the sake of illustration. There are several points of resemblance between the modern thriller and the seventeenth-century revenge play which should help to make the latter accessible to the modern reader. To begin with, if we go back to the lines which I have quoted from *Hamlet*, we shall see how well they fit the thriller too. 'Carnal, bloody, and unnatural acts' well describes a whole sub-group of thrillers in which rapid and violent action seems to exist for its own sake. 'Casual slaughters' aptly summarizes the attitude to murder and mayhem which many modern thrillers share with the revenge play. And 'purposes mistook' provide the mainspring of many of the classics of detective fiction.

A centre of crime and violence is one of the things which link the thriller to the 'tragedy of blood'. Another is the interest in the sheer mechanics of mayhem, the means by which violent crimes or misdeeds are committed. To the Jacobean audience the poisoned picture (*The White Devil*), the poisoned skull (*The Revenger's Tragedy*), and the love-potion (*The Changeling*) had something of the fascination which the elaborately appointed travelling-case of Fleming's 007 has for us today. Contemporary theatre property-lists and other evidence outside of the plays themselves indicate that considerable ingenuity and technical expertise were expended in the staging of such scenes as the cutting off of Alonzo's finger by de Flores in *The Changeling*. And the popularity of such Grand Guignol effects is attested by the fact that they occur in practically all the tragedies of the time, including the very greatest, *Hamlet* and *King Lear*. Jacobean dramatists and their audiences, used to the bear-pit as well as the theatre, were no more squeamish about the details of violence ('deaths put on by cunning and forced cause') than modern thriller writers and their readers.

But the really interesting parallel, or perhaps contrast, is not so much in the outward display of violent action, as in the uses to which that action is put, the relationship between the disordered world of the play or thriller and the larger world of its auditors or readers. In some thrillers, perhaps in most, the violence is an end in itself. It is a mild form of escapism from the routine of urban industrial existence and usually makes no claim to be anything else. Kyd's *Spanish Tragedy* and a host of lesser plays like it show a similar interest in violence. For all his undeniable theatrical skill and occasional insight into character, Kyd has no purpose much deeper than making our hair stand on end (as the publishers of the first printed edition of the play realized when they included as frontispiece a woodcut of the play's most famous and most gruesome scene and also drew attention to this scene in the descriptive title). But in the three plays I have chosen, the violence subserves some purpose outside itself. In two of them, *The Changeling* and *The Revenger's Tragedy*, it is the effect of violence on the moral stature of the characters involved in it which is the centre of the dramatist's interest; and the modern reader may compare the use which Mr Graham Greene or M. Simenon have made of the detective story form. In the third play violent action is emblematic of the moral corruption of the society in which it occurs; and perhaps it would not be wholly inappropriate to mention the novels of Dashiell Hammett or Raymond Chandler. But we are rapidly approaching the limits of utility of our comparison and it is time therefore to abandon it. I hope it has served its main implicit purpose, which was to underline the fact that the revenge play had in its own day the same kind of universal popularity that the thriller has in ours. The drama was in no sense the monopoly of intellectual or coterie writers addressing a highbrow or élite audience; that was one source of its greatness. When, a few years after the period in which our plays come, the drama does become concerned with a single social élite as audience, it loses not only its richness but (perhaps more surprisingly) its subtlety, in the skilful, facile, and largely empty tragi-comedy of Beaumont and Fletcher.

The dramatists' preoccupation with the revenge theme during this period is a reflection of a general interest in the social and ethical implications of revenge which is a feature of the age. L. G. Salingar summarizes the nature of this interest in his essay on 'Tourneur and the Tragedy of Revenge':

The theme of revenge (the 'wild justice' of Bacon's essay) was popular in Elizabethan tragedy because it touched important questions of the day; the social problems of personal honour and the survival of feudal lawlessness; the political problem of tyranny and resistance; and the supreme question of providence, with its provocative contrasts between human vengeance and divine.*

The age lived in a tension between two conflicting attitudes centred on the notion of revenge. On the one hand, the law was unequivocal in condemning private revenge as an attempt by man to usurp the prerogative of God (or its political equivalent, the attempt by powerful individuals to assume the powers of the sovereign). 'Vengeance is mine; I will repay, saith the Lord.' The law of the land and the moralists of the time were united in affirming this viewpoint and on the whole the mass of the people accepted it too. On the other hand the tradition of private revenge, dating from an earlier and more turbulent time when the power of the state to punish crime was neither codified in law nor always effectual, was still very much alive; and it had become linked with certain extreme notions of personal honour which tended to make the avenger appear in a sympathetic light. There were three basic situations when the Christian sanctions against revenge seemed to be neutralized or at least modified in the general consciousness.† The first arose when an injury had been done in a treacherous or dishonourable manner. In such a case, revenge, even if obtained in a treacherous manner, was more or less justified. Secondly, revenge could be extenuated where a wrong had been done, but the victim was unable to obtain legal redress, either through lack of witnesses or because of a loophole in the existing law. Both these points have some bearing on the revenge motif as it is handled in these three plays. But the most striking justification of revenge, and the most important, both from a general point of view and for an understanding of the drama, was the situation of blood-revenge for murder. For

* Pelican Guide to English Literature, Volume 2 – *The Age of Shakespeare*, p. 334.

† See F. T. Bowers: *Elizabethan Revenge Tragedy*, Peter Smith, Gloucester, Mass., 1959.

murder was to the Elizabethan the crime of crimes, a violation of God's commandment the more abhorrent as it appalled Renaissance man by its wanton and final destruction of the possibilities of individual fulfilment. So that contemporary moralists (such as Cornwallis, writing in 1601), while attacking revenge in general, are careful to make an exception in the case of revenge for murder. There was even a current though wholly erroneous idea that a son could not inherit from his murdered father unless and until he avenged the latter's death.*

Thus while the law, backed by religious teaching, made blood-revenge for murder unlawful and sinful, another cluster of feelings in the seventeenth-century mind worked to arouse sympathetic feelings towards the avenger. The character who appeared on the stage dedicated to avenging, by killing, the murder of someone connected to him by blood or marriage had a good deal of the audience's sympathy, to begin with at any rate. He may, as the action proceeds, exhaust this sympathy by the use of treacherous tactics, by employing hired assassins, or by becoming more obsessed with his revenge than with the motive for it. But revenge by murder for murder was not *in itself* wholly condemned by the Elizabethan and Jacobean audience. If we appreciate this point we shall avoid many inappropriate and anachronistic assumptions which may otherwise cloud our understanding of these plays.

It is because the theme of revenge struck a responsive chord in society at large that the playwrights of this period, beginning with Kyd, were so strongly drawn to the Latin tragedies of Seneca which were translated into English between 1559 and 1581. In Seneca we can find many though not all of the features which distinguish the seventeenth century 'tragedy of blood'. (Though T. S. Eliot has drawn attention to the existence of a home-grown variety of

* In 'The Audience and the Revenger of Elizabethan Tragedy', *Studies in Philology*, Volume XXXI, 1934, F. T. Bowers explains how this idea came into being.

domestic crime drama, such as *Arden of Feversham* and *The Yorkshire Tragedy*.*) Plays such as *Thyestes, Medea,* and *Agamemnon* have as their subject matter the great crimes of classical antiquity and incorporate character portrayals of revengers such as Clytemnestra and Medea. The crimes themselves are described with horrifying realism and there are detailed accounts of physical torture (though it is probable that Seneca's plays were intended to be recited rather than acted on the stage). The theme of blood-revenge for murder is heavily emphasized and we also find certain Senecan devices being widely used by his English imitators – characters who unwittingly become accessories to the act of revenge or are tricked into becoming accomplices, the ghosts of the dead clamouring intermittently for revenge and many others.

Thus the Senecan play sets the basic pattern for the Elizabethan revenge tragedy and its five-part structure; Exposition (usually by the ghost, who takes no part in the ensuing action) of the events immediately past which have led up to the situation requiring vengeance; Anticipation, in the form of detailed planning of the revenge by its chief agent; Confrontation of the avenger and his intended victim; Partial Execution of the avenger's plan or temporary thwarting of it; and finally, Completion of the act of vengeance.

In its earlier phase, the English revenge play followed this design. But in the three plays with which we are concerned, the design is complicated and enriched by another strand of ideas and attitudes, mainly deriving from popular English misconceptions about Italy. It is no accident that nearly all revenge plays, including the three in this volume, are set in Italy or Spain (two countries which, as far as his attitude to them was concerned, were hardly distinguished by the seventeenth-century Englishman). Italy was the seed-bed of vice, villainy, and perversion so vast and various that it was all that the right-

* 'Seneca in Elizabethan Translation', *Selected Essays*, p. 81.

17

thinking sober-minded Englishman could do even to imagine it. It is enough for one character to say to another, 'Now you are full Italian', to indicate his perfection in villainy to the contemporary audience. To the Protestant fear of Popery was allied, with no apparent sense of paradox, a popular suspicion of atheism and a Puritan dread of moral contamination, especially in its sexual aspects. (The connexion between 'Venice' and 'venery' is typical.) Add to this the current idea of the Italian as treacherous and vengeful by nature and the view (popularized by works such as Fenton's translation of Guicciardini's *Italian History* in 1579 and widely-read collections of gruesome Italian tales like William Painter's *Palace of Pleasure*, 1567–8) that poisoning was a distinctively Italian accomplishment, and we shall no longer find the Italianate setting of revenge tragedy surprising. If Italy had not existed, Jacobean dramatists would have had to invent it; indeed, many of them did. Webster and Tourneur especially give us a vivid and in many ways accurate portrayal of the Italian scene and character as then conceived by Englishmen. But, as Professor G. K. Hunter has pointed out, it is not the Italy of the seventeenth century, Baroque and Spanish-dominated, that these dramatists describe, but rather Italy of the fifteenth century, based on their reading of Guicciardini. Italy and Italians stand not so much for a real country and its people as for a climate of feeling and action. They are symbols of treachery, corruption, and intrigue, including romantic intrigue, which the English dramatists also found in the Italian and French *novelle* and appropriated to their own use.*

Most of the contemporary attitudes to Italy were crystallized in the epithet 'Machiavellian' and the stage-figure which corresponds to it. The Elizabethan idea of Machiavelli and his political and ethical views had about as much relation to the distinguished Italian statesman and political

* 'English Folly and Italian Vice', *Jacobean Theatre, Stratford-upon-Avon Studies*, I, Arnold, 1960.

theorist as the advertisements encouraging Americans to come to Britain have to contemporary British life. The seventeenth-century English view of Machiavelli and what he stood for was derived mainly from a translation of a French attack on him (Gentillet's *Contre-Machiavel*). Very briefly it can be said that since Marlowe put Machiavel on the stage (in the prologue to the *Jew of Malta*, 1588–9) the Machiavellian figure had been the embodiment of conscious and intricately contrived villainy, usually delighting in its own virtuosity.* Thus Richard III, Iago, and Edmund are typical Machiavellian characters. And in later revenge drama, one of the protagonists, often but not always the avenger, is a recognizably Machiavellian figure. In many of the plays we can see the avenger moving to and fro between the two extremes of sympathetic hero and Machiavellian villain.

Thus the 'Italian influence' accounts for the usual setting of the revenge play and at least in part for one of its chief characters. In the later tragedies, the Machiavellian is also usually a railer against society or 'malcontent'. This point brings me to the last general aspect of these plays which I want to discuss, which is the relationship between revenge tragedy and satire at the turn of the seventeenth century; for in two of these plays the theme of revenge is strongly linked with an attack on the corruption of society, and while social satire is not such a central feature of the third (*The Changeling*) it is by no means entirely absent.

Ordinarily we tend to think of satire as part of comedy, but the close connexion between tragedy and the satirical temper is one of the things which distinguish the drama of these years. There were many reasons for this: the political uncertainty surrounding the succession in the last years of Elizabeth I's reign, leading to instability and disillusion in the first years of King James; the Renaissance emphasis on

* Though in part the Machiavellian figure has an older ancestry, going back to the 'Vice' of medieval Morality drama, as B. Spivack demonstrates in *Shakespeare and the Allegory of Evil*, 1958.

the richness of sensual experience colliding with the 'Machiavellian' cynicism regarding all human experience; and the revival of a medieval notion that the world was running down and civilization on the brink of dissolution.* These ideas are found not only in the drama, but also, for instance, in the work of the Metaphysical poets or in a prose work such as Burton's *Anatomy of Melancholy*. But the new critical spirit, the simultaneous sense of the richness of human capacity and the poverty of human achievement was essentially dramatic, as Patrick Cruttwell brilliantly demonstrates in his book, *The Shakespearean Moment.*† And in drama it can lead either to the compassionate understanding which is the heart of tragedy or the relentless and savage mockery of human enterprise which is satire; but more often it leads to a strange mixture of satire and tragedy, where the two impulses seem to be at war with one another, as in a typical play of the time such as Shakespeare's *Troilus and Cressida* (1601).

A helpful account of the main characteristics of satire as a distinct form of art is given by the American critic Alvin Kernan in *The Cankered Muse.*‡ Its setting, he tells us, is densely crowded with people and things, so that satire is usually found against an urban background. Its personages are grotesque caricatures, distorted by the imperfections which they embody. There is usually some hint of an ideal standard by which to judge their perverted activity, but it is remote or impotent (like the faint gleam of light falling on the shape of the cross in the Madhouse scene of Hogarth's 'The Rake's Progress'). And there is an obsessive concentration on the purely animal aspects of human existence, eating, drinking, defecation, and copulation.

These elements of the satiric landscape are very much a part of the three plays in this volume. Also relevant is the distinctive feature of the satiric plot noted by Kernan,

* See 'The Degeneration of Man and Renaissance Pessimism' by D. C. Allen, *Studies in Philology*, Volume xxxv, 1938.

† Chatto & Windus, 1954. ‡ Yale U.P., 1959.

which is that it shows no development. The satirical hero storms and rails against the world, but all his frenzied outbursts change neither the world nor himself. In the end, he either goes under, like Winston Smith in *Nineteen Eighty-Four*, or escapes, like Gulliver, to live with horses and barely tolerate humanity; and in tragic satire he is destroyed.

But the most immediately important aspect of satire for our present purpose is the personality of the satirical hero himself. (The word 'hero' is used here in a purely formal sense, to denote the chief character.) Kernan distinguishes two aspects of his personality. In his 'public' person, he is blunt, truthful, simple, more or less forced into utterance by the wickedness and hypocrisy of the world about him. But this very need for utterance forces him to adopt violent expression as the only effective protest and thus brings into play the darker 'private' aspect of his character. The urge to tell the whole truth conflicts with the need to paint that truth as black as possible. And thus the satirical hero is led to a kind of sadistic relish in scourging humanity. The simple, plain-speaking moralist becomes a monster of egoism, pride, and cruelty, the zealous reformer is hardly distinguishable from the Sunday-paper sensationalist.

Between these two poles of his personality the satirical hero acts out the drama of his thwarted existence. The reader will see how close one face of the satirist is to the character of the Machiavellian figure already sketched. The union of satirical railer and vengeful schemer is seen in the person of Malevole (Altofronto) in John Marston's *The Malcontent* (1604), a play which set the pattern for later revenge tragedy. In our plays, it is the darker 'private' *persona* of the satirist-hero which is mainly emphasized, in the bitter railings of a Vindice or a Flamineo. And there is a constant source of ironic metaphor, which the dramatists were not slow to exploit, in the fact that the instruments of contemporary medical therapy – caustic acid, emetic, scalpel – are outwardly indistinguishable from the poisoned cup, the sword and the instruments of torture which form the stock-in-trade of the Machiavellian intriguer.*

These three plays, then, are all concerned in one way or another with revenge. Violent crime is their element and they display a fascination with the means by which it is effected. Two of them are centrally and one incidentally concerned with corruption in society. But comprehending all this and moving beyond it, these plays explore the lusts and appetites that drive men to destruction and self-destruction and celebrate the ferocious courage with which victim and villain face extinction. Enough has already been said, perhaps, to suggest how 'modern' they are in idea and attitude. When the reader has attuned himself to what is distinctively of their time in them – a task which is neither difficult nor tedious – he may be surprised to find how much in their tone and temper he can respond to with sympathy and understanding. In their elaborate Renaissance paraphernalia of disguise, poison, and intrigue, these plays speak to us not only of old, unhappy, far-off things but also, and memorably, of familiar matters of today.

II

The Revenger's Tragedy was first published in 1607. It was probably written by Cyril Tourneur† who also wrote *The*

---

* Mary Claire Randolph: 'The Medical Concept in English Renaissance Satiric Theory: Its Possible Relationships and Implications', *Studies in Philology*, Volume xxxviii, 1941. See also Kernan, op. cit.

† I have assumed that Tourneur wrote *The Revenger's Tragedy*, though Middleton's claim has been strongly argued; but the alleged parallels between this play and Middleton's known work seem to me unconvincing. Interested readers will find a convenient summary of recent discussion of the authorship question in Allardyce Nicoll's 'The Revenger's Tragedy and the virtue of anonymity' in *Essays on Shakespeare and Elizabethan Drama in Honour of Hardin Craig*, ed. Richard Hosley, University of Missouri Press, 1962.

Atheist's Tragedy, which is like the former play in some superficial respects, but is generally acknowledged to be inferior to it. Our comparative ignorance of the author, however, need not necessarily be a disadvantage; we can turn it into a virtue if it prompts us to look all the more closely at the play itself.

For there are several things in *The Revenger's Tragedy* which are worth a closer look. Take the characters, for instance. By naturalistic standards they are crude and unconvincing. Yet the reader will find that Vindice, Lussurioso, and the rest of that macabre band, even the unpromising Castiza, exert a strange and growing fascination as the action moves to its bloody end. T. S. Eliot has said that it is necessary not so much to believe in fictional characters as to be aware of them. There can be no doubt of our fascinated awareness of these characters. And since time and time again they violate our ordinary notions of plausibility and credibility, it seems worth while to try and account for some part of the hold they have on us.

Tourneur was sufficiently of his age to set his play in Italy and give his characters Italian names, but his relationship to the older Morality drama is clearly seen in the near-abstract names which he chose – Vindice (Vengeance), Castiza (Chastity), Supervacuo (Over-foolish), Lussurioso (Luxury = Lust), Gratiana (Grace), and so on. Clearly, then, we are to regard these characters not as complex and variable individuals, but as personifications of certain qualities which come into contact with one another in the play. The danger of this approach to character is monotony. To embody a single abstract virtue or vice continuously is to lose something of the variety, the richness, the *humanity* which we look for in character. (*Everyman* is a great play, but it is a masterpiece at a dead end; most Morality plays are tedious for just this reason.) How does Tourneur succeed in making his characters within their own terms alive and convincing?

The general answer is that he does it through a more

developed stage technique and greater sensitiveness to the resources of language than are present in Morality drama. The stage technique shows itself in three devices which heighten our awareness of character. One is the possibility of tension between the abstract quality embodied and the character's attitude to it. In *Everyman*, the notion of Good Deeds, considered in the abstract, is exactly congruent to the stage figure typifying Good Deeds; the stage figure *is* the notion, and that is literally all there is to it. In *The Revenger's Tragedy* on the other hand, one of the richest sources of characterization is the contrast between the idea of revenge (and the cluster of attitudes associated with it, summed up in the first part of this Introduction) and Vindice's changing awareness of it, from a stern embracing of duty to a savage and sadistic lust for destruction. The dramatist also has the advantage here of depicting not an abstract quality but an action or aim, the pursuit of revenge which is by its nature more dynamic and dramatic. What is true of Vindice is also true, though to a lesser extent, of the other leading characters. Thus Gratiana is presented not as the static personification of Grace, but as an instance of the action of Grace in exalting the human spirit, beset by temptation, to a clearer perception of the moral order.

Another aspect of Tourneur's stage technique is what I would call perspective. If all the characters, each embodying a quality, Ambition, Lust, or whatever, were given the same amount of emphasis and attention, all would lose in power and richness, like a group of figures all placed in the centre of the stage and uniformly lit from every side. Detail and variety would be erased and we would have a mechanical parade of abstractions, a dance of death of automatons. But Tourneur has so laid out his action that it has a bright and intense centre – the lust of Lussurioso and the vengeance of Vindice – and a shadowy circumference of related themes and actions – the lust of Spurio and the Duke, the rival ambitions of the brothers, and the

plot to rescue the Duchess's youngest son. This arrangement of characters in depth in relation to the central theme
enhances our sense of their dramatic reality.

Finally, Tourneur constantly involves us as audience in
the drama that he unrolls before us. (The seventeenth-
century theatre, with its straightforward admission that it
was a theatre and not a drawing-room, gave the dramatist
far more opportunities to do this than does the naturalistic
theatre.) From the moment at the very beginning when the
royal procession passes across the stage and Vindice comes
between it and ourselves, we are aware of different levels of
reality in the characters. In relation to the procession, for
instance, Vindice himself acquires a certain measure of
solidity. Again, when Vindice dons his disguise as the
malcontent Piato, we begin to think of the original Vindice
as the 'real' person, and his doings in his new role acquire
another kind of reality.

These are some of the resources of stage-craft which
Tourneur uses to make his characters real and powerful.
But without the vibrant intensity of his language, they
would remain mere devices, to be coldly analysed and
admired. It is the incandescence of his verse which welds
a highly melodramatic plot and primitive characterization
into a play of compelling urgency and power.

There are three dominant impulses behind *The Revenger's
Tragedy*. First there is the revulsion from sin which recalls
the medieval moralist:

Night! Thou that look'st like funeral heralds' fees
Torn down betimes i'th'morning, thou hang'st fitly
To grace those sins that have no grace at all.
Now 'tis full sea a-bed over the world.
There's juggling of all sides, some that were maids
E'en at sunset are now perhaps i'th'toll-book.
This woman in immodest thin apparel
Lets in her friend by water; here a dame
Cunning nails leather hinges to a door
To avoid proclamation.

Now cuckolds are a-coining, apace, apace, apace, apace!
And careful sisters spin that thread i'th'night
That does maintain them and their bawds i'the'day.

Allied to this, there is the mixture of loathing and fascination with which Tourneur regards the life of the senses (represented here mainly by sexual experience and intoxication), which has led critics such as Mr Eliot to see in him little more than an adolescent disgust with life:

Drunken procreation, which begets so many drunkards;
Some fathers dread not – gone to bed in wine – to slide
  from the mother
And cling the daughter-in-law.

. . . and in the morning,
When they are up and dressed, and their mask on,
Who can perceive this? Save that eternal eye
That sees through flesh and all?

(In the sound and placing of two words, 'slide' and 'cling', the whole stealthy action comes alive.)

Lastly there is the Jacobean dramatist's endless delight in the spectacle of the biter bit, 'purposes mistook, fall'n on the inventors' heads'. Almost everyone is involved in a conspiracy and they are all deceived. The Duke conspires to thwart Ambitioso and Supervacuo and to gratify his lust, Lussurioso to deflower Castiza and destroy Spurio, the two princes to destroy Lussurioso and rescue their youngest brother (and also to destroy each other), Spurio to disinherit Lussurioso – the intrigue and counter-intrigue are bewildering in their convolutions. The exceptions, those who are not deceived and do not deceive, are Castiza, the embodiment of purity in a tainted world, and Antonio, the ambiguous representative of justice, impotent and in hiding at first but finally triumphant.

There is one other character who is not deceived, at least not by anybody else, and that is Vindice himself. In the end, his tragedy is that he succeeds only too well. He not only deceives everybody else but also deceives himself, in believing that he could wallow in villainy and remain undefiled. In counterfeiting an instrument of intrigue at the service of corrupt power, he plays his part so expertly that at last there is no difference between the player and the role. When Vindice, having 'sworn allegiance' to Lussurioso, exclaims, 'Now let me burst, I've eaten noble poison', he speaks truer than he knows; the poison works within him, goading him to more and more elaborate refinements of evil, till he can spew it forth only in the final inevitable spasm of self-destruction:

> 'Tis time to die, when we are ourselves our foes.

Almost at the outset Vindice's relish over his anticipated revenge becomes his driving force. The avenger's zeal becomes the artist's delight in his own virtuosity and the malcontent finally compromises his moral integrity:

> I'm lost again! You cannot find me yet;
> I'm in a throng of happy apprehensions.

But for all that, *The Revenger's Tragedy* is a play which is deeply moral and deeply traditional. Much stronger than Tourneur's sense of crime and punishment is his feeling (derived from medieval moral tales in collections such as *The Mirror for Magistrates*) for the downfall of 'greatness', for human pride and overweening ambition reaching their inevitable issue in the grave's decay. The moral coherence of the play resides not so much in the brief assertion of Antonio's authority at the close, which is more like an exhausted cessation of carnage than a restoration of order and sanity, nor even in the fact that everyone, villains included, acknowledges the existence of a universal moral law. (Stage thunder is used as a convention signifying God's wrathful recognition of evil.) It is most clearly evident in Tourneur's vivid, almost sensuous apprehension of two worlds of value which are rendered in terms of

various opposites the most immediately striking of which
is the contrast between 'the bewitching minute', 'the
whispering and withdrawing hour', when sin triumphs
and virtue is dethroned, and the unending vista of damnation

> Does the silkworm expend her yellow labours
> For thee? For thee does she undo herself?
> Are lordships sold to maintain ladyships
> For the poor benefit of a bewitching minute?
> Why does yon fellow falsify high ways
> And put his life between the judge's lips
> To refine such a thing, keeps horse and men
> To beat their valours for her?
> Surely we're all mad people, and they
> Whom we think are, are not – we mistake those;
> 'Tis we are mad in sense, they but in clothes.

Then there are the various images of decay set against
those of changelessness and permanence; chief among these
is the savage contrast between the images of masked and
painted faces and the death's-head's uncompromising
candour. The opposition becomes a confrontation and a
fusion in the tremendous scene where Vindice adorns his
dead lady's skull with an elaborate head-dress and paints
its lips with poison to ensnare and destroy the Duke.
And as a context for these opposing images, there is the oft-
repeated contrast between time-serving and the service of
God ('to be honest is not to be i'th'world', Vindice re-
marks), leading in its turn to the final, most comprehensive
contrast of all – between the shifting disordered round of
earthly existence, especially among the great ones of the
world (symbolized by moonlight processions and masked
revels by flickering torchlight), and the endless peace,
certitude and judgement that follows death; you cannot
deceive worms. In its climactic scenes, *The Revenger's
Tragedy* has a frenetic, panic-stricken kind of rhythm, the
pulse-beat of a world rushing headlong to its final and
inevitable annihilation.

III

We know very little more about John Webster, the author of *The White Devil* (first printed in 1612) than we do about Cyril Tourneur. The year of his birth is unknown. He tells us that he was born free of the Merchant Taylors' Company. By 1602 his dramatic career had begun, as the theatrical manager Philip Henslowe records a payment to him in that year. The last work in which Webster had a share was written in 1625, and in 1634 the dramatist Heywood refers to Webster among other dramatists already dead. Thus, assuming that he was between twenty and thirty when he began writing for the stage, he was born some time in the decade 1570–80. Like many playwrights of his age, Webster wrote mostly in collaboration with other dramatists. Indeed, there are only two tragedies which we can confidently ascribe to Webster's sole authorship, *The White Devil* and *The Duchess of Malfi* (1613–14); but these two are more than enough to secure for their author an important place in English drama.

This opinion is by no means undisputed. Webster's work has produced sharper conflicts of opinion than that of either of the other two dramatists represented here. Judgements of him range from Bernard Shaw's contemptuous dismissal of him as 'Tussaud laureate' to Swinburne's glowing praise:

Except in Aeschylus, in Dante, and in Shakespeare, I at least do not know where to seek for passages which in sheer force of tragic and noble horror . . . may be set against the subtlest, the deepest, the sublimest passages of Webster.

In his own day Webster was not one of the most popular playwrights, as the somewhat disgruntled preface to *The White Devil* shows; and though the revival of interest in Jacobean drama in the twentieth century has certainly renewed interest in Webster, it has not resulted in any widespread acknowledgement of his dramatic distinction;

the balance of critical opinion is, if anything, in favour of Shaw's verdict rather than Swinburne's.

It is not difficult to account for this. Both *The White Devil* and *The Duchess of Malfi* are full of borrowings, echoes of lines, and situations from other writers. Even in an age when literary borrowing was the rule rather than the exception, Webster was an inveterate thieving magpie. We know that he worked from a commonplace-book in which he preserved quotations from his widespread and un-disciplined reading for use in his plays. There has therefore been a tendency to regard Webster merely as a glorified anthologist, an artful arranger of other men's flowers. That this is quite unfair to Webster can be seen by examining the use which he makes of his sources, particularly Florio's translation of Montaigne's *Essays* (1603) and Pettie's translation of Steffano Guazza's *Civil Conversation* (1581).* Nearly always, Webster gives to the original an ironic and dramatically appropriate twist which makes it more than an irrelevant borrowed ornament.

A related, and to my mind equally misdirected, criticism is that Webster's habit of composing from commonplace-books led him to value generalized moral truisms ('sen-tentiae') more than sharply realized individual insights; the result, it is alleged, is that there is no necessary connexion between, say, the moral axioms uttered by Flamineo and the developing action of the play. One answer to this charge is to point out, as Mr John Russell Brown does in the Introduction to his edition of the play,† that Webster's method in the play as a whole is constantly to widen the range of language from an individual event or feeling to its general implications (which is why every scene of love-making or killing has its commentator). Another is to suggest that the moral aphorisms are not intended to

---

* R. W. Dent in *John Webster's Borrowing*, University of California, 1960, gives an exhaustive account of the nature and scope of Webster's indebtedness to other writers.

† Revels Plays, Methuen, 1960.

capture the essence of the various attitudes but to provide succinct (often ironic) summaries of them, like epitaphs. Thus, when Vittoria, at the climax of her trial, says:

> Know this, and let it somewhat raise your spite,
> Through darkness diamonds spread their richest light.

we can see, first, how the speech is appropriate to her proud and independent character, but also how it is true and ironic at the same time. The Court is corrupt and the trial is a sham, for the reasons that Vittoria has given earlier – that judge, jury, and prosecutor are the same, and guilt has been asserted rather than proved. Thus Vittoria's allusion to darkness is justified. Yet we know enough of her by this time to realize that while she may resemble diamonds in the radiance and intensity of her passion, she is very far from resembling them in the relevant point of the comparison – purity. Thus the aphorism comments on the preceding action both directly and ironically, and a similar doubleness applies to many of the moral generalizations in the play. As the Trial scene amply demonstrates, Webster's world is one in which the outward forms of virtue and justice are insisted on, even as the reality is spurned. We need not therefore assume any miraculous transformation when the villains utter high moral truths; they are of a piece with their world, pretending to a virtue which they do not possess, play-acting a moral chorus first for others and finally for themselves.

Yet another criticism of the play centres on the character of Vittoria. How are we to take her? Ian Jack puts the point with admirable succinctness.* Vittoria, he says, is dishonourable; Webster simply makes her behave as if she were honourable and thereby confuses the moral issue.

Now it is certainly true that the Vittoria we are shown at the beginning of the play is no paragon of virtue. She is an adulteress who connives at the murder of her own

* *Scrutiny* xvi, March 1949.

husband. Webster makes no attempt to hide these facts, but neither does he claim our sympathy or admiration for Vittoria *on these grounds*. Rather he shows us a Vittoria who is steadfast in her passion – illicit though it admittedly is – and strong and fearless in standing up to corruption in high places:

> Find me guilty, sever head from body:
> We'll part good friends: I scorn to hold my life
> At yours or any man's entreaty, Sir.

and finally a Vittoria clear-eyed enough to recognize un-flinchingly those elements in her downfall for which she was responsible:

> O, my greatest sin lay in my blood.
> Now my blood pays for it.

and those wherein she was merely a creature of circum-stance:

> O happy they that never saw the court,
> Nor ever knew great men but by report.

There is surely nothing so simple here as a dishonourable character being made to act as if she were honourable. What we have is a combination of qualities – unusual but by no means incredible – some of which repel and some of which attract us; but most readers will feel the undeniable power of the mixture.

The character of Flamineo presents a problem which is somewhat similar. On the one hand, he is the scheming villain with an amoral delight in his own destructive cunning; on the other, he touches tragedy in being more aware of his own nature and those of others than any of the characters among whom he moves. But what does this awareness amount to? Is it merely a Stoic acceptance of death, as many critics have argued? I think there are at least two other facets of Flamineo's self-knowledge which are important. One is his piercing insight into the relation between virtue and wealth, an important subsidiary theme in the play. When his mother condemns him for acting as pander to his sister, he retorts:

> Now, you that stand so much upon your honour,
> . . .
> I would fain know where lies the mass of wealth
> Which you have hoarded for my maintenance,
> That I may bear my beard above the level
> Of my lord's stirrup.

And when Cornelia puts the alternative succinctly to him:

> What? Because we are poor
> Shall we be vicious?

his reply is equally succinct, and, in terms of the world presented by the play, unanswerable:

> Pray, what means have you
> To keep me from the galleys, or the gallows?

Secondly, Flamineo understands that though he is 'free' in being unfettered by orthodox moral values, this is a suicidal freedom since he is utterly bound by the destructive energies of his amoral will. Before he dies, he goes through a rehearsal of death, but both rehearsal and performance are thoroughly authentic. Only in acting out his death can Flamineo find release from the hypocrisy and play-acting of court life to which in life he had been compulsively committed:

> This busy trade of life appears most vain,
> Since rest breeds rest, where all seek pain by pain.

Webster has neither Tourneur's interest in the ironic arrangement of event and character nor Middleton's psychological insight. His principal concern is not with story or person but with an attitude to the world that pervades both plot and character – an attitude compounded of mocking contempt, a sense of the corruption of power ('fame' is almost a synonym for infamy in *The White Devil*) and stoic endurance. Perhaps he is not entirely successful in moulding the disparate elements of the drama

– melodrama, historical incident, generalized moral sentiment, individual personality – into a single whole, and remains a dramatist of great single moments and scenes; for many readers the play will flare into life in the great Trial scene and in the cataclysmic deaths of the two 'white devils' – Vittoria and Flamineo. But for all his echoes and borrowings, Webster's own dramatic voice rings out unique and unmistakable.

IV

The Changeling is the most straightforward and in some ways the most powerful of these three plays. It is the product of a collaboration between Thomas Middleton and William Rowley. Rowley was a hardworking hack with a nose for what the public wanted. His contribution consisted mainly of the opening and closing scenes and the farcical sub-plot whose main function (apart from catering to the contemporary taste for madhouse scenes) is to make crudely explicit the themes of lust in action and self-betrayal which are developed with tragic intensity in the main action.

The credit for most of what we admire and respond to in the play must therefore go to Middleton. He was born in London in 1580, the son of a prosperous bricklayer. He went up to Oxford but probably did not take a degree. Apart from plays, he also produced satires in verse and prose. His early plays were lively London comedies, but he first came into prominence in 1624 with the performance of *A Game at Chess*, a political satire directed against the current activities of the Spanish ambassador in London and the proposed marriage between Prince Charles and the Infanta. Middleton went to prison, but the play created a sensation, running to packed houses for nine days, a record for the time.

Middleton collaborated with most of the dramatists of his day, including Webster, and wrote comedies and tragi-comedies for the children's theatres as well as for the public playhouses. He received commissions from the City authorities to write masques and pageants, and in September 1620 was appointed Chronologer to the City, a post which involved keeping a record of public events. Apart from *The Changeling*, Middleton wrote only one other tragedy, *Women Beware Women*. He was never a success with the critics, though this seems hardly to have troubled him. No folio edition of his works was published, nor was he the subject of commendatory verses or other particular praise in his lifetime. He died in 1627.

In this play, we are much less conscious than in the other two of the Italianate (actually Spanish) setting and the elements of intrigue in the plot, though they are evident especially towards the end – ghosts, dumb shows, virginity tests, and the rest of it. The atmosphere is almost domestic, and reminds us of the native heritage of Jacobean tragedy (see Part I of this Introduction). The emphasis here is not so much on tragic Nemesis as on the interplay between two characters who are drawn together by intense desire on one side and equally intense hatred on the other, and united by their complicity in murder and clandestine passion. The twin centres of psychological interest in *The Changeling* are the growth of De Flores from a wheedling and self-pitying weakling to a character capable not merely of violence but also of protective loyalty, and the gradual degeneration of Beatrice from a dutiful daughter and bride-to-be to a mesmerized accessory in adultery and murder. The heart of the drama is here and Middleton's interest in it is impassioned and single-minded. There are two great scenes from which all the main action arises – Act II, Scene ii, in which Beatrice accepts De Flores' offer of 'service', and Act III, Scene iv, where De Flores confronts her and claims his reward for that service. From this point onward, Beatrice can no longer claim immunity for her transgressions; step by inexorable step she is forced to abandon her naïve belief that she can violate moral laws for her own purposes and escape the consequences of such violation. When, genuinely self-deceived or in momentary panic, she pleads her noble birth as a reason for not yielding herself to De Flores, the latter returns a speedy and contemptuous answer:

> Look but into your conscience, read me there,
> 'Tis a true book, you'll find me there your equal:
> Push, fly not to your birth, but settle you
> In what the act has made you; y'are no more now.
> You must forget your parentage to me,
> Y'are the deed's creature; by that name
> You lost your first condition; and I challenge you,
> As peace and innocency has turned you out,
> And made you one with me.

It is the full implication of the catastrophic union mentioned in the closing lines which *The Changeling* explores in detail. The title alludes not only to Beatrice's change from one kind of person to another, but, as the closing lines of the play make clear, to all the other changes of character in the play (Alsemero, 'a supposed husband', De Flores, 'servant obedience to a master sin', etc.) as well as to the actual changeling of the sub-plot, Antonio.

It has been objected (notably by William Archer in *The Old Drama and the New*) that Middleton's psychological insight into Beatrice's character is inadequate, because no one of her intelligence could fail to see De Flores' ulterior motive. But blindness to all those aspects of a situation except those which are immediately useful to oneself is surely something that is usually found alongside egotism such as Beatrice's. At the very beginning she is preoccupied with means of avoiding the impending marriage with Alonso and marrying Alsemero instead. The latter sees this as evidence of her love for him; De Flores, more realistically, infers from it her essential frailty.

Moreover, we can see in the intensity of Beatrice's initial loathing for De Flores, the inverted image of her subsequent passion for him. And it is psychologically plausible that it is precisely this unacknowledged passion which prevents Beatrice from recognizing the nature of De Flores' demands till they are expressed in all their naked directness by him. Part of her self desires De Flores, but subconsciously she senses the explosive consequences of this desire and will not therefore permit herself to recognize its existence until such recognition is forced on her by external circumstances.

Thus Beatrice's moral myopia is not incompatible with intelligence, though it is incompatible with self-knowledge. And self-knowledge is what Beatrice tragically progresses towards. At the outset she tries to keep her growing awareness of her real character from herself, and this explains to some extent her apparent incapacity to grasp some of De Flores' plainest innuendoes. Then, when she comes to know her true nature, she resorts to stratagem and deception to conceal that knowledge from others, so that she may still preserve the shadow after the substance has been lost; and finally she reaches out towards some kind of tragic acceptance:

> Forgive me Alsemero, all forgive,
> 'Tis time to die when 'tis a shame to live.

As for De Flores, he reminds us most of Iago, not only in his single-minded dedication to evil, but also in his laconic acceptance of consequences and his equation of all passion with lust. He resembles Iago further in that the note of railing against society as a whole is subdued; what we hear more insistently is the strident accent of personal grievance, the sense of injured merit in Iago, the resentment against physical ugliness in De Flores.

The structure of *The Changeling* is simple and consistent, and is in perfect accord with its theme. It has been admirably expounded in an essay by Mr Christopher Ricks,* who shows that the play is built round a series of double meanings in a group of key words – blood, will, act, deed,

* 'The Moral and Poetical Structure of The Changeling', *Essays in Criticism*, July 1960.

and service. In the seventeenth century each of these words had sexual connotations as well as the ordinary ones. De Flores habitually uses them with full awareness of all their meanings while Beatrice is oblivious of their sexual references until forced to recognize them. From this point of view Beatrice's tragic flaw is an unawareness of the full significance of a group of words which are crucial to her moral existence. Each misunderstanding is not only poignantly ironic, but intensely dramatic, in the ordinary theatrical sense. So that *The Changeling*, like the best plays of its age, is good theatre for exactly the same reason that it is great literature.

*

I have tried to show in outline what kind of plays these are, and what sort of assumptions lie behind them, as well as to indicate how each dramatist makes his own personal use of the general form. But what makes these plays worth the twentieth-century reader's attention is not technical brilliance or theatrical virtuosity, though these abound in all of them; it is the vision of man's possibilities and his imperfections, the jarring sense of the disparity between his aspirations and his environment – these are as hauntingly relevant today as they were when these plays were first written. On the surface, the intervening centuries may have dated the language and the plot-situations, as they have made the costumes go out of fashion; in essence, the accents, the habits of mind of the characters, and the tragic situations remain startlingly modern.

University of Sussex   GĀMINI SALGĀDO
June 1964

A NOTE ON TEXTS AND SOURCES

The Revenger's Tragedy: No major source has been found for this play, though Professor G. K. Hunter has suggested that one episode may be derived from Thomas Underdowne's English version of Heliodorus's *Aethiopica* (*An Ethiopian History*, 1587). More recently, L. G. Salingar has discussed Tourneur's possible borrowings from such popular Italian writers as Giraldi and Bandello, either directly or through various English versions.* The play was published in 1607, and the following year the same sheets were issued with a fresh title-page dated 1608. My text is based on the British Museum copy of the 1608 Quarto, though I have consulted other editions, particularly those of Allardyce Nicoll (1929) and Richard Harrier (1963).

The White Devil: The play is based on events which took place in Italy in the late sixteenth century; Webster wrote less than thirty years after the death of the real Vittoria Accoramboni. The exact account from which Webster took the story has not been identified. It is likely that he adapted two or more versions – over a hundred manuscript accounts and six printed versions of the story have been found.†

The play was published in quarto in 1612, and three more quarto editions followed in 1631, 1665 and 1672. There are no major variations between these editions. I have used the 1612 Quarto for my text, but am heavily indebted to the editions of F. L. Lucas (1927) and J. R. Brown (1960), particularly to the latter's discussion of the relationship

* G. K. Hunter: 'A source for The Revenger's Tragedy' (*Review of English Studies*, May 1959). L. G. Salingar: 'The Revenger's Tragedy: Some Possible Sources' (*Modern Language Review*, January 1965).

† See Gunnar Boklund: *The Sources of The White Devil* (Uppsala, 1957).

between the dialogue and the stage-directions, with regard to their probable compositorial history.

The Changeling: The chief source for the main plot is the fourth story in Book I of *The Triumph of God's Revenge against the Crying and Execrable Sin of Wilful and Premeditated Murder*, a collection of gruesome stories by John Reynolds, published in 1621. (It is worth looking at this to see how a great artist transforms his raw material.) A secondary source is *Gerardo, the Unfortunate Spaniard*, a translation from the Spanish by Leonard Digges (1622).

The Changeling was first printed in quarto in 1653, thirty years after it had been licensed for performance. There is a variant of the same year, which differs only in the imprint on the title-page, and an edition of 1668, which may have been printed from the original sheets. My text is based on the British Museum copy of the 1653 Quarto. By far the most comprehensive edition of the play which has yet appeared is that of N. W. Bawcutt (1958); I have also consulted the editions of Dilke and Dyce.

Elizabethan and Jacobean punctuation, even when it is not erratic (as it certainly is in *The Revenger's Tragedy*, where question-marks are scattered with reckless abandon) often obscures the sense to the modern reader. While something is lost when the original spelling is discarded ('murther' has a more murderous look than 'murder'), it is possible to exaggerate the loss; at any rate, the ease of reading and the absence of a bogus 'archaism' in the reader's response are real gains. I have therefore modernized the spelling and punctuation and followed modern practice in changing the lineation, where this seems called for; stage-directions are inserted where necessary. All additions and emendations without Quarto authority are given in brackets and recorded in the Notes, but no variants between the quartos themselves are noted. In the Notes, I have tried to strike a balance between intelligibility and convenience of reading.

G. S.

THE
REVENGERS
TRAGÆDIE

As it hath beene sundry times Acted,
by the Kings Maiesties
Seruants.

AT LONDON.
Printed by G. E l d, and are to be sold at his
house in Fleete-lane at the signe of the
Printers-Presse.
1607.

DRAMATIS PERSONAE

*

DUKE

LUSSURIOSO, the Duke's Son.

SPURIO, his Bastard Son.

AMBITIOSO, the Duchess' eldest Son.

SUPERVACUO, the Duchess' second Son.

JUNIOR, the youngest Son of the Duchess.

VINDICE (Piato)
HIPPOLITO (Carlo) } Brothers, Sons of Gratiana.

ANTONIO
PIERO } Nobles.

DONDOLO, Servant to Castiza.

NENCIO
SORDIDO } followers of Lussurioso.

Nobles, Gentlemen, Judges, Officers, Servants.

DUCHESS

CASTIZA, Sister to Vindice and Hippolito.

GRATIANA, her Mother.

*The Action takes place in Italy, in and around the
Duke's Palace.*

ACT ONE

*

SCENE ONE

Enter VINDICE *(carrying a skull); the* DUKE, DUCHESS,
LUSSURIOSO *his Son,* SPURIO *the Bastard, with a train,
pass over the Stage with Torch-light.*

VINDICE: Duke, royal lecher! Go, grey-haired adultery,
    And thou his son, as impious steeped as he:
    And thou his bastard, true-begot in evil:
    And thou his Duchess, that will do with Devil,
    Four ex'lent characters – O, that marrowless age
    Would stuff the hollow bones with damn'd desires,
    And 'stead of heat kindle infernal fires
    Within the spendthrift veins of a dry Duke,
    A parched and juiceless luxur. O God! One
    That has scarce blood enough to live upon,   10
    And he to riot it like a son and heir?
    O the thought of that
    Turns my abuséd heart-strings into fret.
      [*Addressing Skull.*]
    Thou sallow picture of my poisoned love,
    My study's ornament, thou shell of death,
    Once the bright face of my betrothéd lady,
    When life and beauty naturally filled out
    These ragged imperfections;
    When two heaven-pointed diamonds were set
    In those unsightly rings; – then 'twas a face   20
    So far beyond the artificial shine
    Of any woman's bought complexion
    That the uprightest man, (if such there be,
    That sin but seven times a day) broke custom
    And made up eight with looking after her.
    Oh she was able to ha'made a usurer's son
    Melt all his patrimony in a kiss,

             13. *Fret:* broken music.

45

And what his father fifty yearés told
To have consumed, and yet his suit been cold:
30   But oh accurséd palace!
Thee, when thou wert apparelled in thy flesh,
The old Duke poisoned,
Because thy purer part would not consent
Unto his palsy-lust, for old men lust-full
Do show like young men angry, eager-violent,
Out-bid like their limited performances.
O 'ware an old man hot, and vicious!
'Age as in gold, in lust is covetous.'
Vengeance, thou Murder's quit-rent, and whereby
40   Thou show'st thyself tenant to Tragedy,
Oh keep thy day, hour, minute, I beseech;
For those thou hast determined: hum, whoe'er knew
Murder unpaid? Faith, give Revenge her due
Sh'as kept touch hitherto – be merry, merry
Advance thee, O thou terror to fat folks,
To have their costly three-piled flesh worn off
As bare as this – for banquets, ease and laughter
Can make great men as greatness goes by clay,
But wise men little are more great than they.

    Enter his brother HIPPOLITO.

HIPPOLITO: Still sighing o'er death's vizard.
50   VINDICE: Brother, welcome,
What comfort bring'st thou? How go things at Court?
HIPPOLITO: In silk and silver brother: never braver.
VINDICE: Puh,
Thou play'st upon my meaning. Prithee say
Hast that bald madam, Opportunity,

Yet thought upon's? Speak, are we happy yet?
Thy wrongs and mine are for one scabbard fit.
HIPPOLITO: It may prove happiness.
VINDICE: What is't may prove?
Give me to taste.

39. *Quit-rent:* rent paid in lieu of service by free-holding tenant.
46. *Three-piled:* finest-quality velvet.

46

HIPPOLITO: Give me your hearing then.
You know my place at court.
VINDICE: Ay, the Duke's Chamber,
But 'tis a marvel thou'rt not turned out yet!   60
HIPPOLITO: Faith, I have been shoved at, but 'twas still
    my hap
  To hold by th'Duchess' skirt, you guess at that,
  Whom such a coat keeps up can ne'er fall flat,
  But to the purpose:
  Last evening, predecessor unto this,
  The Duke's son warily enquired for me,
  Whose pleasure I attended: he began
  By policy to open and unhusk me
  About the time and common rumour:
  But I had so much wit to keep my thoughts   70
  Up in their built houses, yet afforded him
  An idle satisfaction without danger;
  But the whole aim and scope of his intent
  Ended in this, conjuring me in private
  To seek some strange-digested fellow forth,
  Of ill-contented nature, either disgraced
  In former times, or by new grooms displaced
  Since his stepmother's nuptials, such a blood,
  A man that were for evil only good;
  To give you the true word, some base-coin'd pan-
    der.   80
VINDICE: I reach you, for I know his heat is such,
  Were there as many concubines as ladies
  He would not be contained, he must fly out:
  I wonder how ill-featured, vile-proportioned
  That one should be, if she were made for woman,
  Whom, at the insurrection of his lust
  He would refuse for once; heart, I think none;
  Next to a skull, tho' more unsound than one
  Each face he meets he strongly dotes upon.
HIPPOLITO: Brother, y'ave truly spoke him.   90
  He knows not you, but I'll swear you know him.

VINDICE: And therefore I'll put on that knave for once,
And be a right man then, a man o'th'time,
For to be honest is not to be i'th'world,
Brother, I'll be that strange-composéd fellow.

HIPPOLITO: And I'll prefer you brother.

VINDICE: Go to then,
The small'st advantage fattens wrongéd men.
It may point out, occasion, if I meet her,
I'll hold her by the fore-top fast enough,

100   Or like the French mole heave up hair and all,
I have a habit that will fit it quaintly.

[*Enter* GRATIANA *and* CASTIZA.]

Here comes our mother.

HIPPOLITO: And sister.

VINDICE: We must coin.
Women are apt, you know, to take false money,
But I dare stake my soul for these two creatures
Only excuse excepted, that they'll swallow
Because their sex is easy in belief.

GRATIANA: What news from Court, son Carlo?

HIPPOLITO: Faith, mother
'Tis whispered there the Duchess' youngest son
Has played a rape on Lord Antonio's wife.

110 GRATIANA: On that religious lady!

CASTIZA: Royal blood! Monster, he deserves to die
If Italy had no more hopes but he.

VINDICE: Sister, y'ave sentenced most direct and true,
The law's a woman, and would she were you.
Mother, I must take leave of you.

GRATIANA: Leave for what?

VINDICE: I intend speedy travel.

HIPPOLITO: That he does, Madam.

GRATIANA: Speedy indeed!

VINDICE: For since my worthy father's funeral
My life's unnatural to me, e'en compelled,

92. *Put on:* assume the guise of.   99. *Fore-top:* forelock.
100. *French mole:* head tumour.   102. *Coin:* feign.

As if I lived now when I should be dead.   120
GRATIANA: Indeed he was a worthy gentleman
  Had his estate been fellow to his mind.
VINDICE: The Duke did much deject him.
GRATIANA: Much!
VINDICE: Too much.
  And through disgrace oft smothered in his spirit
  When it would mount; surely I think he died
  Of discontent, the nobleman's consumption.
GRATIANA: Most sure he did.
VINDICE: Did he? 'Lack – you know all,
  You were his midnight secretary.
GRATIANA: No.
  He was too wise to trust me with his thoughts.
VINDICE [aside]: I' faith then, father, thou wast wise
    indeed   130
  'Wives are but made to go to bed and feed.'
  Come mother, sister: you'll bring me onward, brother?
HIPPOLITO: I will.
VINDICE: I'll quickly turn into another.
    [Exeunt.]

[SCENE TWO]

Enter the old DUKE, LUSSURIOSO *his Son, the* DUCHESS
[SPURIO] *the Bastard, the Duchess' two sons* AMBITIOSO
and SUPERVACUO, *the third her youngest* [JUNIOR]
brought out with Officers for the Rape: two Judges.
DUKE: Duchess, it is your youngest son, we're sorry
  His violent act has e'en drawn blood of honour
  And stained our honours,
  Thrown ink upon the forehead of our state
  Which envious spirits will dip their pens into
  After our death, and blot us in our tombs.
  For that which would seem treason in our lives

    123. *Deject:* bring down; show no favours to.

Is laughter when we're dead; who dares now whisper
That dares not then speak out, and e'en proclaim
10   With loud words and broad pens our closest shame.

FIRST JUDGE: Your Grace hath spoke like to your silver
    years
Full of confirméd gravity; for what is it to have
A flattering false insculption on a tomb,
And in men's hearts reproach? The bowelled corps
May be seared in, but with free tongue I speak,
'The faults of great men through their sear clothes
    break.'

DUKE: They do, we're sorry for't, it is our fate
To live in fear and die to live in hate.
I leave him to your sentence; doom him, lords –
20   The fact is great – whilst I sit by and sigh.

DUCHESS [*kneeling*]: My gracious lord, I pray be merciful,
Although his trespass far exceed his years,
Think him to be your own, as I am yours.
Call him not son in law: the law I fear
Will fall too soon upon his name and him:
Temper his fault with pity!

LUSSURIOSO: Good my lord,
Then 'twill not taste so bitter and unpleasant
Upon the judges' palate, for offences
Gilt o'er with mercy show like fairest women,
30   Good only for their beauties, which washed off,
No sin is uglier.

AMBITIOSO: I beseech your Grace,
Be soft and mild, let not relentless law
Look with an iron forehead on our brother.

SPURIO [*aside*]: He yields small comfort yet, hope he shall
    die,
And if a bastard's wish might stand in force,
Would all the court were turned into a corse.

DUCHESS: No pity yet? Must I rise fruitless then?

14. *Bowelled:* disembowelled (for embalming).
15. *Seared in:* embalmed and coffined.   20. *Fact:* deed (i.e. the crime).

A wonder in a woman. Are my knees
Of such low metal, that without respect –
FIRST JUDGE: Let the offender stand forth: 40
  'Tis the Duke's pleasure that impartial doom
  Shall take first hold of his unclean attempt;
  A rape! Why, 'tis the very core of lust,
  Double adultery.
JUNIOR: So sir.
SECOND JUDGE: And which was worse
  Committed on the lord Antonio's wife,
  That general honest lady; confess my lord
  What moved you to't?
JUNIOR: Why flesh and blood, my lord.
  What should move men unto a woman else?
LUSSURIOSO: Oh do not jest thy doom, trust not an axe
  Or sword too far; the law is a wise serpent   50
  And quickly can beguile thee of thy life;
  Though marriage only has made thee my brother
  I love thee so far, play not with thy death.
JUNIOR: I thank you troth, good admonitions, 'faith,
  If I'd the grace now to make use of them.
FIRST JUDGE: That lady's name has spread such a fair
    wing
  Over all Italy, that if our tongues
  Were sparing toward the fact, judgement itself
  Would be condemned and suffer in men's thoughts.
JUNIOR: Well then 'tis done, and it would please me well   60
  Were it to do again: sure she's a goddess,
  For I'd no power to see her and to live.
  It falls out true in this, for I must die;
  Her beauty was ordained to be my scaffold,
  And yet methinks I might be easier ceast,
  My fault being sport, let me but die in jest.
FIRST JUDGE: This be the sentence –
DUCHESS: O keep't upon your tongue, let it not slip!

---

65. *Ceast:* stopped (i.e. prevented from indulging in lechery). Perhaps
'sess'd' = assessed, judged (Foakes).

Death too soon steals out of a lawyer's lip.
Be not so cruel-wise!

70 FIRST JUDGE:　　　　Your Grace must pardon us,
'Tis but the justice of the law.

DUCHESS:　　　　　　　　The law
Is grown more subtle than a woman should be.

SPURIO [*aside*]: Now, now he dies, rid 'em away.

DUCHESS [*aside*]: O what it is to have an old-cool Duke,
To be as slack in tongue as in performance.

FIRST JUDGE: Confirmed; this be the doom irrevocable.

DUCHESS: Oh!

FIRST JUDGE: Tomorrow early –

DUCHESS:　　　　　　　　Pray be abed my lord.

FIRST JUDGE: Your Grace much wrongs yourself.

AMBITIOSO:　　　　　　　No, 'tis that tongue,
Your too much right does do us too much wrong.

FIRST JUDGE: Let that offender –

80 DUCHESS:　　　　　　　Live and be in health.

FIRST JUDGE: Be on a scaffold –

DUKE:　　　　　　　　Hold, hold my lord.

SPURIO [*aside*]:　　　　　　　　Pox on't,
What makes my dad speak now?

DUKE: We will defer the judgement till next sitting;
In the meantime let him be kept close prisoner:
Guard, bear him hence.

AMBITIOSO [*to* JUNIOR]: Brother, this makes for thee,
Fear not, we'll have a trick to set thee free.

JUNIOR: Brother, I will expect it from you both,
And in that hope I rest.

SUPERVACUO:　　　　Farewell, be merry.
　　Exit [JUNIOR] *with a Guard.*

SPURIO: Delayed, deferred! Nay then, if judgement have
90 Cold blood, flattery and bribes will kill it.

DUKE: About it then, my lords, with your best powers.
More serious business calls upon our hours.
　　Exeunt. DUCHESS [*remains*].

DUCHESS: Was't ever known step-Duchess was so mild

And calm as I? Some now would plot his death
With easy doctors, those loose-living men,
And make his withered Grace fall to his grave
And keep church better.
Some second wife would do this, and dispatch
Her double-loathéd lord at meat, and sleep.
Indeed 'tis true an old man's twice a child;   100
Mine cannot speak, one of his single words
Would quite have freed my youngest dearest son
From death or durance, and have made him walk
With a bold foot upon the thorny law
Whose prickles should bow under him; but 'tis not,
And therefore wedlock faith shall be forgot;
I'll kill him in his forehead, hate there feed,
That wound is deepest, tho' it never bleed.
   [*Enter* SPURIO.]
And here comes he whom my heart points unto,
His bastard son, but my love's true-begot;   110
Many a wealthy letter have I sent him
Swelled up with jewels, and the timorous man
Is yet but coldly kind;
That jewel's mine that quivers in his ear
Mocking his master's chillness and vain fear.
H'as spied me now.
SPURIO: Madam? Your Grace so private?
  My duty on your hand.
DUCHESS: Upon my hand sir? Troth, I think you'd fear
  To kiss my hand too if my lip stood there.
SPURIO: Witness I would not, madam.
   [*Kisses her.*]
DUCHESS: 'Tis a wonder,   120
For ceremony has made many fools.
It is as easy way unto a Duchess
As to a hatted dame – if her love answer –
But that by timorous honours, pale respects,
Idle degrees of fear, men make their ways

123. *Hatted dame:* low-class woman. (Noble ladies wore no hats.)

Hard of themselves. What have you thought of me?

SPURIO: Madam I ever think of you, in duty,
Regard and –

DUCHESS: Puh, upon my love I mean.

SPURIO: I would 'twere love, but 'tis a fouler name
Than lust; you are my father's wife, your Grace may
130   guess now
What I could call it.

DUCHESS: Why, th'art his son but falsely,
'Tis a hard question whether he begot thee.

SPURIO: I'faith 'tis true too; I'm an uncertain man,
Of more uncertain woman; maybe his groom
A'th'stable begot me – you know I know not –
He could ride a horse well, a shrewd suspicion, marry,
He was wondrous tall, he had his length i'faith,
For peeping over half-shut holiday windows,
Men would desire him 'light; when he was afoot,
140   He made a goodly show under a penthouse,
And when he rid, his hat would check the signs
And clatter barbers' basins.

DUCHESS: Nay, set you a-horseback once,
You'll ne'er light off.

SPURIO: Indeed, I am a beggar.

DUCHESS: That's more the sign thou art great –
But to our love:
Let it stand firm both in thought and mind
That the Duke was thy father, as no doubt then
He bid fair for't, thy injury is the more,
For had he cut thee a right diamond
150   Thou hadst been next set in the dukedom's ring
When his worn self, like Age's easy slave
Had dropped out of the collet into th'grave.
What wrong can equal this? Canst thou be tame
And think upon't?

SPURIO: No, mad and think upon't.

140. *Penthouse:* hanging eaves.
152. *Collet:* where stone is set in a ring.

DUCHESS: Who would not be revenged of such a father
    E'en in the worst way? I would thank that sin
    That could most injure him, and be in league with it.
    Oh what a grief 'tis, that a man should live
    But once i'th'world, and then to live a bastard,
    The curse o'the womb, the thief of Nature,   160
    Begot against the seventh commandment,
    Half-damned in the conception, by the justice
    Of that unbribéd everlasting law.
SPURIO: Oh I'd a hot-backed devil to my father!
DUCHESS: Would not this mad e'en patience, make blood
    rough?
    Who but an eunuch would not sin, his bed
    By one false minute disinherited?
SPURIO [aside]: Ay, there's the vengeance that my birth
    was wrapt in.
    I'll be revenged for all; now hate, begin,
    I'll call foul incest but a venial sin.   170
DUCHESS: Cold still? In vain then must a Duchess woo?
SPURIO: Madam, I blush to say what I will do.
DUCHESS: Thence flew sweet comfort; – earnest, and fare-
    well.
    [Kisses him.]
SPURIO: Oh one incestuous kiss picks open hell.
DUCHESS: Faith now old duke, my vengeance shall reach
    high,
    I'll arm thy brow with woman's heraldry.
    Exit.
SPURIO: Duke, thou didst do me wrong, and by thy act
    Adultery is my nature;
    Faith, if the truth were known, I was begot
    After some gluttonous dinner, some stirring dish   180
    Was my first father; when deep healths went round,
    And ladies' cheeks were painted red with wine,
    Their tongues as short and nimble as their heels,

173. *Earnest:* pledge of future favours.
176. *Woman's heraldry:* cuckold's horns.

Uttering words sweet and thick; and when they rose
Were merrily disposed to fall again –
In such a whispering and withdrawing hour,
When base male bawds kept sentinel at stairhead,
Was I stol'n softly; oh – damnation met
The sin of feasts, drunken adultery.
190 I feel it swell me; my revenge is just,
I was begot in impudent wine and lust.
Stepmother, I consent to thy desires;
I love thy mischief well, but I hate thee,
And those three cubs thy sons, wishing confusion
Death and disgrace may be their epitaphs;
As for my brother, the duke's only son
Whose birth is more beholding to report
Than mine, and yet perhaps as falsely sown,
(Women must not be trusted with their own),
200 I'll loose my days upon him, hate all I,
Duke, on thy brow I'll draw my bastardy.
For indeed a bastard by nature should make cuckolds,
Because he is the son of a cuckold-maker.
     Exit.

[SCENE THREE]

Enter VINDICE *and* HIPPOLITO, VINDICE *in disguise
to attend* LUSSURIOSO *the Duke's son.*
VINDICE: What brother, am I far enough from myself?
HIPPOLITO: As if another man had been sent whole
   Into the world, and none wist how he came.
VINDICE: It will confirm me bold: the child o' the court;
   Let blushes dwell i'th'country. Impudence!
   Thou goddess of the palace, mistress of mistresses,
   To whom the costly perfumed people pray,
   Strike thou my forehead into dauntless marble,
   Mine eyes to steady sapphires: turn my visage,

   200. *Loose my days:* spend my time (in working his ruin).

And if I must needs glow, let me blush inward   10
That this immodest season may not spy
That scholar in my cheeks, fool-bashfulness.
That maid in the old time, whose flush of grace
Would never suffer her to get good clothes.
Our maids are wiser, and are less ashamed:
Save Grace the bawd, I seldom here grace named!

HIPPOLITO: Nay brother, you reach out o'th'verge now –
    [*Enter* LUSSURIOSO *attended.*]
'Sfoot, the Duke's son; settle your looks.

VINDICE: Pray let me not be doubted. [*He withdraws.*]

HIPPOLITO: My Lord –

LUSSURIOSO: Hippolito? – Be absent, leave us. 20
    [*Exeunt Attendants.*]

HIPPOLITO: My lord, after long search, wary inquiries
And politic siftings, I made choice of yon fellow,
Whom I guess rare for many deep employments;
This our age swims within him; and if Time
Had so much hair, I should take him for Time,
He is so near kin to this present minute.

LUSSURIOSO: 'Tis enough,
We thank thee: yet words are but great men's blanks,
Gold, tho' it be dumb does utter the best thanks.
    [*Gives him money.*]

HIPPOLITO: Your plenteous honour – an ex'lent fellow my
Lord.   30

LUSSURIOSO: So, give us leave – [*Exit Hippolito.*]
                 Welcome, be not far off,
We must be better acquainted. Push, be bold
With us – thy hand.

VINDICE: With all my heart i'faith!
How dost, sweet musk-cat – when shall we lie together?

17. *Verge:* limit of royal court (*virga* = rod); with possible quibble
on 'beyond virginity'.   22. *Politic:* cunning.
28. *Blanks:* written assurances of payment with blank space for
signature.

LUSSURIOSO [*aside*]: Wondrous knave!
   Gather him into boldness? 'Sfoot, the slave's
   Already as familiar as an ague
   And shakes me at his pleasure. [*To* VINDICE] Friend, I can
   Forget myself in private, but elsewhere
40   I pray do you remember me.
VINDICE: Oh very well sir – I conster myself saucy.
LUSSURIOSO: What hast been,
   Of what profession?
VINDICE: A bone-setter.
LUSSURIOSO: A bone-setter?
VINDICE: A bawd my lord,
   One that sets bones together.
LUSSURIOSO: Notable bluntness!
   Fit, fit for me, e'en trained up to my hand.
   Thou hast been scrivener to much knavery then.
VINDICE: Fool to abundance sir; I have been witness
   To the surrenders of a thousand virgins,
50   And not so little;
   I have seen patrimonies washed apieces,
   Fruit-fields turned into bastards,
   And in a world of acres,
   Not so much dust due to the heir 'twas left to
   As would well gravel a petition.
LUSSURIOSO [*aside*]: Fine villain! Troth, I like him wondrously,
   He's e'en shaped for my purpose. [*To* VINDICE] Then, thou know'st
   I'th'world strange lust?
VINDICE: O Dutch lust! Fulsome lust!
   Drunken procreation, which begets so many drunkards;
   Some father dreads not – gone to bed in wine – to slide from the mother
   And cling the daughter-in-law;

41. *Conster*: construe.   47. *Scrivener*: notary.
55. *Gravel*: to dry ink with sand.   59. *Dutch lust*: drunkenness.

Some uncles are adulterous with their nieces,
Brothers with brothers' wives, O hour of incest!
Any kin now next to the rim o'th'sister
Is man's meat in these days; and in the morning,
When they are up and dressed, and their mask on,
Who can perceive this? Save that eternal eye
That sees through flesh and all? Well, if any thing be
    damned
It will be twelve o'clock at night; that twelve
Will never 'scape,   70
It is the Judas of the hours, wherein
Honest salvation is betrayed to sin.
LUSSURIOSO: In troth it is too, but let this talk glide,
It is our blood to err, tho' hell gaped wide.
Ladies know Lucifer fell, yet still are proud.
Now sir; wert thou as secret as thou art subtle
And deeply fathomed into all estates,
I would embrace thee for a near employment,
And thou shouldst swell in money, and be able
To make lame beggars crouch to thee.
VINDICE: My lord?   80
Secret? I ne'er had that disease o'th'mother
I praise my father: why are men made close
But to keep thoughts in best? I grant you this,
Tell but some woman a secret over night,
Your doctor may find it in the urinal i'th'morning.
But my lord –
LUSSURIOSO: So, thou'rt confirmed in me,
And thus I enter thee.
    [*Gives him gold.*]
VINDICE: This Indian devil
Will quickly enter any man but a usurer;
He prevents that by ent'ring the devil first.
LUSSURIOSO: Attend me: I am past my depth in lust   90
And I must swim or drown. All my desires

    64. *Rim:* limit, edge. Also perhaps womb (Foakes).
    87. *Indian devil:* gold from the Indies.

Are levelled at a virgin, not far from court
To whom I have conveyed by messenger
Many waxed lines, full of my neatest spirit,
And jewels that were able to ravish her
Without the help of man; all which and more
She, foolish chaste, sent back, the messengers
Receiving frowns for answers.

VINDICE: Possible?
   'Tis a rare phoenix who e'er she be;
100 If your desires be such, she so repugnant
   In troth my lord, I'd be revenged and marry her.

LUSSURIOSO: Push! The dowry of her blood and of her
     fortunes
   Are both too mean – good enough to be bad withal.
   I'm one of that number can defend
   Marriage is good: yet rather keep a friend;
   Give me my bed by stealth, there's true delight
   What breeds a loathing in't, but night by night?

VINDICE: A very fine religion!

LUSSURIOSO: Therefore thus,
   I'll trust thee in the business of my heart
110 Because I see thee well experienced
   In this luxurious day wherein we breathe.
   Go thou, and with a smooth enchanting tongue
   Bewitch her ears, and cozen her of all grace.
   Enter upon the portion of her soul,
   Her honour, which she calls her chastity
   And bring it into expense, for honesty
   Is like a stock of money laid to sleep,
   Which ne'er so little broke, does never keep.

VINDICE: You have gi'n't the tang i'faith, my lord.
120 Make known the lady to me, and my brain
   Shall swell with strange invention: I will move it
   Till I expire with speaking, and drop down
   Without a word to save me; – but I'll work –

94. *Waxed:* sealed. *Neatest:* undiluted.   105. *Friend:* mistress.
113. *Cozen:* cheat.   114. *Portion:* inheritance.   116. *Expense:* use.

LUSSURIOSO: We thank thee, and will raise thee: receive
  her name,
  It is the only daughter to Madam
  Gratiana, the late widow.
VINDICE [*aside*]: Oh, my sister, my sister!
LUSSURIOSO: Why dost walk aside?
VINDICE: My lord, I was thinking how I might begin,
  As thus: 'Oh Lady!' – or twenty hundred devices;
  Her very bodkin will put a man in.   130
LUSSURIOSO: Ay, or the wagging of her hair.
VINDICE: No, that shall put you in, my lord.
LUSSURIOSO: Shall't? Why, content. Dost know the
  daughter then?
VINDICE: O ex'lent well by sight.
LUSSURIOSO: That was her brother
  That did prefer thee to us.
VINDICE: My lord, I think so,
  I knew I had seen him somewhere.
LUSSURIOSO: And therefore, prithee let thy heart to him
  Be as a virgin close.
VINDICE: Oh me good Lord!
LUSSURIOSO: We may laugh at that simple age within
  him; –
VINDICE: Ha, ha, ha.   140
LUSSURIOSO: Himself being made the subtle instrument
  To wind up a good fellow.
VINDICE: That's I my lord.
LUSSURIOSO: That's thou
  To entice and work his sister.
VINDICE: A pure novice!
LUSSURIOSO: 'Twas finely managed.
VINDICE: Gallantly carried;
  A pretty-perfumed villain.
LUSSURIOSO: I've bethought me
  If she prove chaste still and immovable,
  Venture upon the mother, and with gifts

          130. *Put a man in:* provide an opening.

61

150 As I will furnish thee begin with her.

VINDICE: O fie, fie, that's the wrong end my lord.
'Tis mere impossible that a mother by any gifts
Should become a bawd to her own daughter!

LUSSURIOSO: Nay then, I see thou'rt but a puny
In the subtle mystery of a woman: –
Why, 'tis held now no dainty dish: the name
Is so in league with age that nowadays
It does eclipse three quarters of a mother.

VINDICE: Does't so my lord?

160 Let me alone then, to eclipse the fourth.

LUSSURIOSO: Why well said, come, I'll furnish thee; but first
Swear to be true in all.

VINDICE: True!

LUSSURIOSO: Nay but swear!

VINDICE: Swear? I hope your honour little doubts my faith.

LUSSURIOSO: Yet for my humour's sake, 'cause I love swearing.

VINDICE: 'Cause you love swearing, – 'slud I will.

LUSSURIOSO: Why enough,
Ere long look to be made of better stuff.

VINDICE: That will do well indeed my lord.

LUSSURIOSO [calling Attendants]: Attend me!
[Exit.]

170 VINDICE: Oh –
Now let me burst, I've eaten noble poison,
We are made strange fellows, brother, innocent villains,
Wilt not be angry when thou hear'st on't, think'st thou?
I'faith, thou shalt. Swear me to foul my sister!
Sword, I durst make a promise of him to thee,
Thou shalt dis-heir him, it shall be thine honour;
And yet, now angry froth is down in me,

154. *Puny*: mere beginner.
157. *So in league with age*: so much in tune with the times.
165. *'Slud*: abbreviation of 'God's blood'.

It would not prove the meanest policy
In this disguise to try the faith of both;
Another might have had the self-same office,   180
Some slave, that would have wrought effectually,
Ay, and perhaps o'er-wrought 'em; therefore I,
Being thought travelled, will apply myself
Unto the self-same form, forget my nature,
As if no part about me were kin to 'em,
So touch 'em, – tho' I durst almost for good
Venture my lands in heaven upon their blood.
 Exit.

[SCENE FOUR]

Enter the discontented Lord ANTONIO, *whose wife the Duchess' younger son ravished; he discovering the body of her dead to certain Lords:* [PIERO] *and* HIPPOLITO.

ANTONIO: Draw nearer lords, and be sad witnesses
 Of a fair comely building newly fall'n,
 Being falsely undermined: violent rape
 Has played a glorious act; behold my lords
 A sight that strikes man out of me.
PIERO: That virtuous lady!
ANTONIO: Precedent for wives!
HIPPOLITO: The blush of many women, whose chaste
 presence
 Would e'en call shame up to their cheeks, and make
 Pale wanton sinners have good colours. –
ANTONIO: Dead!
 Her honour first drunk poison, and her life,   10
 Being fellows in one house, did pledge her honour.
PIERO: O grief of many!
ANTONIO: I mark'd not this before –
 A prayer-book, the pillow to her cheek;
 This was her rich confection, and another

  186. *Touch:* test.   4. *Glorious:* audacious, boastful.

Placed in her right hand, with a leaf tucked up,
Pointing to these words:
Melius virtute mori, quam per dedecus vivere.
True and effectual it is indeed.

HIPPOLITO: My lord, since you invite us to your sorrows,
20   Let's truly taste 'em, that with equal comfort
As to ourselves we may relieve your wrongs;
We have grief too, that yet walks without tongue –
Curae leves loquuntur, majores stupent.

ANTONIO: You deal with truth my lord.
Lend me but your attentions, and I'll cut
Long grief into short words: last revelling night,
When torchlight made an artificial noon
About the court, some courtiers in the mask,
Putting on better faces than their own,
30   Being full of fraud and flattery: amongst whom
The Duchess' youngest son – that moth to honour –
Filled up a room; and with long lust to eat
Into my wearing, amongst all the ladies
Singled out that dear form, who ever lived
As cold in lust as she is now in death,
– Which that step-duchess' monster knew too well –
And therefore in the height of all the revels,
When music was heard loudest, courtiers busiest,
And ladies great with laughter – O vicious minute!
40   Unfit but for relation to be spoke[n] of,
Then with a face more impudent than his vizard
He harried her amidst a throng of panders
That live upon damnation of both kinds,
And fed the ravenous vulture of his lust,
– O death to think on't! – She, her honour forced,
Deemed it a nobler dowry for her name
To die with poison than to live with shame.

HIPPOLITO: A wondrous lady, of rare fire compact;
Sh'as made her name an empress by that act.

50 PIERO: My lord, what judgement follows the offender?

---

43. *Both kinds:* both sexes.

ANTONIO: Faith none, my lord, it cools and is deferred.

PIERO: Delay the doom for rape?

ANTONIO: O you must note who 'tis should die,
   The Duchess' son; she'll look to be a saver,
   'Judgement in this age is near kin to favour.'

HIPPOLITO: Nay then, step forth, thou bribeless officer;
    [*Draws sword.*]
   I bind you all in steel to bind you surely.
   Here let your oaths meet, to be kept and paid,
   Which else will stick like rust and shame the blade:
   Strengthen my vow, that if at the next sitting,   60
   Judgement speak all in gold, and spare the blood
   Of such a serpent, e'en before their seats
   To let his soul out, which long since was found
   Guilty in heaven.

ALL: We swear it and will act it.

ANTONIO: Kind gentlemen, I thank you in mine ire.

HIPPOLITO: 'Twere pity
   The ruins of so fair a monument
   Should not be dipped in the defacer's blood.

PIERO: Her funeral shall be wealthy, for her name
   Merits a tomb of pearl; my lord Antonio,   70
   For this time wipe your lady from your eyes,
   No doubt our grief and yours may one day court it,
   When we are more familiar with Revenge.

ANTONIO: That is my comfort gentlemen, and I joy
   In this one happiness above the rest.
   Which will be called a miracle at last,
   That, being an old man, I'd a wife so chaste.
    Exeunt.

     54. *Saver:* a term derived from various games.
     72. *Court it:* appear at court.

ACT TWO

*

SCENE ONE

Enter CASTIZA, *the sister.*

CASTIZA: How hardly shall that maiden be beset
  Whose only fortunes are her constant thoughts,
  That has no other child's-part but her honour,
  That keeps her low and empty in estate.
  Maids and their honours are like poor beginners,
  Were not sin rich there would be fewer sinners;
  Why had not virtue a revenue? Well
  I know the cause, 'twould have impoverished hell.
    [*Enter* DONDOLO.]
  How now, Dondolo?

10 DONDOLO: Madona, there is one, as they say a thing of
  flesh and blood, a man I take him by his beard, that
  would very desirously mouth to mouth with you.

CASTIZA: What's that?

DONDOLO: Show his teeth in your company.

CASTIZA: I understand thee not.

DONDOLO: Why, speak with you, madona!

CASTIZA: Why, say so, madman, and cut off a great deal
  Of dirty way; had it not been better spoke
  In ordinary words, that one would speak with me?

20 DONDOLO: Ha, ha, that's as ordinary as two shillings, I
  would strive a little to show myself in my place, a
  gentleman-usher scorns to use the phrase and fancy of a
  servingman.

CASTIZA: Yours be your own sir; go direct him hither.
    [*Exit* DONDOLO.]
  I hope some happy tidings from my brother
  That lately travelled, whom my soul affects.
  Here he comes.
    Enter VINDICE, *her brother disguised.*

    3. *Child's-part*: inheritance.   26. *Affects*: loves.

VINDICE: Lady, the best of wishes to your sex;
Fair skins and new gowns. [*Gives her a letter.*]
CASTIZA: Oh they shall thank you, sir.
Whence this?   30
VINDICE: Oh from a dear and worthy friend,
Mighty!
CASTIZA: From whom?
VINDICE: The Duke's son!
CASTIZA: Receive that!
A box o'th'ear to her Brother.
I swore I'd put anger in my hand
And pass the virgin limits of myself
To him that next appeared in that base office
To be his sins' attorney. Bear to him
That figure of my hate upon thy cheek
Whilst 'tis yet hot, and I'll reward thee for't;
Tell him my honour shall have a rich name   40
When several harlots shall share his with shame.
Farewell, commend me to him in my hate!
Exit.
VINDICE: It is the sweetest box that e'er my nose came
nigh,
The finest drawn-work cuff that e'er was worn;
I'll love this blow for ever, and this cheek
Shall still henceforward take the wall of this.
Oh I'm above my tongue! Most constant sister,
In this thou hast right honourable shown;
Many are called by their honour that have none,
Thou art approved for ever in my thoughts.   50
It is not in the power of words to taint thee,
And yet for the salvation of my oath,
As my resolve in that point, I will lay
Hard siege unto my mother, tho' I know
A siren's tongue could not bewitch her so.

35. *Virgin limits:* see note to I. iii. 17.
46. *Take the wall:* have precedence over.
50. *Approved:* proved.

[*Enter* GRATIANA.]

Mass, fitly here she comes. Thanks, my disguise.
Madam, good afternoon.

GRATIANA: Y'are welcome sir.

VINDICE: The next of Italy commends him to you,
Our mighty expectation, the Duke's son.

60 GRATIANA: I think myself much honoured, that he pleases
To rank me in his thoughts.

VINDICE: So may you lady:
One that is like to be our sudden duke –
The crown gapes for him every tide – and then
Commander o'er us all, do but think on him,
How blest were they now that could pleasure him
E'en with any thing almost.

GRATIANA: Ay, save their honour.

VINDICE: Tut, one would let a little of that go too
And ne'er be seen in 't: ne'er be seen in 't, mark you.
I'd wink and let it go.

GRATIANA: Marry but I would not.

VINDICE: Marry but I would I hope, I know you would
70 too,
If you'd that blood now which you gave your daughter;
To her indeed 'tis, this wheel comes about;
That man that must be all this, perhaps ere morning
– For his white father does but mould away –
Has long desired your daughter.

GRATIANA: Desired?

VINDICE: Nay but hear me,
He desires now that will command hereafter,
Therefore be wise, I speak as more a friend
To you than him; Madam, I know you're poor,
80 And 'lack the day, there are too many poor ladies already
Why should you vex the member? 'Tis despised;
Live wealthy, rightly understand the world
And chide away that foolish country girl
Keeps company with your daughter, Chastity.

58. *The next*: in line of succession.

GRATIANA: Oh fie, fie, the riches of the world cannot
  hire
  A mother to such a most unnatural task.
VINDICE: No, but a thousand angels can,
  Men have no power, angels must work you to't.
  The world descends into such base-born evils
  That forty angels can make fourscore devils;   90
  There will be fools still I perceive, still fool[s].
  Would I be poor, dejected, scorned of greatness,
  Swept from the palace, and see other daughters
  Spring with the dew o'th'Court, having mine own
  So much desired and loved – by the Duke's son?
  No, I would raise my state upon her breast
  And call her eyes my tenants, I would count
  My yearly maintenance upon her cheeks:
  Take coach upon her lip, and all her parts
  Should keep men after men, and I would ride   100
  In pleasure upon pleasure.
  You took great pains for her, once when it was,
  Let her requite it now, tho' it be but some;
  You brought her forth, she may well bring you home.
GRATIANA: O heavens! This overcomes me!
VINDICE [aside]: Not, I hope, already?
GRATIANA [aside]: It is too strong for me, men know that
    know us
  We are so weak their words can overthrow us.
  He touched me near-ly, made my virtues 'bate,
  When his tongue struck upon my poor estate.   110
VINDICE [aside]: I e'en quake to proceed, my spirit turns
    edge!
  I fear me she's unmothered, yet I'll venture,
  'That woman is all male whom none can enter' –
  What think you now lady, speak, are you wiser?
  What said advancement to you? Thus it said:
  The daughter's fall lifts up the mother's head!
  Did it not madam? But I'll swear it does

    88-90. *Angels:* gold coins, worth about ten shillings.

In many places: tut, this age fears no man,
''Tis no shame to be bad, because 'tis common'.

GRATIANA: Ay, that's the comfort on't.

120 VINDICE [aside]:   The comfort on't! –
I keep the best for last; can these persuade you
[Showing her gold.]
To forget heaven and –

GRATIANA: Ay, these are they –

VINDICE: Oh!

GRATIANA: That enchant our sex;
These are the means that govern our affections – that woman
Will not be troubled with the mother long
That sees the comfortable shine of you;
I blush to think what for your sakes I'll do!

VINDICE [aside]: O suffering heaven, with thy invisible finger
E'en at this instant turn the precious side

130   Of both mine eyeballs inward, not to see myself.

GRATIANA: Look you sir.

VINDICE: Holla.

GRATIANA: Let this thank your pains.

VINDICE: O you're a kind madam.

GRATIANA: I'll see how I can move.

VINDICE: Your words will sting.

GRATIANA: If she be still chaste, I'll never call her mine.

VINDICE [aside]: Spoke truer than you meant it.

GRATIANA: Daughter Castiza.
[Enter CASTIZA.]

CASTIZA: Madam?

VINDICE: O she's yonder.
Meet her. [Aside] Troops of celestial soldiers guard her heart,
Yon dam has devils enough to take her part.

125. *The mother*: punning on sense of 'hysteria'. Cf. line 239.
128. *Suffering*: permitting.

CASTIZA: Madam, what makes yon evil-officed man
  In presence of you?
GRATIANA: Why?
CASTIZA: He lately brought   140
  Immodest writing sent from the Duke's son
  To tempt me to dishonourable act.
GRATIANA: Dishonourable act? Good honourable fool,
  That wouldst be honest 'cause thou wouldst be so,
  Producing no one reason but thy will;
  And't'as a good report, prettily commended
  But pray by whom? Mean people, ignorant people,
  The better sort I'm sure cannot abide it,
  And by what rule shouldst we square out our lives,
  But by our betters' actions? Oh if thou knew'st   150
  What 'twere to lose it, thou would never keep it:
  But there's a cold curse laid upon all maids,
  While other[s] clip the sun they clasp the shades!
  Virginity is paradise, locked up.
  You cannot come by yourselves without fee.
  And 'twas decreed that man should keep the key.
  Deny advancement, treasure, the Duke's son!
CASTIZA: I cry you mercy. Lady, I mistook you.
  Pray did you see my mother? Which way went you?
  Pray God I have not lost her.
VINDICE [aside]:   Prettily put by.   160
GRATIANA: Are you as proud to me as coy to him?
  Do you not know me now?
CASTIZA: Why, are you she?
  The world's so changed, one shape into another
  It is a wise child now that knows her mother.
VINDICE: Most right, i'faith.
GRATIANA: I owe your cheek my hand
  For that presumption now, but I'll forget it.
  Come, you shall leave these childish 'haviours
  And understand your time. Fortunes flow to you,
  What, will you be a girl?   170

    147. *Mean:* lower-class.   153. *Clip:* embrace.

If all feared drowning that spy waves ashore,
Gold would grow rich and all the merchants poor.

CASTIZA: It is a pretty saying of a wicked one,
But methinks now, it does not show so well
Out of your mouth, – better in his.

VINDICE [aside]: Faith, bad enough in both,
Were I in earnest, as I'll seem no less. –
I wonder lady, your own mother's words
Cannot be taken, nor stand in full force.

180 'Tis honesty you urge; what's honesty?
'Tis but heaven's beggar, and what woman is
So foolish to keep honesty
And be not able to keep herself? No,
Times are grown wiser and will keep less charge.
A maid that has small portion now intends
To break up house and live upon her friends.
How blest are you, you have happiness alone!
Others must fall to thousands, you to one
Sufficient in himself to make your forehead

190 Dazzle the world with jewels, and petitionary people
Start at your presence.

GRATIANA: Oh if I were young, I should be ravish'd!

CASTIZA: Ay, to lose your honour.

VINDICE: 'Slid, how can you lose your honour
To deal with my lord's Grace?
He'll add more honour to it by his title.
Your mother will tell you how.

GRATIANA: That I will.

VINDICE: O think upon the pleasure of the palace,
Secured ease and state, the stirring meats

200 Ready to move out of the dishes
That e'en now quicken when they're eaten!
Banquets abroad by torch-light, music, sports,
Bare-headed vassals, that had ne'er the fortune
To keep on their own hats, but let horns wear 'em!

180. *Honesty:* chastity.
190. *Petitionary people:* people seeking favours.

72

Nine coaches waiting – hurry, hurry, hurry.

CASTIZA: Ay, to the devil.

VINDICE [aside]: Ay, to the devil. – To the Duke, by my
    faith.

GRATIANA: Ay, to the Duke: daughter, you'd scorn to
    think

    O'th'devil, an you were there once.

VINDICE: True, for most there are as proud   210
    As he for his heart, i'faith. –
    Who'd sit at home in a neglected room,
    Dealing her short-lived beauty to the pictures
    That are as useless as old men, when those
    Poorer in face and fortune than herself
    Walk with a hundred acres on their backs,
    Fair meadows cut into green fore-parts? Oh!
    It was the greatest blessing ever happened to women
    When farmers' sons agreed and met again
    To wash their hands and come up gentlemen.   220
    The commonwealth has flourished ever since: –
    Lands that were meat by the rod – that labour's spared –
    Tailors ride down and measure 'em by the yard.
    Fair trees, those comely foretops of the field,
    Are cut to maintain head-tires – much untold.
    All thrives but Chastity, she lies a-cold.
    Nay, shall I come nearer to you? Mark but this:
    Why are there so few honest women, but
    Because 'tis the poorer profession?
    That's accounted best that's best followed;   230
    Least in trade, least in fashion,
    And that's not honesty, believe it; and do
    But note the low and dejected price of it:
    'Lose but a pearl, we search and cannot brook it,
    But that once gone, who is so mad to look it?'

GRATIANA: Troth, he says true.

209. *An:* if.   217. *Fore-parts:* stomachers.
220. *Come up:* to London.   222. *Mete:* measured.
225. *Head-tires:* head-dresses. *Untold:* uncounted.

CASTIZA: False! I defy you both!
    I have endured you with an ear of fire,
    Your tongues have struck hot irons on my face.
    Mother, come from that poisonous woman there.

240 GRATIANA: Where?

CASTIZA: Do you not see her? She's too inward then.
    Slave, perish in thy office! You heavens, please
    Henceforth to make the mother a disease
    Which first begins with me; yet I've outgone you.
    Exit.

VINDICE [*aside*]: O angels, clap your wings upon the skies
    And give this virgin crystal plaudities!

GRATIANA: Peevish, coy, foolish! – But return this
    answer;
    My lord shall be most welcome, when his pleasure
    Conducts him this way. I will sway mine own,

250   Women with women can work best alone.
    Exit.

VINDICE: Indeed I'll tell him so.
    O more uncivil, more unnatural
    Than those base-titled creatures that look downward!
    Why does not heaven turn black, or with a frown
    Undo the world? Why does not earth start up
    And strike the sins that tread upon it? Oh,
    Were't not for gold and women, there would be no
    damnation –
    Hell would look like a lord's great kitchen without fire
    in't.
    But 'twas decreed before the world began,

260   That they should be the hooks to catch at man.
    Exit.

252. *Uncivil:* barbarous.

[SCENE TWO]

Enter LUSSURIOSO *with* HIPPOLITO, VINDICE'*s*
brother.

LUSSURIOSO: I much applaud
　Thy judgement. Thou art well read in a fellow,
　And 'tis the deepest art to study man.
　I know this, which I never learnt in schools,
　The world's divided into knaves and fools.

HIPPOLITO [*aside*]: Knave in your face, my lord - behind
　your back, –

LUSSURIOSO: And I much thank thee, that thou hast
　preferred
　A fellow of discourse well mingled,
　And whose brain time hath seasoned.

HIPPOLITO: 　　　　　　　　　　True, my lord,
　We shall find season once, I hope. [*Aside*] O villain!　10
　To make such an unnatural slave of me, – but –
　[*Enter* VINDICE *disguised.*]

LUSSURIOSO: Mass, here he comes.

HIPPOLITO [*aside*]: And now shall I have free leave to
　depart.

LUSSURIOSO: Your absence – leave us.

HIPPOLITO [*aside*]: 　　　　　Are not my thoughts true?
　I must remove; but brother, you may stay;
　Heart, we are both made bawds a new-found way.
　　Exit.

LUSSURIOSO: Now we're an even number, a third man's
　dangerous,
　Especially her brother; say, be free,
　Have I a pleasure toward?

VINDICE: 　　　　　　　Oh my lord!

LUSSURIOSO: Ravish me in thine answer; art thou rare?　20
　Hast thou beguiled her of salvation
　And rubbed hell o'er with honey? Is she a woman?

VINDICE: In all but in desire.

LUSSURIOSO: Then she's in nothing.
I 'bate in courage now.

VINDICE: The words I brought
Might well have made indifferent honest naught.
A right good woman in these days is changed
Into white money with less labour far;
Many a maid has turned to Mahomet
With easier working; I durst undertake
30 Upon the pawn and forfeit of my life
With half those words to flat a Puritan's wife.
But she is close and good; yet 'tis a doubt
By this time. Oh the mother, the mother!

LUSSURIOSO: I never thought their sex had been a
    wonder
Until this minute; what fruit from the mother?

VINDICE [aside]: Now must I blister my soul, be forsworn
Or shame the woman that received me first.
I will be true; thou liv'st not to proclaim;
Spoke to a dying man, shame has no shame. –
My lord –

LUSSURIOSO: Who's that?

40 VINDICE: Here's none but I, my lord.

LUSSURIOSO: What would thy haste utter?

VINDICE: Comfort.

LUSSURIOSO: Welcome.

VINDICE: The maid being dull, having no mind to travel
Into unknown lands, what did me I straight
But set spurs to the mother; golden spurs
Will put her to a false gallop in a trice.

LUSSURIOSO: Is't possible that in this
The mother should be damned before the daughter?

VINDICE: Oh that's good manners, my lord; the mother
    for
Her age must go foremost, you know.

LUSSURIOSO: Thou'st spoke that true, but where comes in
50   this comfort?

24. *Courage:* spirits.   25. *Naught:* naughty, bad.

VINDICE: In a fine place, my lord, – the unnatural mother
    Did with her tongue so hard beset her honour
    That the poor fool was struck to silent wonder;
    Yet still the maid, like an unlighted taper,
    Was cold and chaste, save that her mother's breath
    Did blow fire on her cheeks. The girl departed
    But the good ancient madam, half mad, threw me
    These promising words, which I took deeply note of:
    'My lord shall be most welcome –'
LUSSURIOSO: 'Faith, I thank her.
VINDICE: '– When his pleasure conducts him this way.'   60
LUSSURIOSO: That shall be soon, i'faith.
VINDICE: 'I will sway mine own.'
LUSSURIOSO: She does the wiser, I commend her for't.
VINDICE: 'Women with women can work best alone.'
LUSSURIOSO: By this light and so they can! Give 'em
    Their due, men are not comparable to 'em.
VINDICE: No, that's true, for you shall have one woman
    Knit more in an hour than any man
    Can ravel again in seven and twenty year.
LUSSURIOSO: Now my desires are happy; I'll make 'em
    free-men now.
    Thou art a precious fellow, 'faith I love thee;   70
    Be wise and make it thy revenue. Beg, leg!
    What office couldst thou be ambitious for?
VINDICE: Office, my lord!
    Marry, if I might have my wish, I would
    Have one that was never begged yet.
LUSSURIOSO: Nay, then thou canst have none.
VINDICE: Yes, my lord,
    I could pick out another office yet.
    Nay, and keep a horse and drab upon't.
LUSSURIOSO: Prithee, good bluntness, tell me.
VINDICE: Why, I would desire but this, my lord;   80
    To have all the fees behind the arras, and all

71. *Beg, leg!*: kneel down to ask a favour.
78. *Drab*: whore.

The farthingales that fall plump about twelve o'clock
At night upon the rushes.

LUSSURIOSO: Thou'rt a mad apprehensive knave;
Dost think to make any great purchase of that?

VINDICE: Oh 'tis an unknown thing my lord: I wonder
'T'as been missed so long!

LUSSURIOSO: Well, this night I'll visit her, and 'tis till
then
A year in my desires. Farewell, attend;
Trust me with thy preferment.
Exit.

90   VINDICE: My loved lord. –
Oh, shall I kill him o'th'wrong-side now? No!
Sword, thou wast never a back-biter yet.
I'll pierce him to his face; he shall die looking upon me;
Thy veins are swelled with lust, this shall unfill 'em;
Great men were gods, if beggars could not kill 'em.
Forgive me, heaven, to call my mother wicked;
Oh lessen not my days upon the earth,
I cannot honour her. By this, I fear me
Her tongue has turned my sister into use.

100   I was a villain not to be forsworn,
To this our lecherous hope, the Duke's son;
For lawyers, merchants, some divines, and all
Count beneficial perjury a sin small.
It shall go hard yet, but I'll guard her honour
And keep the ports sure.
Enter HIPPOLITO.

HIPPOLITO: Brother, how goes the world? I would know
news
Of you, but I have news to tell you.

VINDICE: What, in the name of knavery?

HIPPOLITO: Knavery, 'faith;
This vicious old duke's worthily abused;
110   The pen of his bastard writes him cuckold!

84. *Apprehensive:* quick-witted.
105. *Ports:* gates.   109. *Abused:* deceived.

VINDICE: His bastard?

HIPPOLITO: Pray believe it; he and the duchess
By night meet in their linen; they have been seen
By stair-foot panders.

VINDICE: Oh sin foul and deep!
Great faults are winked at when the Duke's asleep.
See, see, here comes the Spurio.
     [*Enter* SPURIO *with two servants.*]

HIPPOLITO: Monstrous luxur!

VINDICE: Unbraced: two of his valiant bawds with him.
O, there's a wicked whisper, – hell is in his ear.
Stay, let's observe his passage.
     [*They withdraw.*]

SPURIO: Oh, but are you sure on't?

SERVANT: My lord, most sure on't, for 'twas spoke by one   120
That is most inward with the Duke's son's lust
That he intends within this hour to steal
Unto Hippolito's sister, whose chaste life
The mother has corrupted for his use.

SPURIO: Sweet word, sweet occasion! 'Faith then, brother,
I'll disinherit you in as short time
As I was when I was begot in haste,
I'll damn you at your pleasure – precious deed!
After your lust, oh 'twill be fine to bleed.
Come, let our passing out be soft and wary.   130
     Exeunt.

VINDICE: Mark, there, there, that step now, to the
     Duchess;
This their second meeting writes the Duke cuckold
With new additions, his horns newly revived:
Night! Thou that look'st like funeral heralds' fees
Torn down betimes i'th'morning, thou hang'st fitly
To grace those sins that have no grace at all.
Now 'tis full sea a-bed over the world,
There's juggling of all sides; some that were maids

116. *Unbraced:* without doublet; in his shirt.
134. *Fees:* 'pheaze', hangings.

79

E'en at sunset are now perhaps i'th'toll-book.
140 This woman in immodest thin apparel
Lets in her friend by water; here a dame
Cunning nails leather hinges to a door
To avoid proclamation.
Now cuckolds are a-coining, apace, apace, apace, apace!
And careful sisters spin that thread i'th'night
That does maintain them and their bawds i'th'day.

HIPPOLITO: You flow well, brother!

VINDICE: Puh, I'm shallow yet,
Too sparing and too modest; shall I tell thee?
If every trick were told that's dealt by night,
150 There are few here that would not blush outright.

HIPPOLITO: I am of that belief too. Who's this comes?
[*Enter* LUSSURIOSO.]

VINDICE: The Duke's son up so late? Brother, fall back
And you shall learn some mischief. [HIPPOLITO *withdraws.*] – My good lord.

LUSSURIOSO: Piato, why, the man I wished for! Come,
I do embrace this season for the fittest
To taste of that young lady.

VINDICE [*aside*]:   Heart and hell!

HIPPOLITO [*aside*]: Damned villain!

VINDICE [*aside*]: I ha' no way now to cross it, but to kill
him.

LUSSURIOSO: Come, only thou and I.

VINDICE: My lord, my lord.

160 LUSSURIOSO: Why dost thou start us?

VINDICE: I'd almost forgot – the bastard!

LUSSURIOSO: What of him?

VINDICE: This night, this hour – this minute, now –

LUSSURIOSO: What? What?

VINDICE: Shadows the duchess –

LUSSURIOSO: Horrible word!

VINDICE: And like strong poison eats
Into the duke your father's forehead.

139. *Toll-book:* list of horses on sale at a fair.

LUSSURIOSO: Oh!

VINDICE: He makes horn royal.

LUSSURIOSO: Most ignoble slave!

VINDICE: This is the fruit of two beds.

LUSSURIOSO: I am mad.

VINDICE: That passage he trod warily.

LUSSURIOSO: He did?

VINDICE: And hushed his villains every step he took.

LUSSURIOSO: His villains? I'll confound them.   170

VINDICE: Take 'em finely, finely now.

LUSSURIOSO: The duchess' chamber-door shall not control me.

   Exeunt [all but HIPPOLITO].

HIPPOLITO: Good, happy, swift! There's gunpowder
i'th'court,

Wildfire at midnight; in this heedless fury

He may show violence to cross himself.

I'll follow the event.

   Exit.

[SCENE THREE]

   [DUKE *and* DUCHESS *discovered in bed.*]

   Enter again [LUSSURIOSO *and* VINDICE].

LUSSURIOSO: Where is that villain?

VINDICE: Softly my lord, and you may take 'em twisted.

LUSSURIOSO: I care not how!

VINDICE: Oh, 'twill be glorious

To kill 'em doubled, when they're heaped; be soft, my
lord.

LUSSURIOSO: Away, my spleen is not so lazy; thus and
thus

I'll shake their eyelids ope, and with my sword

Shut 'em again for ever. –

   [*Approaching bed.*]

               Villain! Strumpet!

DUKE: You upper guard, defend us!

DUCHESS: Treason, treason!

DUKE: Oh take me not in sleep!

10   I have great sins; I must have days,
    Nay, months dear son, with penitential heaves,
    To lift 'em out, and not to die unclear.
    O, thou wilt kill me both in heaven and here.

LUSSURIOSO: I am amazed to death!

DUKE: Nay, villain traitor,
    Worse than the foulest epithet, now I'll grip thee
    E'en with the nerves of wrath, and throw thy head
    Amongst the lawyers! Guard!

      Enter NOBLES *and Sons* [*with* HIPPOLITO].

FIRST NOBLE: How comes the quiet of your grace disturbed?

DUKE: This boy, that should be myself after me,
20   Would be myself before me, and in heat
    Of that ambition, bloodily rushed in,
    Intending to depose me in my bed.

SECOND NOBLE: Duty and natural loyalty forfend!

DUCHESS: He called his father villain, and me strumpet,
    A word that I abhor to 'file my lips with.

AMBITIOSO: That was not so well done, brother.

LUSSURIOSO: I am abused –
    I know there's no excuse can do me good.

VINDICE [*aside to* HIPPOLITO]: 'Tis now good policy to
    be from sight;
30   His vicious purpose to our sister's honour
    Is crossed beyond our thought.

HIPPOLITO: You little dreamt his father slept here.

VINDICE: Oh 'twas far beyond me,
    But since it fell so, without fright-full word[s],
    Would he had killed him, 'twould have eased our
    swords.

      [VINDICE *and* HIPPOLITO *flee.*]

DUKE: Be comforted our duchess, he shall die.

25. *'File:* defile.

LUSSURIOSO: Where's this slave-pander now? Out of
   mine eye?
   Guilty of this abuse.
    Enter SPURIO *with his villains.*
SPURIO: Y'are villains, fablers,
   You have knaves' chins and harlots' tongues, you lie   40
   And I will damn you with one meal a day.
FIRST SERVANT: O good my lord!
SPURIO: 'Sblood! You shall never sup.
SECOND SERVANT: O I beseech you sir.
SPURIO: To let my sword
   Catch cold so long and miss him.
FIRST SERVANT: Troth, my lord,
   'Twas his intent to meet there.
SPURIO: Heart, he's yonder!
   Ha, what news here? Is the day out o'th'socket
   That it is noon at midnight? – the court up?
   How comes the guard so saucy with his elbows?
LUSSURIOSO: The bastard here?
   Nay then, the truth of my intent shall out.   50
   My lord and father, hear me.
DUKE: Bear him hence.
LUSSURIOSO: I can with loyalty excuse –
DUKE: Excuse? To prison with the villain!
   Death shall not long lag after him.
SPURIO [*aside*]: Good, i'faith, then 'tis not much amiss.
LUSSURIOSO: Brothers, my best release lies on your
   tongues;
   I pray, persuade for me.
AMBITIOSO: It is our duties; make yourself sure of us.
SUPERVACUO: We'll sweat in pleading.
LUSSURIOSO: And I may live to thank you.   60
    Exeunt [LUSSURIOSO *and guards*].
AMBITIOSO [*aside*]: No, thy death shall thank me better.
SPURIO [*aside*]: He's gone; I'll after him
   And know his trespass, seem to bear a part
   In all his ills, but with a Puritan heart.

Exit [SPURIO *and villains*].

AMBITIOSO [*aside*]: Now brother, let our hate and love be
    woven
  So subtly together, that in speaking one
  Word for his life, we may make three for his death;
  The craftiest pleader gets most gold for breath.

SUPERVACUO: Set on, I'll not be far behind you, brother.

70 DUKE: Is't possible a son
  Should be disobedient as far as the sword?
  It is the highest, he can go no farther.

AMBITIOSO: My gracious lord, take pity –

DUKE: Pity, boys?

AMBITIOSO: Nay, we'd be loath to move your Grace too
    much;
  We know the trespass is unpardonable,
  Black, wicked and unnatural.

SUPERVACUO: In a son, oh monstrous!

AMBITIOSO: Yet, my lord,
  A duke's soft hand strokes the rough head of law
  And makes it lie smooth.

DUKE: But my hand shall n'er do't.

AMBITIOSO: That, as you please, my lord.

80 SUPERVACUO: We must needs confess
  Some father would have entered into hate
  So deadly pointed, that before his eyes
  He would have seen the execution sound
  Without corrupted favour.

AMBITIOSO: But my lord,
  Your Grace may live the wonder of all times
  In pardoning that offence which never yet
  Had face to beg a pardon.

DUKE: Honey, how's this?

AMBITIOSO: Forgive him good my lord, he's your own
    son,
  And I must needs say, 'twas the vilelier done.

SUPERVACUO: He's the next heir, yet this true reason
90   gathers,

None can possess that dispossess their fathers.
Be merciful. –

DUKE [*aside*]:   Here's no stepmother's wit;
I'll try 'em both upon their love and hate.

AMBITIOSO: Be merciful – altho' –

DUKE: You have prevailed.
My wrath like flaming wax hath spent itself;
I know 'twas but some peevish moon in him. –
Go, let him be released.

SUPERVACUO [*aside*]:   'Sfoot, how now, brother?

AMBITIOSO: Your Grace doth please to speak beside your
     spleen;
I would it were so happy.

DUKE: Why, go release him.

SUPERVACUO: O my good lord, I know the fault's too
     weighty   100
And full of general loathing, too inhuman,
Rather by all men's voices, worthy death.

DUKE: 'Tis true too; here then, receive this signet:
Doom shall pass, direct it to the judges: he shall die
Ere many days. Make haste.

AMBITIOSO: All speed that may be
We could have wished his burden not so sore,
We knew your Grace did but delay before.
     Exeunt.

DUKE: Here's Envy with a poor thin cover o'er 't
Like scarlet hid in lawn, easily spied through.
This their ambition by the mother's side   110
Is dangerous, and for safety must be purged.
I will prevent their envies. Sure, it was
But some mistaken fury in our son
Which these aspiring boys would climb upon;
He shall be released suddenly.
     Enter NOBLES.

FIRST NOBLE: Good morning to your Grace.

96. *Moon*: lunatic notion.
109. *Lawn*: fine white linen.

DUKE: Welcome, my lords.
[*They kneel.*]

SECOND NOBLE: Our knees shall take away the office of
Our feet for ever,
Unless your Grace bestow a father's eye
120 Upon the clouded fortunes of your son,
And in compassionate virtue grant him that
Which makes e'en mean men happy – liberty.

DUKE [*aside*]: How seriously their loves and honours woo
For that which I am about to pray them do.
– Rise, my lords, your knees sign his release:
We freely pardon him.

FIRST NOBLE: We owe your Grace much thanks, and he
much duty.
Exeunt.

DUKE: It well becomes that judge to nod at crimes
That does commit greater himself and lives.
130 I may forgive a disobedient error,
That expect pardon for adultery
And in my old days am a youth in lust.
Many a beauty have I turned to poison
In the denial, covetous of all.
Age hot is like a monster to be seen:
My hairs are white, and yet my sins are green.

ACT THREE

*

[SCENE ONE]

Enter AMBITIOSO *and* SUPERVACUO.

SUPERVACUO: Brother, let my opinion sway you once,
    I speak it for the best, – to have him die
    Surest and soonest. If the signet come
    Unto the judges' hands, why then his doom
    Will be deferred till sittings and court-days,
    Juries and further; faiths are bought and sold,
    Oaths in these days are but the skin of gold.

AMBITIOSO: In troth, 'tis true too.

SUPERVACUO: Then let's set by the judges
    And fall to the officers; 'tis but mistaking
    The duke our father's meaning, and where he named   10
    'Ere many days', 'tis but forgetting that
    And have him die i'th'morning.

AMBITIOSO: Excellent!
    Then am I heir – duke in a minute.

SUPERVACUO [*aside*]:   Nay,
    An he were once puffed out, here is a pin
    Should quickly prick your bladder.

AMBITIOSO: Blest occasion!
    He being packed, we'll have some trick and wile
    To wind our younger brother out of prison,
    That lies in for the rape; the lady's dead
    And people's thoughts will soon be buriéd.

SUPERVACUO: We may with safety do't, and live and feed: 20
    The duchess' sons are too proud to bleed.

AMBITIOSO: We are i'faith, to say true. – Come, let's not
    linger,
    I'll to the officers; go you before
    And set an edge upon the executioner.

SUPERVACUO: Let me alone to grind him.
    Exit.

AMBITIOSO: Meet; farewell.
    I am next now, I rise just in that place
    Where thou'rt cut off, upon thy neck, kind brother,
    The falling of one head lifts up another.
        Exit.

[SCENE TWO]

Enter with the NOBLES, LUSSURIOSO *from prison.*
LUSSURIOSO: My lords, I am so much indebted to your
        loves
    For this, – O this delivery.
FIRST NOBLE: But our duties, my lord
    Unto the hopes that grow in you.
LUSSURIOSO: If e'er I live to be myself, I'll thank you.
    O Liberty, thou sweet and heavenly dame!
    But hell, for prison is too mild a name.
        Exeunt.

[SCENE THREE]

Enter AMBITIOSO *and* SUPERVACUO *with* OFFICERS.
AMBITIOSO: Officers, here's the Duke's signet, your firm
        warrant
    Brings the command of present death along with it
    Unto our brother, the Duke's son; we are sorry
    That we are so unnaturally employed
    In such an unkind office, fitter far
    For enemies than brothers.
SUPERVACUO: But you know
    The Duke's command must be obeyed.
FIRST OFFICER: It must and shall, my lord; this morning
        then,
    – So suddenly?
AMBITIOSO: Ay, alas, poor good soul,
10   He must breakfast betimes, the executioner
    Stands ready to put forth his cowardly valour.

SECOND OFFICER: Already?

SUPERVACUO: Already i'faith, – O sir, destruction hies,
And that is least impudent, soonest dies.

FIRST OFFICER: Troth, you say true, my lord; we take
our leaves.
Our office shall be sound; we'll not delay
The third part of a minute.

AMBITIOSO: Therein you show
Yourselves good men and upright officers.
Pray, let him die as private as he may;
Do him that favour, for the gaping people   20
Will but trouble him at his prayers
And make him curse and swear, and so die black.
Will you be so far kind?

FIRST OFFICER: It shall be done, my lord.

AMBITIOSO: Why, we do thank you; if we live to be,
You shall have a better office.

SECOND OFFICER: Your good lordship.

SUPERVACUO: Commend us to the scaffold in our tears.

FIRST OFFICER: We'll weep and do your commendations.
        Exeunt.

AMBITIOSO: Fine fools in office!

SUPERVACUO: Things fall out so fit.

AMBITIOSO: So happily! Come brother, ere next clock
His head will be made serve a bigger block.   30
        Exeunt.

[SCENE FOUR]

        Enter in prison JUNIOR.

JUNIOR: Keeper.

KEEPER: My lord?

JUNIOR: No news lately from our brothers?
Are they unmindful of us?

        30. *Bigger block:* quibble on hat-block.

89

KEEPER: My lord, a messenger came newly in
    And brought this from 'em.
    [*Hands him a letter.*]
JUNIOR: Nothing but paper comforts?
    I looked for my delivery before this,
    Had they been worth their oaths. – Prithee, be from us.
    [*Exit* KEEPER.]
    Now, what say you, forsooth; speak out, I pray:
    [*Reads letter*]: 'Brother, be of good cheer.'
10   'Slud, it begins like a whore, with good cheer.
    'Thou shalt not be long a prisoner.'
    Not five and thirty year, like a bankrupt, – I think so.
    'We have thought upon a device to get thee out by a
      trick.'
    By a trick? Pox o' your trick, an it be so long a-playing!
    'And so rest comforted, be merry and expect it suddenly.'
    Be merry? Hang merry, draw and quarter merry!
    I'll be mad. Is't not strange that a man
    Should lie in a whole month for a woman?
    Well, we shall see how sudden our brothers
20   Will be in their promise; I must expect
    Still a trick. I shall not be long a prisoner.
    [*Enter* KEEPER.]
    How now, what news?
KEEPER: Bad news my lord; I am discharged of you.
JUNIOR: Slave, call'st thou that bad news? I thank you,
    brothers.
KEEPER: My lord, 'twill prove so; here come the officers
    Into whose hands I must commit you.
    [*Exit* KEEPER.]
JUNIOR: Ha, officers? What, why?
    [*Enter* OFFICERS.]
FIRST OFFICER: You must pardon us, my lord,
    Our office must be sound; here is our warrant,
30   The signet from the Duke; you must straight suffer.
JUNIOR: Suffer? I'll suffer you to be gone, I'll suffer you
    To come no more; what would you have me suffer?

SECOND OFFICER: My lord, those words were better
    changed to prayers.
  The time's but brief with you, prepare to die.
JUNIOR: Sure 'tis not so.
THIRD OFFICER: It is too true, my lord.
JUNIOR: I tell you 'tis not, for the Duke my father
    Deferred me till next sitting, and I look
    E'en every minute, threescore times an hour
    For a release, a trick wrought by my brothers.
FIRST OFFICER: A trick my lord? If you expect such
    comfort,   40
    Your hope's as fruitless as a barren woman:
    Your brothers were the unhappy messengers
    That brought this powerful token for your death.
JUNIOR: My brothers? No, no.
SECOND OFFICER: 'Tis most true, my lord.
JUNIOR: My brothers to bring a warrant for my death?
    How strange this shows!
THIRD OFFICER: There's no delaying time.
JUNIOR: Desire 'em hither, call 'em up, my brothers!
    They shall deny it to your faces.
FIRST OFFICER: My lord,
    They're far enough by this, at least at court,
    And this most strict command they left behind 'em   50
    When grief swum in their eyes, they showed like
    brothers,
    Brim-full of heavy sorrow: but the Duke
    Must have his pleasure.
JUNIOR: His pleasure?
FIRST OFFICER: These were their last words which my
    memory bears
    'Commend us to the scaffold in our tears.'
JUNIOR: Pox dry their tears, what should I do with tears?
    I hate 'em worse than any citizen's son
    Can hate salt water; here came a letter now,
    New bleeding from their pens, scarce stinted yet, –
    Would I'd been torn in pieces when I tore it;   60

Look, you officious whoresons, words of comfort,
'Not long a prisoner.'
FIRST OFFICER: It says true in that sir, for you must suffer
    presently.
JUNIOR: A villainous Duns upon the letter – knavish
    exposition, –
Look you then here sir: 'We'll get thee out by a trick'
    says he.
SECOND OFFICER: That may hold too sir, for you know
A trick is commonly four cards, which was meant
By us four officers.
JUNIOR: Worse and worse dealing.
FIRST OFFICER: The hour beckons us,
70 The headsman waits, lift up your eyes to heaven.
JUNIOR: I thank you, 'faith; good, pretty-wholesome
    counsel;
I should look up to heaven as you said,
Whilst he behind me cozens me of my head, –
Ay, that's the trick.
THIRD OFFICER: You delay too long, my lord.
JUNIOR: Stay, good Authority's bastards, since I must
Through brothers' perjury die, O let me venom
Their souls with curses.
FIRST OFFICER: Come, 'tis no time to curse.
JUNIOR: Must I bleed then, without respect of sign?
    Well –
80 My fault was sweet sport, which the world approves,
I die for that which every woman loves.
    Exeunt.

[SCENE FIVE]

Enter VINDICE *with* HIPPOLITO *his brother.*
VINDICE: O sweet, delectable, rare, happy, ravishing!
HIPPOLITO: Why what's the matter brother?
VINDICE: O 'tis able

To make a man spring up and knock his forehead
Against yon silver ceiling.

HIPPOLITO: Prithee tell me,
Why may not I partake with you? You vowed once
To give me share to every tragic thought.

VINDICE: By th'Mass, I think I did too;
Then I'll divide it to thee. – The old Duke
Thinking my outward shape and inward heart
Are cut out of one piece – for he that prates his secrets,   10
His heart stands o'th'outside – hires me by price:
To greet him with a lady
In some fit place veiled from the eyes o'th'Court,
Some darkened blushless angle, that is guilty
Of his forefathers' lusts, and great folks' riots,
To which I easily – to maintain my shape –
Consented, and did wish his impudent grace
To meet her here in this unsunnéd lodge,
Wherein 'tis night at noon, and here the rather
Because, unto the torturing of his soul,   20
The bastard and the duchess have appointed
Their meeting too in this luxurious circle,
Which most afflicting sight will kill his eyes
Before we kill the rest of him.

HIPPOLITO: 'Twill i'faith, most dreadfully digested!
I see not how you could have missed me, brother.

VINDICE: True, but the violence of my joy forgot it.

HIPPOLITO: Ay, but where's that lady now?

VINDICE: Oh, at that word
I'm lost again! You cannot find me yet,
I'm in a throng of happy apprehensions.   30
He's suited for a lady; I have took care
For a delicious lip, a sparkling eye, –
You shall be witness, brother;
Be ready, stand with your hat off.
    Exit.

4. *Silver ceiling:* the decorated stage canopy or 'heavens'.
25. *Digested:* contrived.

HIPPOLITO: Troth, I wonder what lady it should be?
 Yet 'tis no wonder, now I think again,
 To have a lady stoop to a duke, that stoops unto his men.
 'Tis common to be common through the world,
 And there's more private common shadowing vices
 Than those who are known both by their names and
40 prices.
 'Tis part of my allegiance to stand bare
 To the Duke's concubine – and here she comes.
  Enter VINDICE *with the skull of his love dressed up in*
  Tires.

VINDICE: Madam, his grace will not be absent long.
 Secret? Ne'er doubt us madam; 'twill be worth
 Three velvet gowns to your ladyship. Known?
 Few ladies respect that disgrace, a poor thin shell!
 'Tis the best grace you have to do it well;
 I'll save your hand that labour, I'll unmask you.
  [*He reveals the skull.*]

HIPPOLITO: Why brother, brother!

50 VINDICE: Art thou beguiled now? Tut, a lady can
 At such – all hid – beguile a wiser man.
 Have I not fitted the old surfeiter
 With a quaint piece of beauty? Age and bare bone
 Are e'er allied in action; here's an eye
 Able to tempt a great man – to serve God;
 A pretty hanging lip, that has forgot now to dissemble;
 Methinks this mouth should make a swearer tremble,
 A drunkard clasp his teeth and not undo 'em
 To suffer wet damnation to run through 'em.
60 Here's a cheek keeps her colour, let the wind go whistle.
 Spout, rain, we fear thee not; be hot or cold,
 All's one with us. And is not he absurd
 Whose fortunes are upon their faces set,
 That fear no other God but wind and wet?

HIPPOLITO: Brother, y'ave spoke that right;
 Is this the form that living shone so bright?

42. S.D. *Tires:* head-dress.

VINDICE: The very same –
  And now methinks I could e'en chide myself
  For doting on her beauty, tho' her death
  Shall be revenged after no common action. –   70
  Does the silk-worm expend her yellow labours
  For thee? For thee does she undo herself?
  Are lordships sold to maintain ladyships
  For the poor benefit of a bewitching minute?
  Why does yon fellow falsify high ways
  And put his life between the judge's lips
  To refine such a thing, keeps horse and men
  To beat their valours for her?
  Surely, we're all mad people, and they
  Whom we think are, are not, – we mistake those;   80
  'Tis we are mad in sense, they but in clothes.
HIPPOLITO: 'Faith, and in clothes too we, – give us our
  due.
VINDICE: Does every proud and self-affecting dame
  Camphor her face for this, and grieve her Maker
  In sinful baths of milk, – when many an infant starves
  For her superfluous outside, – all for this?
  Who now bids twenty pound a night, prepares
  Music, perfumes, and sweetmeats? All are hushed,
  Thou may'st lie chaste now! It were fine, methinks
  To have thee seen at revels, forgetful feasts   90
  And unclean brothels; sure 'twould fright the sinner
  And make him a good coward, put a reveller
  Out of his antic amble,
  And cloy an epicure with empty dishes.
  Here might a scornful and ambitious woman
  Look through and through herself; see, ladies with false
    forms
  You deceive men, but cannot deceive worms. –
  Now to my tragic business. Look you, brother,
  I have not fashioned this only for show
  And useless property; no, it shall bear a part   100

      100. *Property:* theatrical 'prop'.

E'en in its own revenge. This very skull,
Whose mistress the Duke poisoned with this drug,
The mortal curse of the earth, shall be revenged
In the like strain, and kiss his lips to death.
As much as the dumb thing can, he shall feel:
What fails in poison, we'll supply in steel.

HIPPOLITO: Brother, I do applaud thy constant vengeance,
The quaintness of thy malice, – above thought.

VINDICE: So – 'tis laid on: now come, and welcome, Duke,
110   I have her for thee. I protest it, brother,
Methinks she makes almost as fair a sign
As some old gentlewoman in a periwig. [*Masks skull.*]
Hide thy face now for shame; thou hadst need have a mask now.
'Tis vain when beauty flows; but when it fleets,
This would become graves better than the streets.

HIPPOLITO: You have my voice in that.
   [*Noises within.*]
                   Hark, the Duke's come.

VINDICE: Peace, let's observe what company he brings,
And how he does absent 'em, for you know
He'll wish all private. Brother, fall you back a little
With the bony lady.

120 HIPPOLITO: That I will.
   [*He withdraws.*]

VINDICE: So, so; – now nine years' vengeance crowd into a minute.
   [*Enter* DUKE *and* GENTLEMEN.]

DUKE: You shall have leave to leave us, with this charge
Upon your lives: if we be missed by the duchess
Or any of the nobles, to give out
We're privately rid forth.

VINDICE [*aside*]:   Oh happiness!

DUKE: With some few honourable gentlemen, you may say;
You may name those that are away from court.

GENTLEMAN: Your will and pleasure shall be done, my
  lord.
  [*Exeunt* GENTLEMEN.]
VINDICE [*aside*]: 'Privately rid forth!'
  He strives to make sure work on 't.
                                    Your good Grace! 13
DUKE: Piato, well done. Hast brought her? What lady is 't?
VINDICE: 'Faith, my lord,
  A country lady, a little bashful at first,
  As most of them are; but after the first kiss
  My lord, the worst is past with them; your Grace
  Knows now what you have to do;
  Sh'as somewhat a grave look with her, but –
DUKE: I love that best; conduct her.
VINDICE [*aside*]:   Have at all.
DUKE: In gravest looks the greatest faults seem less;
  Give me that sin that's robed in holiness.   14
VINDICE [*aside*]: Back with the torch, brother, raise the
  perfumes.
DUKE: How sweet can a duke breathe? Age has no fault.
  Pleasure should meet in a perfuméd mist.
  Lady, sweetly encountered; I came from court,
  I must be bold with you.
  [*Kisses skull.*]
                        Oh, what's this? Oh!
VINDICE: Royal villain! White devil!
DUKE: Oh!
VINDICE: Brother, place the torch here, that his affrighted
  eye-balls
  May start into those hollows. Duke, dost know
  Yon dreadful vizard? View it well; 'tis the skull
  Of Gloriana, whom thou poisonedst last.   15
DUKE: Oh, 't'as poisoned me!
VINDICE: Didst not know that till now?

> 138. *Have at all:* venture all.
> 146. *White devil:* hypocrite.
> 149. *Vizard:* visage.

DUKE: What are you two?

VINDICE: Villains – all three! The very ragged bone
  Has been sufficiently revenged.

DUKE: Oh Hippolito, call treason!

HIPPOLITO: Yes, my good lord – treason! treason!
  treason!
    Stamping on him.

DUKE: Then I'm betrayed.

VINDICE: Alas, poor lecher! In the hands of knaves,
  A slavish duke is baser than his slaves.

DUKE: My teeth are eaten out.

160 VINDICE: Hadst any left?

HIPPOLITO: I think but few.

VINDICE: Then those that did eat are eaten.

DUKE: O my tongue!

VINDICE: Your tongue? 'Twill teach you to kiss closer,
  Not like a flobbering Dutchman. You have eyes still:
  Look, monster, what a lady hast thou made me
  My once betrothéd wife!

DUKE: Is it thou, villain? Nay then –

VINDICE [*taking off disguise*]: 'Tis I, 'tis Vindice, 'tis I!

HIPPOLITO: And let this comfort thee: our lord and
  father
  Fell sick upon the infection of thy frowns
  And died in sadness; be that thy hope of life.

170 DUKE: Oh!

VINDICE: He had his tongue, yet grief made him die
  speechless.
  Puh, 'tis but early yet; now I'll begin
  To stick thy soul with ulcers, I will make
  Thy spirit grievous sore; it shall not rest,
  But like some pestilent man, toss in thy breast.
  Mark me, duke,
  Thou'rt a renownéd, high and mighty cuckold.

DUKE: Oh!

VINDICE: Thy bastard, thy bastard rides a-hunting in thy
  brow.

DUKE: Millions of deaths!

VINDICE: Nay, to afflict thee more,
Here in this lodge they meet for damnéd clips;   180
Those eyes shall see the incest of their lips.

DUKE: Is there a hell besides this, villains?

VINDICE: Villain?
Nay, heaven is just, scorns are the hires of scorns:
I ne'er knew yet adulterer without horns.

HIPPOLITO: Once ere they die 'tis quitted.

VINDICE: Hark, the music;
Their banquet is prepared, they're coming.

DUKE: Oh, kill me not with that sight!

VINDICE: Thou shalt not lose that sight for all thy
dukedom.

DUKE: Traitors, murderers!

VINDICE: What! Is not thy tongue eaten out yet?   190
Then we'll invent a silence. Brother, stifle the torch.

DUKE: Treason, murder!

VINDICE: Nay, 'faith, we'll have you hushed now with thy
dagger.
Nail down his tongue, and mine shall keep possession
About his heart; if he but gasp he dies,
We dread not death to quittance injuries. Brother,
If he but wink, not brooking the foul object,
Let our two other hands tear up his lids
And make his eyes like comets shine through blood;
When the bad bleeds, then is the tragedy good.   200

HIPPOLITO: Whist, brother, music's at our ear; they
come.

Enter the Bastard [SPURIO] *meeting the* DUCHESS.

SPURIO: Had not that kiss a taste of sin, 'twere sweet.

DUCHESS: Why, there's no pleasure sweet, but it is sinful.

SPURIO: True, such a bitter sweetness fate hath given,
Best side to us is the worst side to heaven.

---

180. *Clips:* embraces.   183. *Hires:* wages.
197. *Wink:* shut his eyes.

DUCHESS: Push, come: 'tis the old Duke, thy doubtful
    father,
  The thought of him rubs heaven in thy way;
  But I protest by yonder waxen fire,
  Forget him, or I'll poison him.

210 SPURIO: Madam, you urge a thought which ne'er had life.
  So deadly do I loathe him for my birth
  That if he took me hasped within his bed,
  I would add murder to adultery
  And with my sword give up his years to death.

DUCHESS: Why, now thou'rt sociable; let's in and feast
  Loud'st music sound: pleasure is Banquet's guest.
    Exeunt.

DUKE: I cannot brook –
    [*Dies*.]

VINDICE: The brook is turned to blood.

HIPPOLITO. Thanks to loud music.

VINDICE: 'Twas our friend indeed.
  'Tis state in music for a duke to bleed.

220 The dukedom wants a head, tho' yet unknown;
  As fast as they peep up, let's cut 'em down.
    Exeunt.

[SCENE SIX]

Enter the DUCHESS' *two sons*, AMBITIOSO *and* SUPER-
VACUO.

AMBITIOSO: Was not his execution rarely plotted?
  We are the Duke's sons now.

SUPERVACUO: Ay, you may thank my policy for that.

AMBITIOSO: Your policy for what?

SUPERVACUO: Why, was't not my invention, brother,
  To slip the judges? And in lesser compass,
  Did not I draw the model of his death,
  Advising you to sudden officers
  And e'en extemporal execution?

      3. *Policy*: cunning.

AMBITIOSO: Heart, 'twas a thing I thought on too.   10
SUPERVACUO: You thought on't too? 'Sfoot, slander not
   your thoughts
   With glorious untruth; I know 'twas from you.
AMBITIOSO: Sir, I say 'twas in my head.
SUPERVACUO: Ay, like your brains then,
   Ne'er to come out as long as you lived.
AMBITIOSO: You'd have the honour on't, forsooth, that
   your wit
   Led him to the scaffold.
SUPERVACUO: Since it is my due,
   I'll publish 't, but I'll ha' 't in spite of you.
AMBITIOSO: Methinks you're much too bold; you should
   a little
   Remember us, brother, next to be honest Duke.
SUPERVACUO [aside]: Ay, it shall be as easy for you to be
   duke   20
   As to be honest, and that's never i'faith.
AMBITIOSO: Well, cold he is by this time, and because
   We're both ambitious, be it our amity
   And let the glory be sharéd equally.
SUPERVACUO: I am content to that.
AMBITIOSO: This night our younger brother shall out
   of prison;
   I have a trick.
SUPERVACUO: A trick! Prithee, what is't?
AMBITIOSO: We'll get him out by a wile.
SUPERVACUO: Prithee, what wile?
AMBITIOSO: No sir, you shall not know it till't be done;
   For then, you'd swear't were yours.
   [Enter OFFICER, bearing a head.]
SUPERVACUO: How now, what's he?
AMBITIOSO: One of the officers. 30
SUPERVACUO: Desiréd news.
AMBITIOSO: How now, my friend?
OFFICER: My lords, under your pardon, I am allotted

12. *Glorious*: boastful. *'Twas from you*: had not occurred to you.

To that desertless office to present you
With the yet bleeding head.

SUPERVACUO [*aside*]:   Ha, ha, excellent.

AMBITIOSO [*aside*]: All's sure our own: brother, canst
weep, think'st thou?
'Twould grace our flattery much; think of some dame,
'Twill teach thee to dissemble.

SUPERVACUO [*aside*]: I have thought; – now for yourself.

AMBITIOSO: Our sorrows are so fluent,
40   Our eyes o'erflow our tongues: words spoke in tears
Are like the murmurs of the waters, the sound
Is loudly heard, but cannot be distinguished.

SUPERVACUO: How died he, pray?

OFFICER: O, full of rage and spleen.

SUPERVACUO: He died most valiantly then; we're glad to
hear it.

OFFICER: We could not woo him once to pray.

AMBITIOSO: He showed himself a gentleman in that:
Give him his due.

OFFICER: But in the stead of prayer
He drew forth oaths.

SUPERVACUO: Then did he pray, dear heart,
Although you understood him not.

OFFICER: My lords,
50   E'en at his last, with pardon be it spoke,
He cursed you both.

SUPERVACUO: He cursed us? 'Las, good soul.

AMBITIOSO: It was not in our powers, but the Duke's
pleasure.
[*Aside*] Finely dissembled o'both sides, sweet fate, –
O happy opportunity!
      Enter LUSSURIOSO.

LUSSURIOSO: Now my lords.

BOTH: Oh!

LUSSURIOSO: Why do you shun me, brothers?
You may come nearer now;

The savour of the prison has forsook me.
I thank such kind lords as yourselves, I'm free.
AMBITIOSO: Alive!
SUPERVACUO: In health!
AMBITIOSO: Released!   60
We were both e'en amazed with joy to see it.
LUSSURIOSO: I am much to thank you.
SUPERVACUO: 'Faith, we spared no tongue unto my lord
    the Duke.
AMBITIOSO: I know your delivery, brother,
Had not been half so sudden but for us.
SUPERVACUO: O how we pleaded!
LUSSURIOSO: Most deserving brothers,
In my best studies I will think of it.
    Exit LUSSURIOSO.
AMBITIOSO: O death and vengeance!
SUPERVACUO: Hell and torments!
AMBITIOSO: Slave, cam'st thou to delude us?
OFFICER: Delude you my lords?
SUPERVACUO: Ay, villain, where's this head now?
OFFICER: Why here, my lord;   70
Just after his delivery, you both came
With warrant from the Duke to behead your brother.
AMBITIOSO: Ay, our brother, the Duke's son.
OFFICER: The Duke's son, my lord, had his release before
    you came.
AMBITIOSO: Whose head's that then?
OFFICER: His whom you left command for, your own
    brother's.
AMBITIOSO: Our brother's? O furies!
SUPERVACUO: Plagues!
AMBITIOSO: Confusions!
SUPERVACUO: Darkness!
AMBITIOSO: Devils!
SUPERVACUO: Fell it out so accursedly?
AMBITIOSO: So damnedly?
SUPERVACUO: Villain, I'll brain thee with it.

80 OFFICER: O my good lord!
    [*Exit* OFFICER.]
SUPERVACUO: The devil overtake thee.
AMBITIOSO: O fatal!
SUPERVACUO: O prodigious to our bloods!
AMBITIOSO: Did we dissemble –
SUPERVACUO: Did we make our tears women for thee?
AMBITIOSO: Laugh and rejoice for thee?
SUPERVACUO: Bring warrant for thy death?
AMBITIOSO: Mock off thy head?
SUPERVACUO: You had a trick, you had a wile, forsooth!
AMBITIOSO: A murrain meet 'em!
    There's none of these wiles that ever come to good:
    I see now there's nothing sure in mortality but mortality.
90   Well, no more words, – 't shall be revenged i'faith
    Come, throw off clouds now, brother; think of ven-
      geance
    And deeper settled hate; sirrah, sit fast,
    We'll pull down all, but thou shalt down at last.
    Exeunt.

ACT FOUR

*

SCENE ONE

Enter LUSSURIOSO *with* HIPPOLITO.

LUSSURIOSO: Hippolito.

HIPPOLITO: My lord –
  Has your good lordship aught to command me in?

LUSSURIOSO: I prithee leave us.

HIPPOLITO: How's this? – come, and leave us?

LUSSURIOSO: Hippolito.

HIPPOLITO: Your honour, I stand ready for any duteous
    employment.

LUSSURIOSO: Heart, what mak'st thou here?

HIPPOLITO [*aside*]: A pretty lordly humour;
  He bids me to be present to depart;
  Something has stung his honour.

LUSSURIOSO: Be nearer, draw nearer: 10
  You are not so good, methinks, I'm angry with you.

HIPPOLITO: With me, my lord? I'm angry with myself
    for't.

LUSSURIOSO: You did prefer a goodly fellow to me,
  'Twas wittily elected, 'twas; I thought
  'Had been a villain, and he proves a knave –
  To me a knave.

HIPPOLITO: I chose him for the best, my lord,
  'Tis much my sorrow if neglect in him
  Breed discontent in you.

LUSSURIOSO: Neglect? 'Twas will: judge of it –   20
  Firmly to tell of an incredible act,
  Not to be thought, less to be spoken of,
  'Twixt my stepmother and the bastard, – oh!
  Incestuous sweets between 'em.

HIPPOLITO: Fie my lord!

LUSSURIOSO: I, in kind loyalty to my father's forehead,
  Made this a desperate arm, and in that fury

Committed treason on the lawful bed
And with my sword e'en razed my father's bosom
30 For which I was within a stroke of death.
HIPPOLITO: Alack! I'm sorry. [*Aside*] 'Sfoot! just upon
the stroke
Jars in my brother; 'twill be villainous music.
    Enter VINDICE.
VINDICE: My honoured lord –
LUSSURIOSO: Away, prithee forsake us! Hereafter we'll
not know thee.
VINDICE: Not know me, my lord! Your lordship cannot
choose. –
LUSSURIOSO: Begone I say; thou art a false knave.
VINDICE: Why, the easier to be known, my lord.
LUSSURIOSO: Push, I shall prove too bitter with a word,
Make thee a perpetual prisoner
40 And lay this ironage upon thee.
VINDICE [*aside*]: Mum,
– For there's a doom would make a woman dumb. –
Missing the bastard next him, the wind's come about;
Now 'tis my brother's turn to stay, mine to go out.
    Exit VINDICE.
LUSSURIOSO: H' 'as greatly moved me.
HIPPOLITO: Much to blame i'faith.
LUSSURIOSO: But I'll recover, to his ruin. – 'Twas told me
lately, –
I know not whether falsely – that you'd a brother.
HIPPOLITO: Who, I? Yes my good lord, I have a brother.
LUSSURIOSO: How chance the court ne'er saw him? Of
what nature?
How does he apply his hours?
50 HIPPOLITO: 'Faith, to curse fates,
Who, as he thinks, ordained him to be poor, –
Keeps at home, full of want and discontent.
LUSSURIOSO [*aside*]: There's hope in him, for discontent
and want

32. *Jars in*: enters discordantly.   40. *Ironage*: fetters.

Is the best clay to mould a villain of. –
Hippolito, wish him repair to us;
If there be aught in him to please our blood
For thy sake we'll advance him and build fair
His meanest fortunes: for it is in us
To rear up towers from cottages.

HIPPOLITO: It is so, my lord; he will attend your honour, 60
But he's a man in whom much melancholy dwells.

LUSSURIOSO: Why, the better: bring him to court.

HIPPOLITO: With willingness and speed.
[*Aside*] Whom he cast off e'en now must now succeed;
Brother, disguise must off,
In thine own shape now I'll prefer thee to him:
How strangely does himself work to undo him.
Exit.

LUSSURIOSO: This fellow will come fitly; he shall kill
That other slave that did abuse my spleen
And made it swell to treason. I have put 70
Much of my heart into him, he must die.
He that knows great men's secrets and proves slight,
That man ne'er lives to see his beard turn white.
Ay, he shall speed him: I'll employ thee, brother;
Slaves are but nails to drive out one another.
He, being of black condition, suitable
To want and ill content, hope of preferment
Will grind him to an edge.
The NOBLES *enter.*

FIRST NOBLE: Good days unto your honour.

LUSSURIOSO: My kind lords, I do return the like. 80

SECOND NOBLE: Saw you my lord the Duke?

LUSSURIOSO: My lord and father – is he from court?

FIRST NOBLE: He's sure from court,
But where, which way his pleasure took we know
not;

72. *Slight:* unreliable.
76. *Black condition:* melancholy disposition.
82. *From:* away from.

Nor can we hear on 't.
[*Enter more* NOBLES.]

LUSSURIOSO: Here come those should tell.
Saw you my lord and father?

THIRD NOBLE: Not since two hours before noon, my
lord,
And then he privately rid forth.

90 LUSSURIOSO: Oh, he's rid forth.

FIRST NOBLE: 'Twas wondrous privately.

SECOND NOBLE: There's none i'th'court had any knowledge on't.

LUSSURIOSO: His Grace is old and sudden; 'tis no treason
To say the Duke my father has a humour
Or such a toy about him; what in us
Would appear light, in him seems virtuous.

THIRD NOBLE: 'Tis oracle, my lord.
Exeunt.

[SCENE TWO]

Enter VINDICE *and* HIPPOLITO, VINDICE *out of his
disguise.*

HIPPOLITO: So so, all's as it should be, y'are your self.

VINDICE: How that great villain puts me to my shifts!

HIPPOLITO: He that did lately in disguise reject thee
Shall, now thou art thy self, as much respect thee.

VINDICE: 'Twill be the quainter fallacy; but brother
'Sfoot, what use will he put me to now, think'st thou?

HIPPOLITO: Nay you must pardon me in that, I know not:
H' 'as some employment for you, but what 'tis
He and his secretary the devil knows best.

10 VINDICE: Well, I must suit my tongue to his desires,
What colour so e'er they be, hoping at last
To pile up all my wishes on his breast.

HIPPOLITO: 'Faith brother, he himself shows the way.

VINDICE: Now the duke is dead, the realm is clad in clay:

His death being not yet known, under his name
The people still are governed. Well, thou his son
Art not long-lived; thou shalt not 'joy his death.
To kill thee then I should most honour thee;
For 'twould stand firm in every man's belief,
Thou'st a kind child and only diedst with grief.   20

HIPPOLITO: You fetch about well, but let's talk in present;
How will you appear in fashion different
As well as in apparel, to make all things possible;
If you be but once tripped, we fall for ever.
It is not the least policy to be doubtful;
You must change tongue – familiar was your first.

VINDICE: Why, I'll bear me in some strain of melancholy
And string myself with heavy-sounding wire,
Like such an instrument that speaks merry things sadly.

HIPPOLITO: Then 'tis as I meant;   30
I gave you out at first in discontent.

VINDICE: I'll turn myself, and then –

HIPPOLITO: 'Sfoot here he comes; hast thought upon't?

VINDICE: Salute him, fear not me.

    [*Enter* LUSSURIOSO.]

LUSSURIOSO: Hippolito.

HIPPOLITO: Your lordship –

LUSSURIOSO: What's he yonder?

HIPPOLITO: 'Tis Vindice, my discontented brother,
Whom, 'cording to your will I've brought to court.

LUSSURIOSO: Is that thy brother? Beshrew me, a good
    presence;
I wonder h' 'as been from the court so long.
Come nearer.   40

HIPPOLITO: Brother, Lord Lussurioso, the Duke['s] son.

LUSSURIOSO: Be more near to us, welcome, nearer yet.

VINDICE: How don you? God you god den.
    Snatches off his hat and makes legs to him.

20. *Kind:* natural. This usage is frequent throughout the play.
25. *Doubtful:* hesitant.
43. *God . . . den:* God give you good day.

LUSSURIOSO: We thank thee.
How strangely such a coarse-homely salute
Shows in the palace, where we greet in fire,
Nimble and desperate tongues. Should we name
God in a salutation, 'twould ne'er be stood on't –
heaven!
Tell me what has made thee so melancholy.

50 VINDICE: Why, going to law.

LUSSURIOSO: Why, will that make a man melancholy?

VINDICE: Yes, to look long upon ink and black buckram.
I went me to law in *Anno Quadragesimo Secundo*, and I
waded out of it in *Anno Sextagesimo Tertio*.

LUSSURIOSO: What, three and twenty years in law?

VINDICE: I have known those that have been five and
fifty, and all about pullin and pigs.

LUSSURIOSO: May it be possible such men should breathe
To vex the terms so much?

60 VINDICE: 'Tis food to some, my lord. There are old men
at the present that are so poisoned with the affectation
of law-words – having had many suits canvassed – that
their common talk is nothing but Barbary Latin: they
cannot so much as pray but in law, that their sins may be
removed with a writ of error, and their souls fetched up
to heaven with a sasarara.

LUSSURIOSO: It seems most strange to me,
Yet all the world meets round in the same bent:
Where the heart's set, there goes the tongue's consent.
70 How dost apply thy studies, fellow?

VINDICE: Study? Why, to think how a great rich man lies
a-dying, and a poor cobbler tolls the bell for him. How
he cannot depart the world, and see the great chest stand
before him; when he lies speechless, how he will point

53–4. *Anno Quadragesimo Secundo*: forty-second year. *Anno Sexta-gesimo Tertio*: sixty-third year.
57. *Pullin*: poultry.   59. *Terms*: legal sessions.
63. *Barbary Latin*: barbarous Latin.
66. *Sasarara*: writ of *certiorari*.

you readily to all the boxes; and when he is past all
memory – as the gossips guess – then thinks he of for-
feitures and obligations; nay, when to all men's hearings
he whirls and rattles in the throat, he's busy threatening
his poor tenants; and this would last me now some seven
years' thinking or thereabouts. But I have a conceit 80
a-coming in picture upon this – I draw it myself – which
i'faith, la, I'll present to your honour; you shall not
choose but like it, for your lordship shall give me
nothing for it.

LUSSURIOSO: Nay, you mistake me then,
For I am published bountiful enough.
Let's taste of your conceit.

VINDICE: In picture, my lord?

LUSSURIOSO: Ay, in picture.

VINDICE: Marry, this it is – 'A usuring Father to be
boiling in hell, and his Son and heir with a Whore 90
dancing over him.'

HIPPOLITO [*aside*]: H'as pared him to the quick.

LUSSURIOSO: The conceit's pretty i'faith,
But take't upon my life 'twill ne'er be liked.

VINDICE: No? Why, I'm sure the whore will be liked well
enough.

HIPPOLITO [*aside*]: Ay, if she were out o'th'picture he'd
like her then himself.

VINDICE: And as for the son and heir, he shall be an
eyesore to no young revellers, for he shall be drawn in
cloth-of-gold breeches.

LUSSURIOSO: An thou hast put my meaning in the
pockets   100
And canst not draw that out, my thought was this,
To see the picture of a usuring father
Boiling in hell, our rich men would ne'er like it.

VINDICE: O true, I cry you heart'ly mercy. I know the
reason, for some of them had rather be damned indeed
than damned in colours.

80. *Conceit:* conception.

LUSSURIOSO [*aside*]: A parlous melancholy! H'as wit
  enough
  To murder any man, and I'll give him means. –
  I think thou art ill moneyed.
VINDICE: Money, ho, ho!
110 'T'as been my want so long, 'tis now my scoff.
  I've e'en forgot what colour silver's of.
LUSSURIOSO [*aside*]: It hits as I could wish.
VINDICE: I get good clothes
  Of those that dread my humour, and for table-room
  I feed on those that cannot be rid of me.
LUSSURIOSO: Somewhat to set thee up withal.
  [*Gives him gold.*]
VINDICE: O mine eyes!
LUSSURIOSO: How now, man?
VINDICE: Almost struck blind;
  This bright unusual shine to me seems proud,
  I dare not look till the sun be in a cloud.
LUSSURIOSO [*aside*]: I think I shall affect his melancholy. –
  How are they now?   .
120 VINDICE: The better for your asking.
LUSSURIOSO: You shall be better yet if you but fasten
  Truly on my intent; now y'are both present,
  I will unbrace such a close private villain
  Unto your vengeful swords, the like ne'er heard of,
  Who hath disgraced you much and injured us.
HIPPOLITO: Disgraced us, my lord?
LUSSURIOSO: Ay, Hippolito.
  I kept it here till now that both your angers
  Might meet him at once.
VINDICE: I'm covetous
  To know the villain.
LUSSURIOSO: You know him, that slave pander
130 Piato, whom we threatened last
  With irons in perpetual prisonment.
VINDICE [*aside*]: All this is I.

119. *Affect*: like.

HIPPOLITO: Is't he my lord?

LUSSURIOSO: I'll tell you – you first preferred him to me.

VINDICE: Did you, brother?

HIPPOLITO: I did indeed.

LUSSURIOSO: And the ingrateful villain,
To quit that kindness, strongly wrought with me,
Being – as you see – a likely man for pleasure,
With jewels to corrupt your virgin sister.

HIPPOLITO: O villain!

VINDICE: He shall surely die that did it.

LUSSURIOSO: I, far from thinking any virgin harm,   140
Especially knowing her to be as chaste
As that part which scarce suffers to be touched –
Th'eye – would not endure him.

VINDICE: Would you not, my lord?
'Twas wondrous honourably done.

LUSSURIOSO: But with some fine frowns kept him out.

VINDICE [*aside*]: Out, slave!

LUSSURIOSO: What did me he? But in revenge of that
Went of his own free will to make infirm
Your sister's honour, whom I honour with my soul   150
For chaste respect, and not prevailing there
– As 'twas but desperate folly to attempt it, –
In mere spleen, by the way, waylays your mother,
Whose honour being coward – as it seems –
Yielded by little force.

VINDICE: Coward indeed!

LUSSURIOSO: He, proud of this advantage – as he thought –
Brought me these news for happy; but I – heaven forgive me for't!

VINDICE: What did your Honour?

LUSSURIOSO: In rage pushed him from me
Trampled beneath his throat, spurned him, and bruised:
Indeed, I was too cruel, to say troth.   160

HIPPOLITO: Most nobly managed!

VINDICE [*aside*]: Has not heaven an ear? Is all the lightning
    wasted?

LUSSURIOSO: If I now were so impatient in a modest
    cause,
    What should you be?

VINDICE: Full mad; he shall not live
    To see the moon change.

LUSSURIOSO: He's about the palace;
    Hippolito, entice him this way, that thy brother
    May take full mark of him.

HIPPOLITO: Heart! – That shall not need, my lord;
    I can direct him so far.

LUSSURIOSO: Yet, for my hate's sake,
170   Go wind him this way; I'll see him bleed myself.

HIPPOLITO [*aside*]: What now, brother?

VINDICE [*aside*]: Nay, e'en what you will; y'are put to it,
    brother.

HIPPOLITO [*aside*]: An impossible task, I'll swear,
    To bring him hither that's already here.
      Exit HIPPOLITO.

LUSSURIOSO: Thy name? I have forgot it.

VINDICE: Vindice, my lord.

LUSSURIOSO: 'Tis a good name, that.

VINDICE: Ay, a Revenger.

LUSSURIOSO: It does betoken courage; thou shouldst be
    valiant
    And kill thine enemies.

VINDICE: That's my hope, my lord.

LUSSURIOSO: This slave is one.

VINDICE: I'll doom him.

180 LUSSURIOSO: Then I'll praise thee.
    Do thou observe me best, and I'll best raise thee.
      Enter HIPPOLITO.

VINDICE: Indeed I thank you.

LUSSURIOSO: Now Hippolito, where's the slave pander?

HIPPOLITO: Your good lordship

           181. *Observe:* serve.

Would have a loathsome sight of him, much offensive;
He's not in case now to be seen, my lord.
The worst of all the deadly sins is in him;
That beggarly damnation, drunkenness.

LUSSURIOSO: Then he's a double slave.

VINDICE [aside]: 'Twas well conveyed, upon a sudden wit. 190

LUSSURIOSO: What, are you both
Firmly resolved? I'll see him dead myself.

VINDICE: Or else let not us live.

LUSSURIOSO: You may direct your brother to take note
of him.

HIPPOLITO: I shall.

LUSSURIOSO: Rise but in this and you shall never fall.

VINDICE: Your Honour's vassals.

LUSSURIOSO [aside]: This was wisely carried;
Deep policy in us makes fools of such –
Then must a slave die, when he knows too much. 200
        Exit LUSSURIOSO.

VINDICE: O thou Almighty patience! 'tis my wonder
That such a fellow, impudent and wicked,
Should not be cloven as he stood,
Or with a secret wind burst open!
Is there no thunder left, or is't kept up
In stock for heavier vengeance? [Thunder.] There it goes!

HIPPOLITO: Brother, we lose ourselves.

VINDICE: But I have found it,
'Twill hold, 'tis sure; thanks, thanks to any spirit
That mingled it 'mongst my inventions.

HIPPOLITO: What is 't?

VINDICE: 'Tis sound and good, thou shalt partake it: 210
I'm hired to kill myself.

HIPPOLITO: True

VINDICE: Prithee, mark it:
And the old Duke being dead, but not conveyed,
For he's already missed too, and you know,
Murder will peep out of the closest husk.

HIPPOLITO: Most true.

VINDICE: What say you then to this device:
  If we dressed up the body of the Duke –
HIPPOLITO: In that disguise of yours –
VINDICE: Y'are quick, y'ave reached it.
HIPPOLITO: I like it wondrously.
VINDICE: And being in drink, as you have published him,
220 To lean him on his elbow, as if sleep had caught him,
  Which claims most interest in such sluggish men.
HIPPOLITO: Good, yet – but here's a doubt:
  We, thought by the Duke's son to kill that pander,
  Shall, when he is known, be thought to kill the Duke.
VINDICE: Neither, O thanks! It is substantial.
  For that disguise being on him which I wore,
  It will be thought I, which he calls the pander,
  Did kill the Duke, and fled away in his
  Apparel, leaving him so disguised
  To avoid swift pursuit.
230 HIPPOLITO: Firmer and firmer.
VINDICE: Nay doubt not, 'tis in grain, I warrant it
  Hold colour.
HIPPOLITO: Let's about it.
VINDICE: But by the way too, now I think on't, brother,
  Let's conjure that base devil out of our mother.
    Exeunt.

[SCENE THREE]

Enter the DUCHESS *arm in arm with the Bastard: he
seemeth lasciviously to her; after them, enter* SUPER-
VACUO, *running with a rapier; his brother* [AMBITIOSO]
stops him.

SPURIO: Madam, unlock yourself; should it be seen
  Your arm would be suspected.
DUCHESS: Who is't that dares suspect or this or these?
  [*Kissing him.*]
  May not we deal our favours where we please?

SPURIO: I'm confident you may.
   Exeunt.
AMBITIOSO: 'Sfoot brother, hold.
SUPERVACUO: Woul't let the bastard shame us?
AMBITIOSO: Hold, hold, brother! There's fitter time than
   now.
SUPERVACUO: Now, when I see it.
AMBITIOSO: 'Tis too much seen already.
SUPERVACUO: Seen and known.
   The nobler she's, the baser is she grown.   10
AMBITIOSO: If she were bent lasciviously – the fault
   Of mighty women that sleep soft, – O death,
   Must she needs choose such an unequal sinner,
   To make all worse?
SUPERVACUO: A bastard, the Duke's bastard! Shame
   heaped on shame!
AMBITIOSO: O our disgrace!
   Most women have small waist the world throughout,
   But their desires are thousand miles about.
SUPERVACUO: Come, stay not here, let's after and prevent,
   Or else they'll sin faster than we'll repent.   20
   Exeunt.

[SCENE FOUR]

Enter VINDICE *and* HIPPOLITO *bringing out their
Mother, one by one shoulder and the other by the other, with
daggers in their hands.*

VINDICE: O thou for whom no name is bad enough!
GRATIANA: What means my sons? What, will you murder
   me?
VINDICE: Wicked, unnatural parent!
HIPPOLITO: Fiend of women!
GRATIANA: Oh, are sons turned monsters? Help!
VINDICE: In vain.

GRATIANA: Are you so barbarous to set iron nipples
Upon the breast that gave you suck?

VINDICE: That breast
Is turned to quarlèd poison.

GRATIANA: Cut not your days for't; am not I your
mother?

10 VINDICE: Thou dost usurp that title now by fraud,
For in that shell of mother breeds a bawd.

GRATIANA: A bawd? O name far loathsomer than hell!

HIPPOLITO: It should be so, knew'st thou thy office well.

GRATIANA: I hate it.

VINDICE: Ah, is't possible? Thou only – you powers on
high,
That women should dissemble when they die!

GRATIANA: Dissemble?

VINDICE: Did not the duke's son direct
A fellow of the world's condition hither,
That did corrupt all that was good in thee,
20 Made thee uncivilly forget thyself
And work our sister to his lust?

GRATIANA: Who? I?
That had been monstrous! I defy that man
For any such intent; none lives so pure
But shall be soiled with slander.
Good son, believe it not.

VINDICE: Oh, I'm in doubt
Whether I'm myself or no!
Stay, let me look again upon this face.
Who shall be saved when mothers have no grace?

HIPPOLITO: 'Twould make one half despair.

VINDICE: I was the man.
30 Defy me now, let's see! Do't modestly.

GRATIANA: O hell unto my soul!

VINDICE: In that disguise I, sent from the Duke's son,
Tried you, and found you base metal,
As any villain might have done.

8. *Quarlèd:* curdled.

GRATIANA: O no, no tongue but yours could have
bewitched me so.

VINDICE: O nimble in damnation, quick in tune!
There is no devil could strike fire so soon. –
I am confuted in a word.

GRATIANA: Oh sons, forgive me! To my self I'll prove
more true.
You that should honour me, I kneel to you.   40
[*Kneels, weeping.*]

VINDICE: A mother to give aim to her own daughter!

HIPPOLITO: True, brother; how far beyond nature 'tis,
Tho' many mothers do't!

VINDICE: Nay, an you draw tears once, go you to bed;
Wet will make iron blush and change to red.
Brother, it rains; 'twill spoil your dagger, house it.

HIPPOLITO: 'Tis done.

VINDICE: I'faith, 'tis a sweet shower, it does much good:
The fruitful grounds and meadows of her soul
Has been long dry; pour down, thou blessed dew!   50
Rise, mother; troth, this shower has made you higher.

GRATIANA: O you heavens, take this infectious spot out of
my soul!
I'll rinse it in seven waters of mine eyes.
Make my tears salt enough to taste of grace;
To weep is to our sex naturally given,
But to weep truly, that's a gift from heaven.

VINDICE: Nay, I'll kiss you now. Kiss her, brother,
Let's marry her to our souls, wherein's no lust,
And honourably love her.

HIPPOLITO: Let it be.

VINDICE: For honest women are so seld and rare   60
'Tis good to cherish those poor few that are.
Oh you of easy wax! Do but imagine,
Now the disease has left you, how leprously
That office would have clinged unto your forehead.
All mothers that had any graceful hue

65. Graceful hue: touch of (divine) grace.

Would have worn masks to hide their face at you.
It would have grown to this – at your foul name,
Green-coloured maids would have turned red with shame.

HIPPOLITO: And then, our sister full of hire and baseness!

70 VINDICE: There had been boiling lead again.
Duke's son's great concubine!
A drab of state, a cloth o'silver slut,
To have her train borne up, and her soul trail i'th'dirt.

HIPPOLITO: Great, too miserably great! Rich to be
eternally wretched.

VINDICE: O common madness!
Ask but the thriving'st harlot in cold blood,
She'd give the world to make her honour good.
Perhaps you'll say: but only to the Duke's son
In private. Why, she first begins with one

80 Who afterward[s] to thousand proves a whore:
'Break ice in one place, it will crack in more.'

GRATIANA: Most certainly applied.

HIPPOLITO: Oh brother, you forget our business.

VINDICE: And well remembered; joy's a subtle elf;
I think man's happiest when he forgets himself.
Farewell, once dried, now holy-watered mead,
Our hearts wear feathers, that before wore lead.

GRATIANA: I'll give you this: that one I never knew
Plead better for and 'gainst the devil, than you.

90 VINDICE: You make me proud on't.

HIPPOLITO: Commend us in all virtue to our sister.

VINDICE: Ay, for the love of heaven, to that true maid.

GRATIANA: With my best words.

VINDICE: Why, that was motherly said.
    Exeunt.

GRATIANA: I wonder now what fury did transport me.
I feel good thoughts begin to settle in me.
Oh, with what forehead can I look on her
Whose honour I've so impiously beset.
– And here she comes.
    [*Enter* CASTIZA.]

CASTIZA: Now, mother, you have wrought with me so strongly
That what for my advancement, as to calm   100
The trouble of your tongue, I am content.
GRATIANA: Content to what?
CASTIZA: To do as you have wished me,
To prostitute my breast to the Duke's son
And put myself to common usury.
GRATIANA: I hope you will not so.
CASTIZA: Hope you I will not?
That's not the hope you look to be saved in.
GRATIANA: Truth, but it is.
CASTIZA: Do not deceive yourself.
I am as you, e'en out of marble wrought.
What would you now? Are you not pleased yet with me?
You shall not wish me to be more lascivious   110
Than I intend to be.
GRATIANA: Strike not me cold.
CASTIZA: How often have you charged me on your blessing
To be a curséd woman? When you knew
Your blessing had no force to make me lewd,
You laid your curse upon me. That did more;
The mother's curse is heavy – where that fights,
Sons set in storm, and daughters lose their lights.
GRATIANA: Good child, dear maid, if there be any spark
Of heavenly intellectual fire within thee,
O let my breath revive it to a flame!   120
Put not all out with woman's wilful follies.
I am recovered of that foul disease
That haunts too many mothers; kind, forgive me.
Make me not sick in health. If then
My words prevailed when they were wickedness,
How much more now, when they are just and good!
CASTIZA: I wonder what you mean. Are not you she
For whose infect persuasions I could scarce

123. *Kind:* kin (also Nature generally?).

Kneel out my prayers, and had much ado
130   In three hours' reading, to untwist so much
Of the black serpent as you wound about me?

GRATIANA: 'Tis unfruitful, held tedious, to repeat what's
    past;
I'm now your present mother.

CASTIZA: Push, now 'tis too late.

GRATIANA: Bethink again, thou know'st not what thou
    say'st.

CASTIZA: No? Deny advancement, treasure, the Duke's son?

GRATIANA: O see, I spoke those words and now they
    poison me.
What will the deed do then?
Advancement? True, as high as shame can pitch.
For treasure — whoe'er knew a harlot rich,
140   Or could build by the purchase of her sin
An hospital to keep their bastards in?
The Duke's son — oh, when women are young courtiers,
They are sure to be old beggars.
To know the miseries most harlots taste,
Thou'dst wish thyself unborn when thou'rt unchaste.

CASTIZA: O mother, let me twine about your neck
And kiss you till my soul melt on your lips.
— I did but this to try you.

GRATIANA: O speak truth.

CASTIZA: Indeed, I did not; for no tongue has force
150   To alter me from honest.
If maidens would, men's words could have no power;
A virgin honour is a crystal tower
Which, being weak, is guarded with good spirits;
Until she basely yields, no ill inherits.

GRATIANA: O happy child! Faith and thy birth hath
    saved me.
'Mongst thousand daughters, happiest of all others,
Be thou a glass for maids, and I for mothers.
    Exeunt.

154. *Inherits:* takes possession of.

[ACT FIVE]

*

[SCENE ONE]

Enter VINDICE *and* HIPPOLITO, [*with the Duke's corpse.*]

VINDICE: So, so, he leans well; take heed you wake him not, brother.

HIPPOLITO: I warrant you my life for yours.

VINDICE: That's a good lay, for I must kill myself. Brother, that's I: [*Pointing to corpse*] that sits for me: do you mark it. And I must stand ready here to make away myself yonder. I must sit to be killed, and stand to kill myself. I could vary it not so little as thrice over again; 't'as some eight returns, like Michaelmas Term.

HIPPOLITO: That's enow, o'conscience.

VINDICE: But sirrah, does the Duke's son come single?   10

HIPPOLITO: No, there's the hell on't. His faith's too feeble to go alone; he brings flesh-flies after him, that will buzz against supper time and hum for his coming out.

VINDICE: Ah, the fly-flop of vengeance beat 'em to pieces! Here was the sweetest occasion, the fittest hour to have made my revenge familiar with him, – show him the body of the Duke his father, and how quaintly he died, like a politician, in hugger-mugger, made no man acquainted with it, – and in catastrophe slain him over his father's breast! And oh, I'm mad to lose such a sweet opportunity!   20

HIPPOLITO: Nay, push, prithee be content. There's no remedy present. May not hereafter times open in as fair faces as this?

VINDICE: They may, if they can paint so well.

HIPPOLITO: Come now, to avoid all suspicion let's forsake this room and be going to meet the Duke's son.

18. *Politician:* intriguer. *Hugger-mugger:* secrecy.
19. *Catastrophe:* conclusion and climax (of a play).

VINDICE: Content, I'm for any weather. Heart, step close;
here he comes.

Enter LUSSURIOSO.

HIPPOLITO: My honoured lord.

LUSSURIOSO: Oh me! You both present?

30 VINDICE: E'en newly my lord, just as your lordship
entered now. About this place we had notice given he
should be, but in some loathsome plight or other.

HIPPOLITO: Came your honour private?

LUSSURIOSO: Private enough for this: only a few
Attend my coming out.

HIPPOLITO [*aside*]: Death rot those few.

LUSSURIOSO: Stay, yonder's the slave.

VINDICE: Mass, there's the slave indeed, my lord.
Aside] 'Tis a good child; he calls his father slave.

LUSSURIOSO: Ay, that's the villain, the damned villain;
40   softly.
Tread easy.

VINDICE: Push, I warrant you, my lord
We'll stifle in our breaths.

LUSSURIOSO: That will do well.
Base rogue, thou sleepest thy last. [*Aside*] 'Tis policy
To have him killed in's sleep, for if he waked
He would betray all to them.

VINDICE: But my lord –

LUSSURIOSO: Ha, – what say'st?

VINDICE: Shall we kill him now he's drunk?

LUSSURIOSO: Ay, best of all.

VINDICE: Why, then he will ne'er live to be sober.

LUSSURIOSO: No matter, let him reel to hell.

VINDICE: But being so full of liquor, I fear he will put out
50   all the fire.

LUSSURIOSO: Thou art a mad beast.

VINDICE [*aside*]: And leave none to warm your lordship's
gols withal; for he that dies drunk falls into hell-fire like
a bucket o'water, qush, qush.

52. *Gols:* hands.

LUSSURIOSO: Come, be ready; nake your swords, think
   of your wrongs.
  This slave has injured you.

VINDICE: Troth, so he has, – and he has paid well for't.

LUSSURIOSO: Meet with him now.

VINDICE: You'll bear us out, my lord?

LUSSURIOSO: Puh, am I a lord for nothing, think you?
  Quickly now.

VINDICE [*stabbing Duke's corpse*]: Sa, sa, sa!

                        Thump, there he lies.

LUSSURIOSO: Nimbly done! Ha! Oh villains, murderers!
  'Tis the old Duke my father.

VINDICE: That's a jest.

LUSSURIOSO: What – stiff and cold already?
  O pardon me to call you from your names –
  'Tis none of your deed. That villain Piato,
  Whom you thought now to kill, has murdered him
  And left him thus disguised.

HIPPOLITO: And not unlikely.

VINDICE: O rascal, was he not ashamed
  To put the Duke into a greasy doublet?   70

LUSSURIOSO: He has been cold and stiff – who knows how
   long?

VINDICE [*aside*]: Marry, that do I.

LUSSURIOSO: No words, I pray, of any thing intended.

VINDICE: Oh my lord.

HIPPOLITO: I would fain have your lordship think that we
  Have small reason to prate.

LUSSURIOSO: 'Faith, thou sayest true. I'll forthwith send
   to court
  For all the nobles, bastard, duchess, all –
  How here by miracle we found him dead
  And in his raiment that foul villain fled.   80

VINDICE: That will be the best way my lord, to clear
  Us all; let's cast about to be clear.

55. *Nake:* unsheath.
61. *Sa, sa, sa:* expression used in fencing. (French 'Ça'.)

LUSSURIOSO: Ho, Nencio, Sordido, and the rest!
   Enter all [his SERVANTS].
FIRST [SERVANT]: My lord?
SECOND [SERVANT]:   My lord?
LUSSURIOSO: Be witnesses of a strange spectacle. –
   Choosing for private conference that sad room,
   We found the Duke my father 'gealed in blood.
FIRST [SERVANT]: My lord the Duke! Run, hie thee
   Nencio –
90   Startle the court by signifying so much.
   [*Exit* NENCIO.]
VINDICE [*aside*]: Thus much by wit a deep Revenger can,
   When murder's known, to be the clearest man.
   We're farthest off, and with as bold an eye
   Survey his body, as the standers-by.
LUSSURIOSO: My royal father, too basely let blood
   By a malevolent slave!
HIPPOLITO [*aside*]: Hark, he calls thee slave again.
VINDICE [*aside*]:   H'as lost, he may.
LUSSURIOSO: Oh sight! Look hither, see, his lips are
   gnawn
   With poison.
100 VINDICE: How? – His lips? By th'Mass, they be.
   O villain! O rogue! O slave! O rascal!
HIPPOLITO [*aside*]: O good deceit, he quits him with like
   terms.
[VOICES WITHIN]: Where? Which way?
   [*Enter* AMBITIOSO *and* SUPERVACUO, *with Courtiers.*]
AMBITIOSO: Over what roof hangs this prodigious comet
   In deadly fire.
LUSSURIOSO: Behold, behold, my lords!
   The Duke my father's murdered by a vassal
   That owes this habit and here left disguised.
   [*Enter* DUCHESS *and* SPURIO.]
DUCHESS: My lord and husband!

86. *Room:* place.   102. *Quits:* pays back.
107. *Owes:* owns. *Habit:* garment.

[FIRST NOBLE]:   Reverend Majesty.

[SECOND NOBLE]: I have seen these clothes often attending on him.

VINDICE [*aside*]: That nobleman has been i'th'country, for
he does not lie.   110

SUPERVACUO [*aside*]: Learn of our mother, let's dissemble
too.

I am glad he's vanished; so I hope are you.

AMBITIOSO [*aside*]: Ay, you may take my word for't.

SPURIO [*aside*]: Old dad dead?

I, one of his cast sins, will send the fates

Most hearty commendations by his own son;

I'll tug in the new stream till strength be done.

LUSSURIOSO: Where be those two that did affirm to us

My lord the duke was privately rid forth?

FIRST [NOBLE]: O pardon us my lords, he gave that
charge   120

Upon our lives, if he were missed at court

To answer so; he rode not anywhere

We left him private with that fellow here.

VINDICE: Confirmed.

LUSSURIOSO: O heavens, that false charge was his death!

Impudent beggars! Durst you to our face

Maintain such a false answer? Bear him straight

To execution.

FIRST [NOBLE]: My lord!

LUSSURIOSO: Urge me no more.

In this the excuse may be called half the murder.

VINDICE: You've sentenced well.

                                    Away, see it be done.   130

[*Exit* FIRST NOBLE *under guard.*]

VINDICE [*aside*]: Could you not stick? See what confession
doth –

Who would not lie when men are hanged for truth?

HIPPOLITO [*aside*]: Brother, how happy is our vengeance!

VINDICE [*aside*]:   Why, it hits

Past the apprehension of indifferent wits.

LUSSURIOSO: My lord, let post-horse be sent
Into all places to entrap the villain.

VINDICE [*aside*]: Post-horse! Ha, ha!

NOBLE: My lord, we're something bold to know our
duty:
Your father's accidentally departed;
140   The titles that were due to him meet you.

LUSSURIOSO: Meet me? I'm not at leisure my good lord,
I've many griefs to dispatch out o'th'way.
[*Aside*] Welcome, sweet titles. – Talk to me, my lords,
Of sepulchres and mighty emperors' bones;
That's thought for me.

VINDICE [*aside*]:   So, one may see by this
How foreign markets go:
Courtiers have feet o'th'nines, and tongues o'th'twelves,
They flatter dukes and dukes flatter themselves.

NOBLE: My lord, it is your shine must comfort us.

150 LUSSURIOSO: Alas, I shine in tears, like the sun in April.

NOBLE: You're now my lord's Grace.

LUSSURIOSO: My lord's Grace! I perceive you'll have it so.

NOBLE: 'Tis but your own.

LUSSURIOSO: Then heavens give me grace to be so.

VINDICE [*aside*]: He prays well for himself.

NOBLE [*to* DUCHESS]: Madam, all sorrows
Must run their circles into joys; no doubt
But time will make the murderer bring forth himself.

VINDICE [*aside*]: He were an ass then, i' faith.

160 NOBLE: In the mean season,
Let us bethink the latest funeral honours
Due to the Duke's cold body, – and withal
Calling to memory our new happiness,
Spread in his royal son; – lords, gentlemen,
Prepare for revels.

VINDICE [*aside*]:   Revels!

NOBLE: Time hath several falls;
Griefs lift up joys, feasts put down funerals.

       146. *Foreign markets:* abandoned titles.

LUSSURIOSO: Come then my lords, my favours to you all.
  [*Aside*] The duchess is suspected foully bent;
  I'll begin dukedom with her banishment.   170
    Exeunt [LUSSURIOSO] NOBLES *and* DUCHESS.
HIPPOLITO [*aside*]: Revels!
VINDICE [*aside*]:   Ay, that's the word, we are firm yet;
  Strike one strain more, and then we crown our wit.
    Exeunt Brothers.

SPURIO [*aside*]: Well, have at the fairest mark,
  So said the Duke when he begot me;
  And if I miss his heart or near about
  Then have at any – a bastard scorns to be out.
    [*Exit.*]
SUPERVACUO: Not'st thou that Spurio, brother?
AMBITIOSO: Yes, I note him to our shame.
SUPERVACUO: He shall not live; his hair shall not grow
      much longer.
  In this time of revels, tricks may be set afoot.   180
  Seest thou yon new moon? It shall outlive
  The new duke by much; this hand shall dispossess him,
  Then we're mighty.
  A mask is treason's licence, that build upon;
  'Tis murder's best face when a vizard's on.
    Exit SUPERVACUO.
AMBITIOSO: Is't so? 'Tis very good.
  And do you think to be Duke then, kind brother?
  I'll see fair play; drop one, and there lies t'other.
    Exit AMBITIOSO.

[SCENE TWO]

Enter VINDICE *and* HIPPOLITO *with* PIERO *and other*
LORDS.
VINDICE: My lords, be all of music! Strike old griefs into
    other countries

185. *Vizard:* mask.

That flow in too much milk and have faint livers,
Not daring to stab home their discontents.
Let our hid flames break out, as fire, as lightning,
To blast this villainous dukedom vexed with sin;
Wind up your souls to their full height again!

PIERO: How?

FIRST [LORD]: Which way?

[SECOND LORD]: Any way; our wrongs are such

10   We cannot justly be revenged too much.

VINDICE: You shall have all enough: revels are toward,
And those few nobles that have long suppressed you
Are busied to the furnishing of a mask
And do affect to make a pleasant tail on't.
The masking suits are fashioning; now comes in
That which must glad us all – we too take pattern
Of all those suits, the colour, trimming, fashion,
E'en to an undistinguished hair almost:
Then, entering first, observing the true form,

20   Within a strain or two we shall find leisure
To steal our swords out handsomely,
And when they think their pleasure sweet and good,
In midst of all their joys they shall sigh blood.

PIERO: Weightily, effectually!

THIRD [LORD]:   Before the tother maskers come –

VINDICE: We're gone, all done and past.

PIERO: But how for the Duke's guard?

VINDICE: Let that alone;
By one and one their strengths shall be drunk down.

HIPPOLITO: There are five hundred gentlemen in the action
That will apply themselves, and not stand idle.

30 PIERO: Oh let us hug our bosoms!

VINDICE: Come my lords,
Prepare for deeds, let other times have words.

Exeunt.

14. *Affect:* wish.
30. *Hug our bosoms:* be determined and keep our own counsel.

[SCENE THREE]

*In a dumb show, the possessing of the young Duke
[LUSSURIOSO], with all his Nobles: then sounding music.
A furnished table is brought forth: then enters the DUKE and
his NOBLES to the banquet. A blazing star appeareth.*

[FIRST] NOBLE: Many harmonious hours and choicest
   pleasures
Fill up the royal numbers of your years.

LUSSURIOSO: My lords, we're pleased to thank you, tho'
   we know
'Tis but your duty, now to wish it so.

[SECOND] NOBLE: That shine makes us all happy.

THIRD NOBLE: His grace frowns.

SECOND NOBLE: Yet we must say he smiles.

FIRST NOBLE: I think we must.

LUSSURIOSO [*aside*]: That foul, incontinent duchess we
   have banished;
The bastard shall not live: after these revels
I'll begin strange ones; he and the stepsons
Shall pay their lives for the first subsidies.   10
We must not frown so soon, else't'ad been now.

FIRST NOBLE: My gracious lord, please you prepare for
   pleasure,
The mask is not far off.

LUSSURIOSO: We are for pleasure.
Beshrew thee! What art thou mad'st me start?
Thou hast committed treason. – A blazing star!

FIRST NOBLE: A blazing star! O where, my lord?

LUSSURIOSO: Spy out.

SECOND NOBLE: See, see, my lords, a wondrous dreadful
   one!

LUSSURIOSO: I am not pleased at that ill-knotted fire,
That bushing-flaring star: – am not I Duke?

S.D. *Possessing:* coronation. *Furnished:* laid for banqueting.

20 It should not quake me now; had it appeared
Before it, I might then have justly feared.
But yet, they say whom art and learning weds,
When stars wear locks, they threaten great men's heads.
Is it so? You are read, my lords.

FIRST NOBLE: May it please your Grace,
It shows great anger.

LUSSURIOSO: That does not please our grace.

SECOND NOBLE: Yet here's the comfort, my lord; many
times,
When it seems most, it threatens farthest off.

LUSSURIOSO: 'Faith, and I think so too.

30 FIRST NOBLE: Beside, my lord,
You're gracefully established with the loves
Of all your subjects: and for natural death,
I hope it will be threescore years a-coming.

LUSSURIOSO: True. – No more but threescore years?

FIRST NOBLE: Fourscore I hope, my lord.

SECOND NOBLE: And fivescore, I.

THIRD NOBLE: But 'tis my hope, my lord, you shall ne'er
die.

LUSSURIOSO: Give me thy hand, these others I rebuke;
He that hopes so is fittest for a duke.
– Thou shalt sit next me. Take your places, lords,
40 We're ready now for sports, let 'em set on.
You thing! We shall forget you quite anon.

THIRD NOBLE: I hear 'em coming, my lord.

Enter the Mask of Revengers, the two Brothers [VINDICE
and HIPPOLITO] *and two Lords more.*

LUSSURIOSO: Ah 'tis well.

[*Aside.*] Brothers, and bastard, you dance next in hell.
*The Revengers dance. At the end, steal out their swords, and
these four kill the four at the table, in their chairs. It thunders.*

VINDICE: Mark, thunder!
Dost know thy cue, thou big-voiced crier?
Dukes' groans are thunder's watch words.

21. *Before it:* before he became duke.

HIPPOLITO: So, my lords, you have enough.
VINDICE: Come, let's away – no lingering.
HIPPOLITO: Follow, go!
    Exeunt. [VINDICE *remains.*]
VINDICE: No power is angry when the lustful die:
  When thunder claps, heaven likes the tragedy.   50
    Exit VINDICE.
LUSSURIOSO: Oh! Oh!
    Enter the other Mask of intended murderers, Stepsons
    [AMBITIOSO *and* SUPERVACUO]*; Bastard; and a fourth*
    man, coming in dancing; the Duke [LUSSURIOSO] *recovers*
    a little in voice and groans – calls 'A guard, treason!'. At
    which they all start out of their measure, and turning towards
    the table, they find them all to be murdered.
SPURIO: Whose groan was that?
LUSSURIOSO: Treason! A guard!
AMBITIOSO: How now? All murdered!
SUPERVACUO: Murdered!
FOURTH [LORD]: And those his nobles?
AMBITIOSO [*aside*]: Here's a labour saved;
  I thought to have sped him. 'Sblood! How came this?
SUPERVACUO: Then I proclaim myself! Now I am Duke.
AMBITIOSO: Thou duke! Brother, thou liest!
    [*He slays* SUPERVACUO.]
SPURIO: Slave, so dost thou!
    [*He slays* AMBITIOSO.]
FOURTH [LORD]: Base villain, hast thou slain my lord and
  master?   60
    [*He slays* SPURIO.]
    Enter the first men [VINDICE, HIPPOLITO *and the two*
    LORDS.]
VINDICE: Pistols! Treason! Murder! Help, guard my lord
  the Duke!
    [*Enter* ANTONIO *with a Guard.*]
HIPPOLITO: Lay hold upon this traitor!
    [*They seize* FOURTH LORD.]
        51. S.D. *Measure*: dance.

LUSSURIOSO: Oh!

VINDICE: Alas, the Duke is murdered!

HIPPOLITO: And the nobles.

VINDICE: Surgeons, surgeons! [*Aside*] Heart, does he
   breathe so long?

ANTONIO: A piteous tragedy! Able to wake
An old man, 's eyes bloodshot.

LUSSURIOSO: Oh!

VINDICE: Look to my lord the Duke. [*Aside*] A vengeance
   throttle him. –

Confess, thou murderous and unhallowed man,
Didst thou kill all these?

FOURTH [LORD]:   None but the bastard, I.

70 VINDICE: How came the Duke slain then?

FOURTH [LORD]: We found him so.

LUSSURIOSO: O villain!

VINDICE: Hark!

LUSSURIOSO: Those in the mask did murder us.

VINDICE: Law! You now, sir.

O marble impudence! Will you confess now?

FOURTH [LORD]: 'Sblood! Tis all false.

ANTONIO: Away with that foul monster
Dipped in a prince's blood.

FOURTH [LORD]:   Heart, tis a lie!

ANTONIO: Let him have bitter execution.

   [*Exit* FOURTH LORD *under guard*.]

VINDICE [*aside*]: New marrow! – No, I cannot be expressed. –

How fares my lord the Duke?

80 LUSSURIOSO: Farewell to all:
He that climbs highest has the greatest fall.
 – My tongue is out of office.

VINDICE: Air gentlemen, air!

   [*Whispering to* LUSSURIOSO] Now thou'lt not prate on't –
   'twas Vindice murdered thee.

LUSSURIOSO: Oh!

     79. *Expressed:* in the sense of squeezed out.

134

VINDICE: Murdered thy father.

LUSSURIOSO: Oh!

VINDICE: And I am he – tell nobody.

 [LUSSURIOSO *dies.*]

 So, so, the Duke's departed.

ANTONIO: It was a deadly hand that wounded him.

 The rest, ambitious who should rule and sway   90

 After his death, were so made all away.

VINDICE: My lord was unlikely.

HIPPOLITO: Now the hope

 Of Italy lies in your reverend years.

VINDICE: Your hair will make the silver age again,

 When there was fewer but more honest men.

ANTONIO: The burden's weighty and will press age
 down;

 May I so rule that heaven may keep the crown.

VINDICE: The rape of your good lady has been 'quited

 With death on death.

ANTONIO: Just is the law above.   100

 But of all things it puts me most to wonder

 How the old Duke came murdered.

VINDICE: Oh my lord.

ANTONIO: It was the strangeliest carried; I not heard of
 the like.

HIPPOLITO: 'Twas all done for the best, my lord.

VINDICE: All for your Grace's good. We may be bold to
 speak it now.

 'Twas somewhat witty carried, tho' we say it;

 'Twas we two murdered him.

ANTONIO: You two?

VINDICE: None else i'faith, my lord. Nay, 'twas well
 managed.

ANTONIO: Lay hands upon those villains!

VINDICE: How! On us?

ANTONIO: Bear 'em to speedy execution.   110

VINDICE: Heart, was't not for your good, my lord?

   92. *Unlikely:* unpromising.

ANTONIO: My good? Away with 'em! – Such an old man
 as he!
 You that would murder him would murder me.
VINDICE: Is't come about?
HIPPOLITO: 'Sfoot brother, you begun.
VINDICE: May not we set as well as the Duke's son?
 Thou hast no conscience – are we not revenged?
 Is there one enemy left alive amongst those?
 'Tis time to die when we are ourselves our foes.
 When murd'rers shut deeds close, this curse does seal
 'em:
120 If none disclose 'em, they themselves reveal 'em.
 This murder might have slept in tongueless brass
 But for ourselves, and the world died an ass.
 Now I remember too, here was Piato
 Brought forth a knavish sentence once: –
 No doubt, said he, but time
 Will make the murderer bring forth himself.
 'Tis well he died, he was a witch.
 And now my lord, since we are in for ever –
 This work was ours, which else might have been slipped,
130 And if we list, we could have nobles clipped
 And go for less than beggars; but we hate
 To bleed so cowardly. We have enough
 I'faith, we're well, our mother turned, our sister true,
 We die after a nest of dukes. – Adieu.
  Exeunt [VINDICE *and* HIPPOLITO *under guard*]
ANTONIO. How subtly was that murder closed. Bear up
 Those tragic bodies. 'Tis a heavy season;
 Pray heaven their blood may wash away all treason.
  [*Exeunt* OMNES.]

THE
WHITE DIVEL,

OR,

The Tragedy of *Paulo Giordano Ursini*, Duke of *Brachiano*,

With

The Life and Death of Vittoria Corombona the famous Venetian Curtizan.

Acted by the Queenes Maiesties Seruants.

Written by IOHN WEBSTER.

Non inferiora secutus.

LONDON,
Printed by *N.O.* for *Thomas Archer*, and are to be sold at his Shop in Popes head Pallace, neere the Royall Exchange. 1612.

TO THE READER

*

In publishing this tragedy, I do but challenge to myself that liberty, which other men have taken before me; not that I affect praise by it, for, *nos haec novimus esse nihil*, only, since it was acted in so dull a time of winter, presented in so open and black a theatre, that it wanted (that which is the only grace and setting-out of a tragedy) a full and understanding auditory; and that since that time I have noted, most of the people that come to that playhouse resemble those ignorant asses (who, visiting stationers' shops, their use is not to inquire for good books, but new books), I present it to the general view with this confidence: 10

> *Nec rhoncos metues maligniorum,*
> *Nec scombris tunicas dabis molestas.*

If it be objected this is no true dramatic poem, I shall easily confess it, *non potes in nugas dicere plura meas, ipse ego quam dixi*; willingly, and not ignorantly, in this kind have I faulted: For should a man present to such an auditory, the most sententious tragedy that ever was written, observing all the critical laws, as height of style, and gravity of person, 20 enrich it with the sententious *Chorus*, and, as it were life and death, in the passionate and weighty *Nuntius*: yet after all this divine rapture, *O dura messorum ilia*, the breath that comes from the uncapable multitude is able to poison it; and, ere it be acted, let the author resolve to fix to every scene this of *Horace*:

> *– Haec hodie porcis comedenda relinques.*

To those who report I was a long time in finishing this tragedy, I confess I do not write with a goose-quill winged with two feathers; and if they will needs make it my fault, 30 I must answer them with that of *Euripides* to *Alcestides*, a tragic writer: *Alcestides* objecting that *Euripides* had only, in three days composed three verses, whereas himself had written three hundred: Thou tellest truth (quoth he), but here's the difference, thine shall only be read for three days, whereas mine shall continue three ages.

Detraction is the sworn friend to ignorance: for mine own part, I have ever truly cherished my good opinion of other men's worthy labours, especially of that full and
40 heightened style of *Mr Chapman*, the laboured and understanding works of *Mr Jonson*, the no less worthy composures of the both worthily excellent *Mr Beaumont* and *Mr Fletcher*; and lastly (without wrong last to be named), the right happy and copious industry of *Mr Shakespeare*, *Mr Dekker* and *Mr Heywood*, wishing what I write may be read by their light: protesting that, in the strength of mine own judgement, I know them so worthy, that though I rest silent in my own work, yet to most of theirs I dare (without flattery) fix that of *Martial*:

50   *– non norunt haec monumenta mori.*

DRAMATIS PERSONAE

*

MONTICELSO, a Cardinal; afterwards Pope PAUL IV.

FRANCISCO DE MEDICI, Duke of Florence; in the last Act disguised as MULINASSAR, a Moor.

BRACHIANO, otherwise PAULO GIORDANO URSINI, Duke of Brachiano, Husband first of ISABELLA, and later of VITTORIA.

GIOVANNI – his Son by ISABELLA.

LODOVICO (Lodowick), in love with ISABELLA; later a conspirator in the pay of FRANCISCO.

ANTONELLI
GASPARO } his Friends; later fellow-conspirators.

CARLO
PEDRO } BRACHIANO's attendants, secretly in league with FRANCISCO.

CAMILLO, Husband to VITTORIA; cousin to MONTICELSO.

HORTENSIO, one of BRACHIANO's Officers.

MARCELLO, an Attendant of FRANCISCO, and Brother to VITTORIA.

FLAMINEO, his Brother; Secretary to BRACHIANO.

ISABELLA, Sister to FRANCISCO DE MEDICI, and first wife of BRACHIANO.

VITTORIA COROMBONA, a Venetian Lady; first married to CAMILLO, afterwards to BRACHIANO.

CORNELIA, Mother to VITTORIA, FLAMINEO, and MARCELLO.

ZANCHE, a Moor, Servant to VITTORIA.

Ambassadors, Courtiers, Lawyers, Officers, Physicians, Conjurer, Armourer, Attendants.

Matron of the House of Convertites, Ladies.

The action takes place in Italy, first at Rome and, in the final act, in Padua.

[ACT ONE]

*

[SCENE ONE]

Enter COUNT LODOVICO, ANTONELLI, *and*
GASPARO.

LODOVICO: Banish'd?

ANTONELLI: It grieved me much to hear the sentence.

LODOVICO: Ha, ha, O Democritus, thy gods
That govern the whole world! – Courtly reward
And punishment! Fortune's a right whore:
If she give aught, she deals it in small parcels,
That she may take away all at one swoop.
This 'tis to have great enemies, God 'quite them:
Your wolf no longer seems to be a wolf
Than when she's hungry.

GASPARO: You term those enemies,
Are men of princely rank.

LODOVICO: Oh, I pray for them: 10
The violent thunder is adored by those
Are pash'd in pieces by it.

ANTONELLI: Come my lord,
You are justly doomed; look but a little back
Into your former life: you have in three years
Ruined the noblest earldom –

GASPARO: Your followers
Have swallowed you, like mummia, and being sick
With such unnatural and horrid physic,
Vomit you up i'th'kennel.

ANTONELLI: All the damnable degrees   20
Of drinking[s] have you staggered through. One citizen,
Is lord of two fair manors, called you master

5. *Parcels:* portions.
17. *Mummia:* pitch used for embalming, hence embalmed flesh;
both were approved medicines.
19. *Kennel:* gutter.

143

Only for caviare.

GASPARO: Those noblemen
Which were invited to your prodigal feasts,
– Wherein the phoenix scarce could 'scape your throats –
Laugh at your misery, as fore-deeming you
An idle meteor which drawn forth the earth
Would be soon lost i'the air.

ANTONELLI: Jest upon you,
And say you were begotten in an earthquake,
You have ruined such fair lordships.

30 LODOVICO: Very good.
This well goes with two buckets: I must tend
The pouring out of either.

GASPARO: Worse than these,
You have acted certain murders here in Rome,
Bloody and full of horror.

LODOVICO: 'Las, they were flea-bitings:
Why took they not my head then?

GASPARO: O my lord,
The law doth sometimes mediate, thinks it good
Not ever to steep violent sins in blood:
This gentle penance may both end your crimes,
And in the example better these bad times.

40 LODOVICO: So; but I wonder then some great men 'scape
This banishment: there's Paulo Giordano Orsini,
The Duke of Brachiano, now lives in Rome,
And by close pandarism seeks to prostitute
The honour of Vittoria Corombona, –
Vittoria, she that might have got my pardon
For one kiss to the duke.

ANTONELLI: Have a full man within you:
We see that trees bear no such pleasant fruit
There where they grew first, as where they are new set.

50 Perfumes, the more they are chafed the more they render
Their pleasing scents, and so affliction

31. *Tend:* wait on.
33. *Acted:* executed or brought about.

Expresseth virtue fully, whether true
Or else adulterate.

LODOVICO: Leave your painted comforts;
I'll make Italian cut-works in their guts
If ever I return.

GASPARO: O sir.

LODOVICO: I am patient;
I have seen some ready to be executed
Give pleasant looks, and money, and grown familiar
With the knave hangman; so do I; I thank them,
And would account them nobly merciful
Would they dispatch me quickly.

ANTONELLI: Fare you well, 60
We shall find time, I doubt not, to repeal
Your banishment.

LODOVICO: I am ever bound to you.
  A Sennet sounds.
This is the world's alms; pray make use of it.
Great men sell sheep, thus to be cut in pieces,
When first they have shorn them bare and sold their
  fleeces.
  Exeunt.

[SCENE TWO]

Enter BRACHIANO, CAMILLO, FLAMINEO, VITTORIA
  [*and Attendants*].

BRACHIANO: Your best of rest.

VITTORIA: Unto my lord the duke,
The best of welcome. More lights: attend the duke.
  [*Exeunt* CAMILLO *and* VITTORIA.]

BRACHIANO: Flamineo.

FLAMINEO: My lord.

BRACHIANO: Quite lost, Flamineo.

52. *Expresseth:* in the sense of 'squeezes out'.
53. *Painted comforts:* false comforts. A common phrase.
54. *Cut-works:* openwork embroidery.

FLAMINEO: Pursue your noble wishes, I am prompt
As lightning to your service. O my lord!
[*Whispers*] The fair Vittoria, my happy sister
Shall give you present audience – Gentlemen,
Let the caroche go on, and 'tis his pleasure
You put out all your torches and depart.
[*Exeunt Attendants.*]

BRACHIANO: Are we so happy?

10 FLAMINEO: Can it be otherwise?
Observed you not tonight my honoured lord
Which way soe'er you went she threw her eyes?
I have dealt already with her chambermaid,
Zanche the Moor, and she is wondrous proud
To be the agent for so high a spirit.

BRACHIANO: We are happy above thought, because 'bove
merit.

FLAMINEO: 'Bove merit! We may now talk freely: 'bove
merit! What is't you doubt? Her coyness? That's but the
superficies of lust most women have; yet why should
20 ladies blush to hear that named, which they do not fear
to handle? O they are politic; they know our desire is
increased by the difficulty of enjoying; whereas satiety
is a blunt, weary and drowsy passion. If the buttery-
hatch at court stood continually open, there would be
nothing so passionate crowding, nor hot suit after the
beverage.

BRACHIANO: Oh, but her jealous husband –

FLAMINEO: Hang him; a gilder that hath his brains
perished with quicksilver is not more cold in the liver.
30 The great barriers moulted not more feathers than he
hath shed hairs, by the confession of his doctor. An

8. *Caroche:* stately coach.
23. *Buttery:* storeroom for drinks and provisions.
30. *Barriers:* waist-high partitions separating pike and sword
duellists. *Feathers:* plumes from combatants' helmets.
31. *Shed hairs:* been treated for venereal disease.

Irish gamester that will play himself naked, and then
wage all downward, at hazard, is not more venturous.
So unable to please a woman that like a Dutch doublet,
all his back is shrunk into his breeches.
Shroud you within this closet, good my lord;
Some trick now must be thought on to divide
My brother-in-law from his fair bed-fellow.

BRACHIANO: Oh, should she fail to come –

FLAMINEO: I must not have your lordship thus unwisely 40
amorous, – I myself have loved a lady and pursued her
with a great deal of under-age protestation, whom some
three or four gallants that have enjoyed would with all
their hearts have been glad to have been rid of. 'Tis
just like a summer bird-cage in a garden: the birds that
are without despair to get in, and the birds that are
within despair and are in a consumption for fear they
shall never get out. Away, away, my lord.

    [*Exit* BRACHIANO.]
    Enter CAMILLO.

See here he comes. This fellow by his apparel
Some men would judge a politician,   50
But call his wit in question, you shall find it
Merely an ass in's foot-cloth. – How now, brother?
What, travailing to bed to your kind wife?

CAMILLO: I assure you brother, no. My voyage lies
More northerly, in a far colder clime.
I do not well remember I protest
When I last lay with her.

FLAMINEO: Strange you should lose your count.

CAMILLO: We never lay together, but ere morning
There grew a flaw between us.

FLAMINEO: 'T had been your part 60
To have made up that flaw.

33. *All downward:* testicles.
34. *Dutch doublet:* close-fitting doublet, with very full breeches.
52. *Foot-cloth:* a low hanging cloth laid over a horse to protect
rider from mud and dust.

CAMILLO: True, but she loathes
I should be seen in't.

FLAMINEO: Why, sir, what's the matter?

CAMILLO: The duke your master visits me – I thank him,
And I perceive how, like an earnest bowler,
He very passionately leans that way
He should have his bowl run.

FLAMINEO: I hope you do not think –

CAMILLO: That nobleman bowl booty? Faith, his cheek
Hath a most excellent bias, it would fain
Jump with my mistress.

FLAMINEO: Will you be an ass,
70   Despite your Aristotle, or a cuckold,
Contrary to your Ephemerides
Which shows you under what a smiling planet
You were first swaddled?

CAMILLO: Pew wew, sir, tell not me
Of planets nor of Ephemerides;
A man may be made cuckold in the daytime
When the stars' eyes are out.

FLAMINEO: Sir, good-bye you;
I do commit you to your pitiful pillow
Stuffed with horn-shavings.

CAMILLO: Brother!

FLAMINEO: God refuse me,
80   Might I advise you now, your only course
Were to lock up your wife.

CAMILLO: 'Twere very good.

FLAMINEO: Bar her the sight of revels.

CAMILLO: Excellent.

FLAMINEO: Let her not go to church, but, like a hound

67. *Booty:* a term in bowls where two players combine for the disadvantage of a third.

67–9. A series of bowling terms. *Cheek:* Brachiano's cheek, as well as the round side of a bowl. *Bias:* weighted side of a bowl, also inclination. *Jump with:* run up against. With a quibble on 'lie with'. *Mistress:* small white ball (jack) at which bowls are aimed.

In leon at your heels.

CAMILLO: 'Twere for her honour.

FLAMINEO: And so you should be certain in one fort-
night,
Despite her chastity or innocence,
To be cuckolded, which yet is in suspense:
This is my counsel, and I ask no fee for't.

CAMILLO: Come, you know not where my nightcap
wrings me.

FLAMINEO: Wear it a'th'old fashion, let your large ears 90
come through, it will be more easy – nay, I will be bitter
– bar your wife of her entertainment: women are more
willingly and more gloriously chaste, when they are
least restrained of their liberty. It seems you would be a
fine capricious, mathematically jealous coxcomb; take
the height of your own horns with a Jacob's staff afore
they are up. These politic enclosures for paltry mutton
makes more rebellion in the flesh than all the provocative
electuaries doctors have uttered since last jubilee.

CAMILLO: This doth not physic me.   100

FLAMINEO: It seems you are jealous: I'll show you the
error of it by a familiar example: I have seen a pair of
spectacles fashioned with such perspective art, that lay
down but one twelve pence a'th'board, 'twill appear as
if there were twenty; now should you wear a pair of
these spectacles, and see your wife tying her shoe, you
would imagine twenty hands were taking up of your
wife's clothes, and this would put you into a horrible
causeless fury.

CAMILLO: The fault there sir, is not in the eyesight.   110

FLAMINEO: True, but they that have the yellow jaundice
think all objects they look on to be yellow. Jealousy is
worser, her fits present to a man, like so many bubbles

84. *Leon:* leash.
96. *Jacob's staff:* an instrument for measuring heights.
97. *Mutton:* slang for loose women.
99. *Provocative electuaries:* aphrodisiacs.

in a basin of water, twenty several crabbed faces, many times makes his own shadow his cuckold-maker.

Enter [VITTORIA] COROMBONA.

See she comes; what reason have you to be jealous of this creature? What an ignorant ass or flattering knave might he be counted, that should write sonnets to her eyes, or call her brow the snow of Ida, or ivory of

120   Corinth, or compare her hair to the blackbird's bill, when 'tis liker the blackbird's feather? This is all. Be wise, I will make you friends and you shall go to bed together. Marry, look you, it shall not be your seeking, do you stand upon that by any means: walk you aloof, I would not have you seen in't. – Sister – my lord attends you in the banqueting-house – your husband is wondrous discontented.

VITTORIA: I did nothing to displease him; I carved to him at supper-time.

130 FLAMINEO: (You need not have carved him, in faith; they say he is a capon already. – I must now seemingly fall out with you.) Shall a gentleman so well descended as Camillo (a lousy slave, that within this twenty years rode with the black guard in the duke's carriage 'mongst spits and dripping-pans) –

CAMILLO: Now he begins to tickle her.

FLAMINEO: An excellent scholar (one that hath a head filled with calves' brains without any sage in them,) come crouching in the hams to you for a night's lodging?

140   (That hath an itch in 's hams, which like the fire at the glass-house hath not gone out this seven years). Is he not a courtly gentleman? (when he wears white satin, one would take him by his black muzzle to be no other creature than a maggot). You are a goodly foil, I confess,

130. *Carved*: castrated.
131. *Capon*: castrated cock, hence eunuch.
134. *Black guard*: kitchen menials; a common phrase.
138. *Calf*: young fool.
141. *Glass-house*: glass-factory.
144. *Foil*: a thin metal leaf placed under a gem to enhance its lustre.

well set out (but covered with a false stone – yon counterfeit diamond).

CAMILLO: He will make her know what is in me.

FLAMINEO [*aside to* VITTORIA]: Come, my lord attends
you; thou shalt go to bed to my lord.

CAMILLO: Now he comes to't.   150

FLAMINEO: With a relish as curious as a vintner going to
taste new wine. [*To* CAMILLO] I am opening your case
hard.

CAMILLO: A virtuous brother, o'my credit.

FLAMINEO: He will give thee a ring with a philosopher's
stone in it.

CAMILLO: Indeed I am studying alchemy.

FLAMINEO: Thou shalt lie in a bed stuffed with turtle's
feathers, swoon in perfumed linen like the fellow was
smothered in roses. So perfect shall be thy happiness, 160
that as men at sea think land and trees and ships go that
way they go, so both heaven and earth shall seem to go
your voyage. Shalt meet him, 'tis fix'd, with nails of
diamonds to inevitable necessity.

VITTORIA [*aside to* FLAMINEO]: How shall's rid him
hence?

FLAMINEO [*aside to* VITTORIA]: I will put brees in 's tail,
set him gadding presently. [*To* CAMILLO] I have almost
wrought her to it, I find her coming, but, might I
advise you now, for this night I would not lie with her,
I would cross her humour to make her more humble. 170

CAMILLO: Shall I, shall I?

FLAMINEO: It will show in you a supremacy of judgement.

CAMILLO: True, and a mind differing from the tumultuary
opinion; for *quae negata, grata.*

FLAMINEO: Right: you are the adamant shall draw her to
you, though you keep distance off.

166. *Brees:* gadflies.   167. *Presently:* at once.
168. *Coming:* complaisant.   173. *Tumultuary:* haphazard.
174. *Quae . . . grata:* what is denied is desired.

CAMILLO: A philosophical reason.

FLAMINEO: Walk by her a'th'nobleman's fashion, and tell her you will lie with her at the end of the progress.

180 CAMILLO: Vittoria, I cannot be induced, or as a man would say, incited –

VITTORIA: To do what, sir?

CAMILLO: To lie with you tonight. Your silkworm useth to fast every third day, and the next following spins the better. Tomorrow at night I am for you.

VITTORIA: You'll spin a fair thread, trust to't.

FLAMINEO: But do you hear, I shall have you steal to her chamber about midnight.

CAMILLO: Do you think so? Why look you brother, 190 because you shall not think I'll gull you, take the key, lock me into the chamber, and say you shall be sure of me.

FLAMINEO: In troth I will, I'll be your jailer once, – But have you ne'er a false door?

CAMILLO: A pox on't, as I am a Christian! Tell me tomorrow how scurvily she takes my unkind parting.

FLAMINEO: I will.

CAMILLO: Didst thou not mark the jest of the silkworm? Good-night – in faith, I will use this trick often.

200 FLAMINEO: Do, do, do.

Exit CAMILLO.

So, now you are safe. Ha, ha, ha, thou entanglest thyself in thine own work like a silkworm.

Enter BRACHIANO.

Come sister, darkness hides your blush. Women are like curst dogs: civility keeps them tied all daytime, but they are let loose at midnight, then they do most good or most mischief. – My lord, my lord!

BRACHIANO: Give credit: I could wish time would stand still

179. *Progress:* state visit.
204. *Curst:* vicious. *Civility:* good social feeling.
207. *Give credit:* believe me.

And never end this interview, this hour,
But all delight doth itself soon'st devour.

> ZANCHE *brings out a carpet, spreads it, and lays on it two*
> *fair cushions. Enter* CORNELIA [*listening unseen*].

Let me into your bosom, happy lady,   210
Pour out, instead of eloquence, my vows.
Loose me not madam, for if you forego me,
I am lost eternally.

VITTORIA: Sir, in the way of pity,
I wish you heart-whole.

BRACHIANO: You are a sweet physician.

VITTORIA: Sure, sir, a loathéd cruelty in ladies
Is as to doctors many funerals:
It takes away their credit.

BRACHIANO: Excellent creature.
We call the cruel fair, what name for you
That are so merciful?

ZANCHE: See now they close.

FLAMINEO: Most happy union.   220

CORNELIA [*aside*]: My fears are fall'n upon me: oh my heart!
My son the pander! Now I find our house
Sinking to ruin. Earthquakes leave behind,
Where they have tyranniz'd, iron, or lead, or stone,
But – woe to ruin – violent lust leaves none.

BRACHIANO: What value is this jewel?

VITTORIA: 'Tis the ornament
Of a weak fortune.

BRACHIANO: In sooth, I'll have it; nay, I will but change
My jewel for your jewel.

FLAMINEO: Excellent,
His jewel for her jewel, – well put in, duke.   230

BRACHIANO: Nay, let me see you wear it.

VITTORIA: Here, sir?

BRACHIANO: Nay lower, you shall wear my jewel lower.

FLAMINEO: That's better: she must wear his jewel lower.

VITTORIA: To pass away the time, I'll tell your grace
A dream I had last night.

BRACHIANO: Most wishedly.

VITTORIA: A foolish idle dream: –
Methought I walked about the mid of night
Into a churchyard, where a goodly yew-tree
Spread her large root in ground: under that yew,
240   As I sat sadly leaning on a grave,
Chequered with cross-sticks, there came stealing in
Your duchess and my husband; one of them
A pickaxe bore, th'other a rusty spade,
And in rough terms they 'gan to challenge me
About this yew.

BRACHIANO: That tree?

VITTORIA: This harmless yew.
They told me my intent was to root up
That well-grown yew, and plant i'the stead of it
A withered blackthorn; and for that they vowed
To bury me alive. My husband straight
250   With pickaxe 'gan to dig, and your fell duchess
With shovel, like a Fury, voided out
The earth and scattered bones: Lord, how methought
I trembled! And yet for all this terror
I could not pray.

FLAMINEO: No, the devil was in your dream.

VITTORIA: When to my rescue there arose methought,
A whirlwind, which let fall a massy arm
From that strong plant,
And both were struck dead by that sacred yew
In that base shallow grave that was their due.

260 FLAMINEO: Excellent devil!
She hath taught him in a dream
To make away his duchess and her husband.

BRACHIANO: Sweetly shall I interpret this your dream.
You are lodged within his arms who shall protect you
From all the fevers of a jealous husband,
From the poor envy of our phlegmatic duchess.

266. *Envy:* malice, as well as the modern sense of 'jealousy'.
Phlegmatic: of a cold, dull temper.

I'll seat you above law, and above scandal,
Give to your thoughts the invention of delight,
And the fruition; nor shall government
Divide me from you longer than a care   270
To keep you great: you shall to me at once
Be dukedom, health, wife, children, friends and all.

CORNELIA [*advancing*]: Woe to light hearts, they still fore-
run our fall!

FLAMINEO: What Fury raised thee up? Away, away!
Exit ZANCHE.

CORNELIA: What make you here my lord, this dead of
night?
Never dropped mildew on a flower here
Till now.

FLAMINEO: I pray, will you go to bed then,
Lest you be blasted?

CORNELIA: O that this fair garden
Had with all poisoned herbs of Thessaly   280
At first been planted, made a nursery
For witchcraft, rather than a burial plot
For both your honours!

VITTORIA: Dearest mother, hear me.

CORNELIA: Oh, thou dost make my brow bend to the earth
Sooner than nature! See the curse of children!
In life they keep us frequently in tears,
And in the cold grave leave us in pale fears.

BRACHIANO: Come, come, I will not hear you.

VITTORIA: Dear my lord.

CORNELIA: Where is thy duchess now, adulterous duke?
Thou little dream'd'st this night she's come to Rome.   290

FLAMINEO: How? Come to Rome?

VITTORIA: The duchess!

BRACHIANO: She had been better –

CORNELIA: The lives of princes should like dials move,
Whose regular example is so strong,
They make the times by them go right or wrong.

286. *Frequently*: incessantly.   293. *Dials*: sun-dials.

FLAMINEO: So, have you done?

CORNELIA: Unfortunate Camillo!

VITTORIA [*kneeling*]: I do protest, if any chaste denial,
If anything but blood could have allayed
His long suit to me –

300 CORNELIA [*kneeling*]: I will join with thee,
To the most woeful end e'er mother kneeled –
If thou dishonour thus thy husband's bed,
Be thy life short as are the funeral tears
In great men's –

BRACHIANO: Fie, fie, the woman's mad.

CORNELIA: Be thy act Judas-like – betray in kissing:
May'st thou be envied during his short breath,
And pitied like a wretch after his death!

VITTORIA: O me accursed!

Exit VITTORIA.

FLAMINEO: Are you out of your wits? My lord
I'll fetch her back again.

310 BRACHIANO: No, I'll to bed:
Send Doctor Julio to me presently. –
Uncharitable woman! thy rash tongue
Hath raised a fearful and prodigious storm;
Be thou the cause of all ensuing harm.

Exit BRACHIANO.

FLAMINEO: Now, you that stand so much upon your
honour,
Is this a fitting time a'night think you,
To send a duke home without e'er a man?
I would fain know where lies the mass of wealth
Which you have hoarded for my maintenance,

320 That I may bear my beard out of the level
Of my lord's stirrup.

CORNELIA: What? Because we are poor
Shall we be vicious?

FLAMINEO: Pray what means have you
To keep me from the galleys, or the gallows?
My father proved himself a gentleman,

Sold all's land, and, like a fortunate fellow,
Died ere the money was spent. You brought me up
At Padua I confess, where I protest,
For want of means – the University judge me –
I have been fain to heel my tutor's stockings,
At least seven years; conspiring with a beard,   330
Made me a graduate; then to this duke's service:
I visited the court, whence I returned
More courteous, more lecherous by far,
But not a suit the richer. And shall I,
Having a path so open and so free
To my preferment, still retain your milk
In my pale forehead? No, this face of mine
I'll arm and fortify with lusty wine
'Gainst shame and blushing.

CORNELIA: O that I ne'er had borne thee!

FLAMINEO: So would I;   340
I would the common'st courtesan in Rome
Had been my mother, rather than thyself.
Nature is very pitiful to whores,
To give them but few children, yet those children
Plurality of fathers – they are sure
They shall not want. Go, go,
Complain unto my great lord cardinal,
Yet may be he will justify the act.
Lycurgus wondered much men would provide
Good stallions for their mares, and yet would suffer   350
Their fair wives to be barren.

CORNELIA: Misery of miseries!

   Exit CORNELIA.

FLAMINEO: The duchess come to court! I like not that. –
We are engaged to mischief and must on;
As rivers to find out the ocean
Flow with crook bendings beneath forced banks,
Or as we see, to aspire some mountain's top,

356. *Crook:* crooked. *Forced:* perhaps 'fabricated' (Brown).
357. *Aspire:* mount up to.

The way ascends not straight, but imitates
The subtle foldings of a winter's snake,
360 So who knows policy and her true aspect,
Shall find her ways winding and indirect.
  Exit.

[ACT TWO]

*

[SCENE ONE]

Enter FRANCISCO DE MEDICI, CARDINAL MONTI-
CELSO, MARCELLO, ISABELLA, *young* GIOVANNI,
with Attendants.

FRANCISCO: Have you not seen your husband since you
    arrived?

ISABELLA: Not yet, sir.

FRANCISCO: Surely he is wondrous kind;
    If I had such a dove-house as Camillo's,
    I would set fire on't, were't but to destroy
    The polecats that haunt to it – My sweet cousin!

GIOVANNI: Lord uncle, you did promise me a horse
    And armour.

FRANCISCO: That I did, my pretty cousin.
    Marcello, see it fitted.

MARCELLO: My lord, the duke is here.

FRANCISCO: Sister, away;   10
    You must not yet be seen.

ISABELLA: I do beseech you
    Entreat him mildly, let not your rough tongue
    Set us at louder variance; all my wrongs
    Are freely pardoned; and I do not doubt,
    As men, to try the precious unicorn's horn
    Make of the powder a preservative circle
    And in it put a spider, so these arms
    Shall charm his poison, force it to obeying
    And keep him chaste from an infected straying.

FRANCISCO: I wish it may. Begone.

    Exit [ISABELLA].
    Enter BRACHIANO *and* FLAMINEO.

                      Void the chamber.   20

    Exeunt FLAMINEO, MARCELLO, GIOVANNI, *and*
    Attendants.

You are welcome; will you sit? I pray my lord,
Be you my orator, my heart's too full;
I'll second you anon.

MONTICELSO: Ere I begin,
Let me entreat your grace forego all passion
Which may be raised by my free discourse.

BRACHIANO: As silent as i'th'church – you may proceed.

MONTICELSO: It is a wonder to your noble friends,
That you, [that] have as 'twere entered the world
With a free sceptre in your able hand,
30   And have to th'use of nature well applied
High gifts of learning, should in your prime age
Neglect your awful throne for the soft down
Of an insatiate bed. O my lord,
The drunkard after all his lavish cups
Is dry, and then is sober; so at length,
When you awake from this lascivious dream,
Repentance then will follow, like the sting
Placed in the adder's tail. Wretched are princes
When fortune blasteth but a petty flower
40   Of their unwieldy crowns, or ravisheth
But one pearl from their sceptre; but alas!
When they to wilful shipwreck loose good fame,
All princely titles perish with their name.

BRACHIANO: You have said, my lord –

MONTICELSO: Enough to give you taste
How far I am from flattering your greatness.

BRACHIANO: Now you that are his second, what say you?
Do not like young hawks fetch a course about;
Your game flies fair, and for you.

FRANCISCO: Do not fear it:
I'll answer you in your own hawking phrase. –
50   Some eagles that should gaze upon the sun
Seldom soar high, but take their lustful ease,
Since they from dunghill birds their prey can seize. –
You know Vittoria?

BRACHIANO: Yes.

FRANCISCO: You shift your shirt there,
When you retire from tennis?

BRACHIANO: Happily.

FRANCISCO: Her husband is lord of a poor fortune,
Yet she wears cloth of tissue.

BRACHIANO: What of this?
Will you urge that, my good lord cardinal,
As part of her confession at next shrift,
And know from whence it sails?

FRANCISCO: She is your strumpet –

BRACHIANO: Uncivil sir, there's hemlock in thy breath   60
And that black slander. Were she a whore of mine
All thy loud cannons, and thy borrowed Switzers,
Thy galleys, nor thy sworn confederates,
Durst not supplant her.

FRANCISCO: Let's not talk on thunder. –
Thou hast a wife, our sister; would I had given
Both her white hands to death, bound and locked fast
In her last winding sheet, when I gave thee
But one.

BRACHIANO: Thou hadst given a soul to God then.

FRANCISCO: True:
Thy ghostly father, with all's absolution,   70
Shall ne'er do so by thee.

BRACHIANO: Spit thy poison –

FRANCISCO: I shall not need, lust carries her sharp whip
At her own girdle. – Look to't, for our anger
Is making thunderbolts.

BRACHIANO: Thunder? In faith,
They are but crackers.

FRANCISCO: We'll end this with the cannon.

BRACHIANO: Thou'lt get naught by it but iron in thy
    wounds,
And gunpowder in thy nostrils.

54. *Happily:* commonly 'haply'.
56. *Cloth of tissue:* rich cloth.
62. *Switzers:* Swiss mercenaries.

FRANCISCO: Better that
Than change perfumes for plasters.

BRACHIANO: Pity on thee!
'Twere good you'd show your slaves, or men con-
80   demned,
Your new-ploughed forehead. – Defiance! – And I'll
    meet thee,
Even in a thicket of thy ablest men.

MONTICELSO: My lords, you shall not word it any further
Without a milder limit.

FRANCISCO: Willingly.

BRACHIANO: Have you proclaimed a triumph, that you
    bait
A lion thus?

MONTICELSO: My lord!

BRACHIANO: I am tame, I am tame sir.

FRANCISCO: We send unto the duke for conference
'Bout levies 'gainst the pirates, my lord duke
Is not at home: we come ourself in person,
90   Still my lord duke is busied. But we fear
When Tiber to each prowling passenger
Discovers flocks of wild ducks, then my lord –
'Bout moulting time I mean – we shall be certain
To find you sure enough and speak with you.

BRACHIANO: Ha?

FRANCISCO: A mere tale of a tub, my words are idle.
But to express the sonnet by natural reason,
    Enter GIOVANNI.
When stags grow melancholic you'll find the season –

MONTICELSO: No more my lord, here comes a champion
Shall end the difference between you both;

81. *New-ploughed:* newly-furrowed (with anger).
92. *Wild ducks:* prostitutes.
93. *Moulting time:* mating season.
95. *Tale of a tub:* a cock-and-bull story; also allusion to sweating-tub used in treating venereal disease.
96. *Express ... reason:* put it simply. *Sonnet:* any short poem, usually amatory.

Your son, the Prince Giovanni. See my lords,   100
What hopes you store in him; this is a casket
For both your crowns, and should be held like dear.
Now is he apt for knowledge; therefore know
It is a more direct and even way
To train to virtue those of princely blood,
By examples than by precepts: if by examples,
Whom should he rather strive to imitate
Than his own father? Be his pattern then,
Leave him a stock of virtue that may last,
Should fortune rend his sails, and split his mast.   110

BRACHIANO: Your hand, boy: growing to a soldier?

GIOVANNI: Give me a pike.

FRANCISCO: What, practising your pike so young, fair coz?

GIOVANNI: Suppose me one of Homer's frogs, my lord,
Tossing my bulrush thus. Pray sir, tell me,
Might not a child of good discretion
Be leader to an army?

FRANCISCO: Yes cousin, a young prince
Of good discretion might.

GIOVANNI: Say you so?
Indeed I have heard 'tis fit a general
Should not endanger his own person oft,   120
So that he make a noise, when he's a-horseback
Like a Dansk drummer, – Oh 'tis excellent!
He need not fight, methinks his horse as well
Might lead an army for him; if I live
I'll charge the French foe in the very front
Of all my troops, the foremost man.

FRANCISCO: What! What!

GIOVANNI: And will not bid my soldiers up, and follow,
But bid them follow me.

BRACHIANO: Forward lapwing!
He flies with the shell on's head.

FRANCISCO: Pretty cousin!

109. *Stock:* (i) store, (ii) line of ancestors.
128. *Lapwing:* emblem of precocity.

163

130 GIOVANNI: The first year, uncle, that I go to war,
All prisoners that I take, I will set free,
Without their ransom.

FRANCISCO: Ha, without their ransom!
How then will you reward your soldiers,
That took those prisoners for you?

GIOVANNI: Thus, my lord:
I'll marry them to all the wealthy widows
That fall that year.

FRANCISCO: Why then, the next year following
You'll have no men to go with you to war.

GIOVANNI: Why then I'll press the women to the war,
And then the men will follow.

MONTICELSO: Witty prince!

140 FRANCISCO: See, a good habit makes a child a man,
Whereas a bad one makes a man a beast:
Come, you and I are friends.

BRACHIANO: Most wishedly:
Like bones which broke in sunder and well set,
Knit the more strongly.

FRANCISCO: Call Camillo hither.
You have received the rumour, how Count Lodowick
Is turned a pirate?

BRACHIANO: Yes.

FRANCISCO: We are now preparing
Some ships to fetch him in. –
    [*Enter* ISABELLA.]
Behold your duchess –

150 We now will leave you, and expect from you
Nothing but kind entreaty.

BRACHIANO: You have charmed me.
    Exeunt FRANCISCO, MONTICELSO, [*and*] GIOVANNI.
You are in health, we see.

ISABELLA: And above health,
To see my lord well.

BRACHIANO: So: I wonder much
What amorous whirlwind hurried you to Rome.

ISABELLA: Devotion my lord.

BRACHIANO: Devotion?
  Is your soul charged with any grievous sin?

ISABELLA: 'Tis burdened with too many, and I think
  The oftener that we cast our reckonings up,
  Our sleeps will be the sounder.

BRACHIANO: Take your chamber.

ISABELLA: Nay, my dear lord, I will not have you angry. 160
  Doth not my absence from you, now two months
  Merit one kiss?

BRACHIANO: I do not use to kiss:
  If that will dispossess your jealousy,
  I'll swear it to you.

ISABELLA: Oh my loved lord,
  I do not come to chide: my jealousy?
  I am to learn what that Italian means;
  You are as welcome to these longing arms
  As I to you a virgin.

BRACHIANO: Oh, your breath!
  Out upon sweetmeats and continued physic,
  The plague is in them!

ISABELLA: You have oft for these two lips 170
  Neglected cassia or the natural sweets
  Of the spring-violet: they are not yet much withered.
  My lord, I should be merry: these your frowns
  Show in a helmet lovely, but on me,
  In such a peaceful interview, methinks
  They are too too roughly knit.

BRACHIANO: O dissemblance!
  Do you bandy factions 'gainst me? Have you learnt
  The trick of impudent baseness to complain
  Unto your kindred?

ISABELLA: Never, my dear lord.

BRACHIANO: Must I be hunted out? Or was't your trick 180

----

166. *Am to learn*: am ignorant of.
171. *Cassia*: a fragrant shrub.
177. *Bandy factions*: form leagues.

165

To meet some amorous gallant here in Rome
That must supply our discontinuance?

ISABELLA: I pray sir, burst my heart, and in my death
Turn to your ancient pity, though not love.

BRACHIANO: Because your brother is the corpulent duke,
That is, the great duke, 'sdeath, I shall not shortly
Racket away five hundred crowns at tennis,
But it shall rest 'pon record! I scorn him
Like a shaved Polack: all his reverend wit
190   Lies in his wardrobe; he's a discreet fellow
When he's made up in his robes of state. –
Your brother, the great duke, because h' 'as galleys,
And now and then ransacks a Turkish fly-boat,
(Now all the hellish furies take his soul!)
First made this match: accursèd be the priest
That sang the wedding-mass, and even my issue!

ISABELLA: Oh, too too far you have cursed!

BRACHIANO: Your hand I'll kiss, –
This is the latest ceremony of my love.
Henceforth I'll never lie with thee; by this,
200   This wedding-ring, I'll ne'er more lie with thee!
And this divorce shall be as truly kept
As if the judge had doomed it. Fare you well:
Our sleeps are severed.

ISABELLA: Forbid it the sweet union
Of all things blessed! Why, the saints in heaven
Will knit their brows at that.

BRACHIANO: Let not thy love
Make thee an unbeliever; this my vow
Shall never, on my soul, be satisfied
With my repentance: let thy brother rage
Beyond a horrid tempest or sea-fight,
My vow is fixed.

210 ISABELLA: O, my winding-sheet,
Now shall I need thee shortly! Dear my lord,

193. *Fly-boat:* pinnace.
207. *Satisfied:* put away.

Let me hear once more, what I would not hear –
Never?

BRACHIANO: Never.

ISABELLA: Oh my unkind lord, may your sins find mercy,
As I upon a woeful widowed bed
Shall pray for you, if not to turn your eyes
Upon your wretched wife and hopeful son,
Yet that in time you'll fix them upon heaven.

BRACHIANO: No more; go, go, complain to the great
duke.   220

ISABELLA: No my dear lord, you shall have present
witness
How I'll work peace between you. I will make
Myself the author of your curséd vow –
I have some cause to do it, you have none, –
Conceal it I beseech you, for the weal
Of both your dukedoms, that you wrought the means
Of such a separation, let the fault
Remain with my supposéd jealousy, –
And think with what a piteous and rent heart
I shall perform this sad ensuing part.   230

    Enter FRANCISCO, FLAMINEO, MONTICELSO [*and*]
    MARCELLO.

BRACHIANO: Well, take your course. – My honourable
brother!

FRANCISCO: Sister! – This is not well, my lord. – Why,
sister! –
She merits not this welcome.

BRACHIANO: Welcome, say?
She hath given a sharp welcome.

FRANCISCO: Are you foolish?
Come, dry your tears: is this a modest course
To better what is naught, to rail and weep?
Grow to a reconcilement, or by heaven,
I'll ne'er more deal between you.

ISABELLA: Sir, you shall not;
No, though Vittoria upon that condition

Would become honest.

240 FRANCISCO: Was your husband loud
Since we departed?

ISABELLA: By my life sir, no, –
I swear by that I do not care to lose.
Are all these ruins of my former beauty
Laid out for a whore's triumph?

FRANCISCO: Do you hear?
Look upon other women, with what patience
They suffer these slight wrongs, with what justice
They study to requite them; – take that course.

ISABELLA: O that I were a man, or that I had power
To execute my apprehended wishes!
I would whip some with scorpions.

250 FRANCISCO: What! Turned Fury?

ISABELLA: To dig the strumpet's eyes out, let her lie
Some twenty months a-dying, to cut off
Her nose and lips, pull out her rotten teeth,
Preserve her flesh like mummia, for trophies
Of my just anger! Hell, to my affliction,
Is mere snow-water. By your favour, sir, –
Brother, draw near, and my lord cardinal, –
Sir, let me borrow of you but one kiss;
Henceforth I'll never lie with you, by this,
This wedding-ring.

260 FRANCISCO: How? Ne'er more lie with him?

ISABELLA: And this divorce shall be as truly kept
As if in throngéd court a thousand ears
Had heard it, and a thousand lawyers' hands
Sealed to the separation.

BRACHIANO: Ne'er lie with me?

ISABELLA: Let not my former dotage
Make thee an unbeliever; this my vow
Shall never, on my soul, be satisfied
With my repentance: – *manet alta mente repostum.*

---

240. *Honest:* chaste.
250. *Scorpions:* probably knotted whips.

FRANCISCO: Now by my birth, you are a foolish, mad,
  And jealous woman.
BRACHIANO: You see 'tis not my seeking.   270
FRANCISCO: Was this your circle of pure unicorn's horn
  You said should charm your lord? Now horns upon
    thee,
  For jealousy deserves them! Keep your vow
  And take your chamber.
ISABELLA: No sir, I'll presently to Padua,
  I will not stay a minute.
MONTICELSO: Oh good madam!
BRACHIANO: 'Twere best to let her have her humour;
  Some half-day's journey will bring down her stomach
  And then she'll turn in post.
FRANCISCO: To see her come
  To my lord cardinal for a dispensation   280
  Of her rash vow will beget excellent laughter.
ISABELLA: Unkindness, do thy office; poor heart, break, –
  'Those are the killing griefs, which dare not speak.'
    Exit.
MARCELLO: Camillo's come, my lord.
    Enter CAMILLO.
FRANCISCO: Where's the commission?
MARCELLO: 'Tis here.
FRANCISCO: Give me the signet.
FLAMINEO [*to* BRACHIANO]: My lord, do you mark
  their whispering? I will compound a medicine out of
  their two heads, stronger than garlic, deadlier than   290
  stibium: the cantharides, which are scarce seen to stick
  upon the flesh when they work to the heart, shall not do
  it with more silence or invisible cunning.
    Enter Doctor [JULIO].
BRACHIANO: About the murder?

272. *Horns upon thee:* may your husband be unfaithful.
279. *Turn in post:* return post-haste.
291. *Stibium:* antimony, used as a poison. *Cantharides:* Spanish
fly.

FLAMINEO: They are sending him to Naples, but I'll send him to Candy. Here's another property too.

BRACHIANO: Oh, the doctor –

FLAMINEO: A poor quack-salving knave, my lord, one that should have been lashed for's lechery, but that he
300 confessed a judgement, had an execution laid upon him, and so put the whip to a *non plus*.

DOCTOR: And was cozened, my lord, by an arranter knave than myself, and made pay all the colourable execution.

FLAMINEO: He will shoot pills into a man's guts shall make them have more ventages than a cornet or a lamprey; he will poison a kiss; and was once minded, for his masterpiece, because Ireland breeds no poison, to have prepared a deadly vapour in a Spaniard's fart that should have poisoned all Dublin.

310 BRACHIANO: Oh Saint Anthony's fire!

DOCTOR: Your secretary is merry my lord.

FLAMINEO: O thou curséd antipathy to nature! Look, his eye's bloodshot like a needle a chirurgeon stitcheth a wound with. – Let me embrace thee toad, and love thee, O thou abhominable, loathsome gargarism, that will fetch up lungs, lights, heart, and liver, by scruples!

BRACHIANO: No more. – I must employ thee, honest doctor:
    You must to Padua, and by the way
    Use some of your skill for us.

DOCTOR: Sir, I shall.

320 BRACHIANO: But for Camillo?

FLAMINEO: He dies this night by such a politic strain,
    Men shall suppose him by 's own engine slain.
    But for your duchess' death –

DOCTOR: I'll make her sure.

---

296. *To Candy:* to death (see Additional Notes). *Property:* instrument.
302. *Cozened:* cheated.   303. *Colourable:* plausible.
313. *Chirurgeon:* surgeon.   315. *Gargarism:* gargle.
322. *Engine:* means, contrivance.

BRACHIANO: Small mischiefs are by greater made secure.

FLAMINEO: Remember this, you slave, – when knaves
come to preferment, they rise as gallowses are raised in
the Low Countries, one upon another's shoulders.

Exeunt [BRACHIANO, FLAMINEO, *and* DOCTOR
JULIO].

MONTICELSO: Here is an emblem, nephew, pray peruse it:
'Twas thrown in at your window.

CAMILLO: At my window?
Here is a stag my lord, hath shed his horns,   330
And for the loss of them the poor beast weeps:
The word, *Inopem me copia fecit.*

MONTICELSO: That is,
Plenty of horns hath made him poor of horns.

CAMILLO: What should this mean?

MONTICELSO: I'll tell you; 'tis given out
You are a cuckold.

CAMILLO: Is it given out so?
I had rather such report as that, my lord,
Should keep within doors.

FRANCISCO: Have you any children?

CAMILLO: None, my lord.

FRANCISCO: You are the happier: –
I'll tell you a tale.

CAMILLO: Pray, my lord.

FRANCISCO: An old tale.   340
Upon a time Phoebus, the god of light,
Or him we call the sun, would need be marriéd.
The gods gave their consent, and Mercury
Was sent to voice it to the general world.
But what a piteous cry there straight arose
Amongst smiths and felt-makers, brewers and cooks,
Reapers and butter-women, amongst fishmongers
And thousand other trades, which are annoyed
By his excessive heat! 'Twas lamentable.

326. *Gallowses:* felons condemned to the gallows.
332. *Word:* motto.

350 They came to Jupiter all in a sweat,
And do forbid the banns. A great fat cook
Was made their speaker, who entreats of Jove
That Phoebus might be gelded; for if now,
When there was but one sun, so many men
Were like to perish by his violent heat,
What should they do if he were marriéd
And should beget more, and those children
Make fireworks like their father? – So say I;
Only I will apply it to your wife:
360 Her issue, should not providence prevent it,
Would make both nature, time, and man repent it.
MONTICELSO: Look you cousin,
Go change the air for shame; see if your absence
Will blast your cornucopia. – Marcello
Is chosen with you joint commissioner,
For the relieving our Italian coast
From pirates.
MARCELLO: I am much honoured in 't.
CAMILLO: But, sir,
Ere I return, the stag's horns may be sprouted,
Greater than these are shed.
MONTICELSO: Do not fear it,
I'll be your ranger.
370 CAMILLO: You must watch i'th'nights,
Then's the most danger.
FRANCISCO: Farewell good Marcello:
All the best fortunes of a soldier's wish
Bring you a-shipboard.
CAMILLO: Were I not best, now I am turned soldier,
Ere that I leave my wife, sell all she hath
And then take leave of her?
MONTICELSO: I expect good from you,
Your parting is so merry.

363. *Go . . . air:* leave this place.
364. *Cornucopia:* horn of plenty.
370. *Ranger:* gamekeeper (with a quibble on 'libertine').

172

CAMILLO: Merry, my lord, o'th'captain's humour right –
  I am resolvéd to be drunk this night.
    [*Exeunt* CAMILLO *and* MARCELLO.]
FRANCISCO: So, – 'twas well fitted, now shall we discern 380
  How his wished absence will give violent way
  To Duke Brachiano's lust.
MONTICELSO: Why, that was it;
  To what scorned purpose else should we make choice
  Of him for a sea-captain? And besides,
  Count Lodowick which was rumoured for a pirate,
  Is now in Padua.
FRANCISCO: Is't true?
MONTICELSO: Most certain:
  I have letters from him, which are suppliant
  To work his quick repeal from banishment;
  He means to address himself for pension
  Unto our sister duchess.
FRANCISCO: Oh, 'twas well! 390
  We shall not want his absence past six days.
  I fain would have the Duke Brachiano run
  Into notorious scandal, for there's naught
  In such cursed dotage, to repair his name,
  Only the deep sense of some deathless shame.
MONTICELSO: It may be objected I am dishonourable
  To play thus with my kinsman; but I answer,
  For my revenge I'd stake a brother's life,
  That being wronged, durst not avenge himself.
FRANCISCO: Come to observe this strumpet.
MONTICELSO: Curse of greatness, – 400
  Sure he'll not leave her.
FRANCISCO: There's small pity in't:
  Like mistletoe on sere elms spent by weather,
  Let him cleave to her and both rot together.
    Exeunt.

390. *Sister:* courtesy title.

[SCENE TWO]

Enter BRACHIANO *with one in the habit of a Conjurer.*

BRACHIANO: Now sir, I claim your promise: 'tis dead
   midnight,
 The time prefixed to show me by your art
 How the intended murder of Camillo
 And our loathed duchess grow to action.
CONJURER: You have won me by your bounty to a deed
 I do not often practise. Some there are,
 Which by sophistic tricks, aspire that name
 Which I would gladly lose, of Nigromancer;
 As some that use to juggle upon cards,
10 Seeming to conjure, when indeed they cheat;
 Others that raise up their confederate spirits
 'Bout windmills, and endanger their own necks
 For making of a squib; and some there are
 Will keep a curtal to show juggling tricks
 And give out 'tis a spirit; besides these,
 Such a whole ream of almanac-makers, figure-flingers, –
 Fellows indeed, that only live by stealth,
 Since they do merely lie about stolen goods, –
 They'd make men think the devil were fast and loose,
20 With speaking fustian Latin. Pray sit down,
 Put on this nightcap sir, 'tis charmed, – and now
 I'll show you by my strong commanding art
 The circumstance that breaks your duchess' heart.

A DUMB SHOW.

Enter suspiciously JULIO *and another: they draw a curtain
where* BRACHIANO'S *picture is; they put on spectacles of
glass, which cover their eyes and noses, and then burn perfumes
afore the picture, and wash the lips of the picture; that done,*

12. *Windmills:* fanciful projects.   14. *Curtal:* docked horse.
16. *Figure-flingers:* casters of horoscopes.
20. *Fustian:* bombastic.

quenching the fire, and putting off their spectacles, they depart laughing.

Enter ISABELLA *in her night-gown, as to bedward, with lights, after her,* COUNT LODOVICO, GIOVANNI, *and others waiting on her: she kneels down as to prayers, then draws the curtain of the picture, does three reverences to it, and kisses it thrice; she faints, and will not suffer them to come near it; dies; sorrow expressed in* GIOVANNI, *and in* COUNT LODOVICO. *She is conveyed out solemnly.*

BRACHIANO: Excellent! Then she's dead.

CONJURER: She's poisoned
By the fumed picture. 'Twas her custom nightly,
Before she went to bed, to go and visit
Your picture, and to feed her eyes and lips
On the dead shadow: Doctor Julio,
Observing this, infects it with an oil,
And other poisoned stuff, which presently   30
Did suffocate her spirits.

BRACHIANO: Methought I saw
Count Lodowick there.

CONJURER: He was, and by my art,
I find he did most passionately dote
Upon your duchess. Now turn another way,
And view Camillo's far more politic fate.
Strike louder music from this charmèd ground,
To yield, as fits the act, a tragic sound!

THE SECOND DUMB SHOW.

Enter FLAMINEO, MARCELLO, CAMILLO, *with four more as captains: they drink healths, and dance; a vaulting horse is brought into the room;* MARCELLO *and two more whispered out of the room, while* FLAMINEO *and* CAMILLO *strip themselves into their shirts, as to vault; compliment who shall begin; as* CAMILLO *is about to vault,* FLAMINEO *pitcheth him upon his neck, and, with the help of the rest, writhes his neck about; seems to see if it be broke, and lays*

30. *Presently:* immediately.   35. *Politic:* ingeniously contrived.

him folded double, as 'twere under the horse; makes shows to call for help; MARCELLO *comes in, laments, sends for the Cardinal and Duke, who comes forth with armed men; wonder at the act; commands the body to be carried home; apprehends* FLAMINEO, MARCELLO, *and the rest, and go as 'twere to apprehend* VITTORIA.

BRACHIANO: 'Twas quaintly done; but yet each circumstance
I taste not fully.

CONJURER: Oh, 'twas most apparent:
40   You saw them enter, charged with their deep healths
To their boon voyage; and, to second that,
Flamineo calls to have a vaulting horse
Maintain their sport; the virtuous Marcello
Is innocently plotted forth the room;
Whilst your eye saw the rest, and can inform you
The engine of all.

BRACHIANO: It seems Marcello and Flamineo
Are both committed.

CONJURER: Yes, you saw them guarded;
And now they are come with purpose to apprehend
50   Your mistress, fair Vittoria; we are now
Beneath her roof: 'twere fit we instantly
Make out by some back postern.

BRACHIANO: Noble friend,
You bind me ever to you: this shall stand
As the firm seal annexéd to my hand;
It shall enforce a payment.

CONJURER: Sir, I thank you.
    Exit BRACHIANO.
Both flowers and weeds spring, when the sun is warm,
And great men do great good, or else great harm.
    Exit.

38. *Quaintly:* cleverly.   41. *Boon voyage:* bon voyage.
46. *Engine:* contrivance.
54. *Annexed . . . hand:* affixed to my signature.

[ACT THREE]

*

[SCENE ONE]

Enter FRANCISCO *and* MONTICELSO, *their Chancellor and Register.*

FRANCISCO: You have dealt discreetly, to obtain the presence
Of all the grave lieger ambassadors
To hear Vittoria's trial.

MONTICELSO: 'Twas not ill,
For sir, you know we have naught but circumstances
To charge her with, about her husband's death:
Their approbation, therefore, to the proofs
Of her black lust shall make her infamous
To all our neighbouring kingdoms. I wonder
If Brachiano will be here?

FRANCISCO: Oh, fie!
'Twere impudence too palpable.   10
      Exeunt.
      Enter FLAMINEO *and* MARCELLO *guarded, and a Lawyer.*

LAWYER: What, are you in by the week? So – I will try
now whether thy wit be close prisoner – methinks none
should sit upon thy sister, but old whore-masters –

FLAMINEO: Or cuckolds; for your cuckold is your most
terrible tickler of lechery. Whore-masters would serve;
for none are judges at tilting, but those that have been
old tilters.

LAWYER: My lord duke and she have been very private.

FLAMINEO: You are a dull ass; 'tis threatened they have
been very public.   20

LAWYER: If it can be proved they have but kissed one
another –

2. *Lieger*: resident.
11. *In . . . week*: trapped (usually applied to infatuation).
18. *Private*: intimate.   20. *Public*: (i) open, (ii) unchaste.

177

FLAMINEO: What then?

LAWYER: My lord cardinal will ferret them.

FLAMINEO: A cardinal, I hope, will not catch conies.

LAWYER: For to sow kisses (mark what I say), to sow
kisses is to reap lechery; and I am sure a woman that
will endure kissing is half won.

FLAMINEO: True, her upper part, by that rule; if you will
30 win her nether part too, you know what follows.

LAWYER: Hark! the ambassadors are 'lighted –

FLAMINEO [*aside*]: I do put on this feignéd garb of mirth,
To gull suspicion.

MARCELLO: Oh, my unfortunate sister!
I would my dagger's point had cleft her heart
When she first saw Brachiano: you, 'tis said,
Were made his engine, and his stalking horse,
To undo my sister.

FLAMINEO: I made a kind of path
To her and mine own preferment.

MARCELLO: Your ruin.

40 FLAMINEO: Hum! thou art a soldier,
Followest the great duke, feed'st his victories,
As witches do their serviceable spirits,
Even with thy prodigal blood: what hast got?
But like the wealth of captains, a poor handful,
Which in thy palm thou bear'st, as men hold water;
Seeking to grip it fast, the frail reward
Steals through thy fingers.

MARCELLO: Sir!

FLAMINEO: Thou hast scarce maintenance
To keep thee in fresh chamois.

MARCELLO: Brother!

FLAMINEO: Hear me:
And thus, when we have even poured ourselves

---

25. *Catch conies:* (i) trick gullible folk, (ii) hunt women (coney =
rabbit).

33. *Gull:* deceive.   37. *Engine:* instrument.

48. *Chamois:* jerkins worn under armour.

Into great fights, for their ambition,   50
Or idle spleen, how shall we find reward?
But as we seldom find the mistletoe,
Sacred to physic, on the builder oak,
Without a mandrake by it; so in our quest of gain,
Alas, the poorest of their forced dislikes
At a limb proffers, but at heart it strikes:
This is lamented doctrine.

MARCELLO: Come, come.

FLAMINEO: When age shall turn thee
White as a blooming hawthorn –

MARCELLO: I'll interrupt you: 60
For love of virtue bear an honest heart,
And stride o'er every politic respect,
Which, where they most advance, they most infect.
Were I your father, as I am your brother,
I should not be ambitious to leave you
A better patrimony.

FLAMINEO: I'll think on 't.

Enter SAVOY [AMBASSADOR].

The lord[s] ambassadors.

Here there is a passage of the Lieger AMBASSADORS *over
the stage severally.*

Enter FRENCH AMBASSADOR.

LAWYER: Oh, my sprightly Frenchman! Do you know
him? He's an admirable tilter.

FLAMINEO: I saw him at last tilting: he showed like a   70
pewter candlestick fashioned like a man in armour,
holding a tilting staff in his hand, little bigger than a
candle of twelve i'th'pound.

LAWYER: Oh, but he's an excellent horseman!

FLAMINEO: A lame one in his lofty tricks; he sleeps
a-horseback, like a poulterer.

Enter ENGLISH *and* SPANISH [AMBASSADORS].

LAWYER: Lo you, my Spaniard!

54. *Mandrake:* poisonous plant.   56. *Proffers:* feints.
75. *Lofty tricks:* acrobatics.

179

FLAMINEO: He carries his face in's ruff, as I have seen a
serving-man carry glasses in a cypress hatband, monstrous
80   steady, for fear of breaking; he looks like the claw of a
blackbird, first salted, and then broiled in a candle.
Exeunt.

[SCENE TWO]

The Arraignment of VITTORIA.

Enter FRANCISCO, MONTICELSO, *the six Lieger*
AMBASSADORS, BRACHIANO, VITTORIA, [ZANCHE,
FLAMINEO, MARCELLO,] LAWYER, *and a Guard.*

MONTICELSO: Forbear, my lord, here is no place assigned
you.
This business, by his Holiness, is left
To our examination.
BRACHIANO: May it thrive with you.
Lays a rich gown under him.
FRANCISCO: A chair there for his lordship.
BRACHIANO: Forbear your kindness: an unbidden guest
Should travel as Dutch women go to church,
Bear their stools with them.
MONTICELSO: At your pleasure, sir.
Stand to the table, gentlewoman. Now, signior,
Fall to your plea.
10 LAWYER: *Domine judex, converte oculos in hanc pestem,*
mulierum corruptissimam.
VITTORIA: What's he?
FRANCISCO: A lawyer that pleads against you.
VITTORIA: Pray, my lord, let him speak his usual tongue,
I'll make no answer else.
FRANCISCO: Why, you understand Latin.
VITTORIA: I do, sir, but amongst this auditory
Which come to hear my cause, the half or more
May be ignorant in't.
MONTICELSO: Go on, sir.

79. *Cypress:* crepe.

VITTORIA: By your favour,
  I will not have my accusation clouded
  In a strange tongue: all this assembly
  Shall hear what you can charge me with.
FRANCISCO: Signior,   20
  You need not stand on't much; pray, change your
    language.
MONTICELSO: Oh, for God's sake – Gentlewoman, your
    credit
  Shall be more famous by it.
LAWYER: Well then, have at you.
VITTORIA: I am at the mark, sir; I'll give aim to you,
  And tell you how near you shoot.
LAWYER: Most literated judges, please your lordships
  So to connive your judgements to the view
  Of this debauched and diversivolent woman;
  Who such a black concatenation
  Of mischief hath effected, that to extirp   30
  The memory of't, must be the consummation
  Of her, and her projections –
VITTORIA: What's all this?
LAWYER: Hold your peace!
  Exorbitant sins must have exulceration.
VITTORIA: Surely, my lords, this lawyer here hath
    swallowed
  Some 'pothecaries' bills, or proclamations;
  And now the hard and undigestible words
  Come up, like stones we use give hawks for physic.
  Why, this is Welsh to Latin.
LAWYER: My lords, the woman
  Knows not her tropes, nor figures, nor is perfect   40
  In the academic derivation
  Of grammatical elocution.
FRANCISCO: Sir, your pains
  Shall be well spared, and your deep eloquence

28. *Diversivolent*: strife-desiring.   32. *Projections*: projects.
42. *Elocution*: expression.

Be worthily applauded amongst those
Which understand you.

LAWYER: My good lord.

FRANCISCO: Sir,
Put up your papers in your fustian bag –
    FRANCISCO *speaks this as in scorn.*
Cry mercy, sir, 'tis buckram, and accept
My notion of your learned verbosity.

LAWYER: I most graduatically thank your lordship:
50   I shall have use for them elsewhere.
    [*Exit.*]

MONTICELSO: I shall be plainer with you, and paint out
Your follies in more natural red and white
Than that upon your cheek.

VITTORIA: Oh, you mistake –
You raise a blood as noble in this cheek
As ever was your mother's.

MONTICELSO: I must spare you, till proof cry whore to that.
Observe this creature here, my honoured lords,
A woman of a most prodigious spirit
In her effected.

VITTORIA: Honourable my lord,
60   It doth not suit a reverend cardinal
To play the lawyer thus.

MONTICELSO: Oh, your trade instructs your language!
You see, my lords, what goodly fruit she seems;
Yet like those apples travellers report
To grow where Sodom and Gomorrah stood,
I will but touch her, and you straight shall see
She'll fall to soot and ashes.

VITTORIA: Your envenomed 'pothecary should do't.

MONTICELSO: I am resolved,
70   Were there a second paradise to lose,
This devil would betray it.

46. *Fustian:* (i) coarse cloth, (ii) bombast.
49. *Graduatically:* (i) with deliberate courtesy, (ii) like a graduate.
69. *Resolved:* convinced.

VITTORIA: O poor Charity!
  Thou art seldom found in scarlet.
MONTICELSO: Who knows not how, when several night
    by night
  Her gates were choked with coaches, and her rooms
  Outbraved the stars with several kind of lights;
  When she did counterfeit a prince's court
  In music, banquets, and most riotous surfeits;
  This whore forsooth was holy.
VITTORIA: Ha! Whore! What's that?
MONTICELSO: Shall I expound whore to you? Sure I shall;
  I'll give their perfect character. They are first,   80
  Sweetmeats which rot the eater; in man's nostrils
  Poisoned perfumes. They are cozening alchemy;
  Shipwrecks in calmest weather. What are whores!
  Cold Russian winters, that appear so barren,
  As if that nature had forgot the spring.
  They are the true material fire of hell:
  Worse than those tributes i'th'Low Countries paid,
  Exactions upon meat, drink, garments, sleep,
  Ay, even on man's perdition, his sin.
  They are those brittle evidences of law,   90
  Which forfeit all a wretched man's estate
  For leaving out one syllable. What are whores!
  They are those flattering bells have all one tune,
  At weddings, and at funerals. Your rich whores
  Are only treasuries by extortion filled,
  And emptied by cursèd riot. They are worse,
  Worse than dead bodies which are begged at gallows,
  And wrought upon by surgeons, to teach man
  Wherein he is imperfect. What's a whore!
  She's like the guilty counterfeited coin,   100
  Which, whosoe'er first stamps it, brings in trouble
  All that receive it.
VITTORIA: This character 'scapes me.

    80. *Character*: formal literary portrait.
    89. *Perdition*: prostitution.

MONTICELSO: You, gentlewoman?
Take from all beasts and from all minerals
Their deadly poison –
VITTORIA: Well, what then?
MONTICELSO: I'll tell thee;
I'll find in thee a 'pothecary's shop,
To sample them all.
FRENCH AMBASSADOR: She hath lived ill.
ENGLISH AMBASSADOR: True, but the cardinal's too
bitter.
MONTICELSO: You know what whore is. Next the devil
adultery,
110   Enters the devil murder.
FRANCISCO: Your unhappy husband is dead.
VITTORIA: Oh he's a happy husband
Now he owes nature nothing.
FRANCISCO: And by a vaulting engine.
MONTICELSO: An active plot; he jumped into his grave.
FRANCISCO: What a prodigy was't,
That from some two yards' height, a slender man
Should break his neck!
MONTICELSO: I'th'rushes!
FRANCISCO: And what's more,
Upon the instant lose all use of speech,
120   All vital motion, like a man had lain
Wound up three days. Now mark each circumstance.
MONTICELSO: And look upon this creature was his
wife!
She comes not like a widow; she comes armed
With scorn and impudence: is this a mourning-habit?
VITTORIA: Had I foreknown his death, as you suggest,
I would have bespoke my mourning.
MONTICELSO: Oh you are cunning!
VITTORIA: You shame your wit and judgement,
To call it so. What! Is my just defence
By him that is my judge called impudence?

     121. *Wound up:* shrouded.

Let me appeal then from this Christian court,   130
　　To the uncivil Tartar.
MONTICELSO:　　　　　　See, my lords,
　　She scandals our proceedings.
VITTORIA: Humbly thus,
　　Thus low, to the most worthy and respected
　　Lieger ambassadors, my modesty
　　And womanhood I tender; but withal,
　　So entangled in a curséd accusation,
　　That my defence, of force, like Perseus,
　　Must personate masculine virtue. To the point.
　　Find me but guilty, sever head from body,   140
　　We'll part good friends: I scorn to hold my life
　　At yours, or any man's entreaty, sir.
ENGLISH AMBASSADOR: She hath a brave spirit.
MONTICELSO: Well, well, such counterfeit jewels
　　Make true ones oft suspected.
VITTORIA:　　　　　　　　You are deceived:
　　For know, that all your strict-combinéd heads,
　　Which strike against this mine of diamonds,
　　Shall prove but glassen hammers; they shall break.
　　These are but feignéd shadows of my evils.
　　Terrify babes, my lord, with painted devils,   150
　　I am past such needless palsy. For your names
　　Of 'whore' and 'murderess', they proceed from you,
　　As if a man should spit against the wind,
　　The filth returns in's face.
MONTICELSO: Pray you mistress, satisfy me one question:
　　Who lodged beneath your roof that fatal night
　　Your husband brake his neck?
BRACHIANO:　　　　　　　　That question
　　Enforceth me break silence: I was there.
MONTICELSO: Your business?

130. *Christian*: (i) ecclesiastical, (ii) civilized.
131. *Uncivil*: uncivilized.
146. *Strict-combined*: closely (secretly?) leagued.
149. *Shadows*: often referring to portraits.

BRACHIANO: Why, I came to comfort her,
160 And take some course for settling her estate,
Because I heard her husband was in debt
To you, my lord.

MONTICELSO: He was.

BRACHIANO: And 'twas strangely feared,
That you would cozen her.

MONTICELSO: Who made you overseer?

BRACHIANO: Why, my charity, my charity, which should
flow
From every generous and noble spirit,
To orphans and to widows.

MONTICELSO: Your lust!

BRACHIANO: Cowardly dogs bark loudest: sirrah priest,
I'll talk with you hereafter. Do you hear?
The sword you frame of such an excellent temper,
170 I'll sheathe in your own bowels.
There are a number of thy coat resemble
Your common post-boys.

MONTICELSO: Ha?

BRACHIANO: Your mercenary post-boys;
Your letters carry truth, but 'tis your guise
To fill your mouths with gross and impudent lies.

SERVANT: My lord your gown.

BRACHIANO: Thou liest, 'twas my stool:
Bestow't upon thy master, that will challenge
The rest o'th'household-stuff; for Brachiano
Was ne'er so beggarly to take a stool
Out of another's lodging: let him make
180 Vallance for his bed on't, or a demy foot-cloth
For his most reverend moil. Monticelso,
Nemo me impune lacessit.
[*Exit* BRACHIANO.]

MONTICELSO: Your champion's gone.

VITTORIA: The wolf may prey the better.

FRANCISCO: My lord, there's great suspicion of the murder,

173. *Guise:* habit. 176. *Challenge:* claim. 181. *Moil:* mule.

But no sound proof who did it. For my part,
I do not think she hath a soul so black
To act a deed so bloody; if she have,
As in cold countries husbandmen plant vines,
And with warm blood manure them; even so
One summer she will bear unsavoury fruit,   190
And ere next spring wither both branch and root.
The act of blood let pass; only descend
To matter of incontinence.

VITTORIA: I discern poison
Under your gilded pills.

MONTICELSO: Now the duke's gone, I will produce a
    letter
Wherein 'twas plotted, he and you should meet
At an apothecary's summer-house,
Down by the River Tiber, – view't, my lords, –
Where after wanton bathing and the heat
Of a lascivious banquet – I pray read it,
I shame to speak the rest.

VITTORIA: Grant I was tempted;   200
Temptation to lust proves not the act:
Casta est quam nemo rogavit.
You read his hot love to me, but you want
My frosty answer.

MONTICELSO: Frost i'th'dog-days! Strange!

VITTORIA: Condemn you me for that the duke did love
    me?
So may you blame some fair and crystal river,
For that some melancholic distracted man
Hath drowned himself in't.

MONTICELSO: Truly drowned, indeed.

VITTORIA: Sum up my faults, I pray, and you shall find,
That beauty and gay clothes, a merry heart,   210
And a good stomach to feast, are all
All the poor crimes that you can charge me with.
In faith, my lord, you might go pistol flies,
The sport would be more noble.

MONTICELSO: Very good.

VITTORIA: But take you your course: it seems you've
beggared me first,
And now would fain undo me. I have houses,
Jewels, and a poor remnant of crusadoes;
Would those would make you charitable!

MONTICELSO: If the devil
Did ever take good shape, behold his picture.

220 VITTORIA: You have one virtue left,
You will not flatter me.

FRANCISCO: Who brought this letter?

VITTORIA: I am not compelled to tell you.

MONTICELSO: My lord duke sent to you a thousand
ducats
The twelfth of August.

VITTORIA: 'Twas to keep your cousin
From prison; I paid use for't.

MONTICELSO: I rather think,
'Twas interest for his lust.

VITTORIA: Who says so but yourself? If you be my
accuser,
Pray cease to be my judge: come from the bench;
Give in your evidence 'gainst me, and let these

230 Be moderators. My lord cardinal,
Were your intelligencing ears as long
As to my thoughts, had you an honest tongue,
I would not care though you proclaimed them all.

MONTICELSO: Go to, go to.
After your goodly and vainglorious banquet,
I'll give you a choke-pear.

VITTORIA: O'your own grafting?

MONTICELSO: You were born in Venice, honourably
descended

217. *Crusadoes:* Portuguese coins.
225. *Use:* interest.
231. *Intelligencing:* spying.
236. *Choke-pear:* unpalatable pear; figuratively, severe rebuke.

From the Vitelli: 'twas my cousin's fate, –
Ill may I name the hour, – to marry you;
He bought you of your father.

VITTORIA: Ha?   240

MONTICELSO: He spent there in six months
   Twelve thousand ducats, and, to my acquaintance,
   Received in dowry with you not one julio:
   'Twas a hard pennyworth, the ware being so light.
   I yet but draw the curtain; now to your picture:
   You came from thence a most notorious strumpet,
   And so you have continued.

VITTORIA: My lord –

MONTICELSO: Nay hear me.
   You shall have time to prate. My Lord Brachiano –
   Alas! I make but repetition
   Of what is ordinary and Rialto talk,   250
   And ballated, and would be played o'th'stage,
   But that vice many times finds such loud friends,
   That preachers are charmed silent.
   You, gentlemen, Flamineo and Marcello,
   The Court hath nothing now to charge you with,
   Only you must remain upon your sureties
   For your appearance.

FRANCISCO: I stand for Marcello.

FLAMINEO: And my lord duke for me.

MONTICELSO: For you, Vittoria, your public fault,
   Joined to th'condition of the present time,   260
   Takes from you all the fruits of noble pity,
   Such a corrupted trial have you made
   Both of your life and beauty, and been styled
   No less an ominous fate than blazing stars
   To princes. Hear your sentence: you are confined
   Unto a house of convertites, and your bawd –

243. *Julio:* coin worth about 6*d.*
244. *Light:* (i) in weight, (ii) in morals. A very common pun.
250. *Rialto talk:* town gossip.
251. *Ballated:* made the subject of ballads.

FLAMINEO [*aside*]: Who, I?

MONTICELSO: The Moor.

FLAMINEO [*aside*]: Oh, I am a sound man again.

VITTORIA: A house of convertites, what's that?

MONTICELSO: A house
Of penitent whores.

VITTORIA: Do the noblemen in Rome
270 Erect it for their wives, that I am sent
To lodge there?

FRANCISCO: You must have patience.

VITTORIA: I must first have vengeance!
I fain would know if you have your salvation
By patent, that you proceed thus.

MONTICELSO: Away with her,
Take her hence.

VITTORIA: A rape, a rape!

MONTICELSO: How?

VITTORIA: Yes you have ravished justice,
Forced her to do your pleasure.

MONTICELSO: Fie, she's mad –

VITTORIA: Die with those pills in your most cursèd maw,
Should bring you health! Or while you sit o'th'bench,
Let your own spittle choke you!

280 MONTICELSO: She's turned Fury.

VITTORIA: That the last day of judgement may so find you,
And leave you the same devil you were before!
Instruct me, some good horse-leech, to speak treason:
For since you cannot take my life for deeds,
Take it for words. O woman's poor revenge,
Which dwells but in the tongue! I will not weep;
No, I do scorn to call up one poor tear
To fawn on your injustice: bear me hence
Unto this house of – what's your mitigating title?

290 MONTICELSO: Of convertites.

VITTORIA: It shall not be a house of convertites;
My mind shall make it honester to me

283. *Horse-leech*: blood-sucker.

Than the Pope's palace, and more peaceable
Than thy soul, though thou art a cardinal.
Know this, and let it somewhat raise your spite,
Through darkness diamonds spread their richest light.
    [*Exit* VITTORIA.]
    Enter BRACHIANO.

BRACHIANO: Now you and I are friends, sir, we'll shake hands
In a friend's grave together; a fit place,
Being th'emblem of soft peace, t'atone our hatred.

FRANCISCO: Sir, what's the matter?   300

BRACHIANO: I will not chase more blood from that loved cheek;
You have lost too much already; fare you well.
    [*Exit.*]

FRANCISCO: How strange these words sound! What's the interpretation?

FLAMINEO [*aside*]: Good; this is a preface to the discovery of the duchess' death: he carries it well. Because now I cannot counterfeit a whining passion for the death of my lady, I will feign a mad humour for the disgrace of my sister; and that will keep off idle questions. Treason's tongue hath a villainous palsy in't; I will talk to any man, hear no man, and for a time appear a politic 310 madman.
    [*Exit.*]
    Enter GIOVANNI, COUNT LODOVICO.

FRANCISCO: How now, my noble cousin? What, in black!

GIOVANNI: Yes uncle, I was taught to imitate you
In virtue, and you must imitate me
In colours for your garments. My sweet mother
Is –

FRANCISCO: How? Where?

GIOVANNI: Is there; no, yonder: indeed, sir, I'll not tell you,
For I shall make you weep.

      309. *Palsy:* uncontrolled movement.

FRANCISCO: Is dead?

320 GIOVANNI: Do not blame me now,
    I did not tell you so.

LODOVICO: She's dead, my lord.

FRANCISCO: Dead!

MONTICELSO: Bless'd lady, thou art now above thy woes!
    Will't please your lordships to withdraw a little?
    [*Exeunt* AMBASSADORS.]

GIOVANNI: What do the dead do, uncle? Do they eat,
    Hear music, go a-hunting, and be merry,
    As we that live?

FRANCISCO: No, coz; they sleep.

GIOVANNI: Lord, Lord that I were dead!
    I have not slept these six nights. When do they wake?

FRANCISCO: When God shall please.

330 GIOVANNI: Good God, let her sleep ever
    For I have known her wake an hundred nights,
    When all the pillow where she laid her head
    Was brine-wet with her tears. I am to complain to you,
        sir;
    I'll tell you how they have us'd her now she's dead:
    They wrapped her in a cruel fold of lead,
    And would not let me kiss her.

FRANCISCO: Thou didst love her.

GIOVANNI: I have often heard her say she gave me suck,
    And it should seem by that she dearly loved me,
    Since princes seldom do it.

340 FRANCISCO: Oh, all of my poor sister that remains!
    Take him away for God's sake!
    [*Exit* GIOVANNI *attended.*]

MONTICELSO: How now, my lord?

FRANCISCO: Believe me, I am nothing but her grave;
    And I shall keep her blessed memory
    Longer than thousand epitaphs.
    [*Exeunt.*]

[SCENE THREE]

Enter FLAMINEO *as distracted,* [MARCELLO, *and* LODOVICO].

FLAMINEO: We endure the strokes like anvils or hard steel,
Till pain itself make us no pain to feel.
Who shall do me right now? Is this the end of service?
I'd rather go weed garlic; travel through France, and
be mine own ostler; wear sheep-skin linings, or shoes
that stink of blacking; be entered into the list of the
forty thousand pedlars in Poland.

Enter SAVOY [AMBASSADOR].

Would I had rotted in some surgeon's house at Venice,
built upon the pox as well as on piles, ere I had served
Brachiano!   10

SAVOY AMBASSADOR: You must have comfort.

FLAMINEO: Your comfortable words are like honey: they
relish well in your mouth that's whole, but in mine that's
wounded, they go down as if the sting of the bee were
in them. Oh they have wrought their purpose cunningly,
as if they would not seem to do it of malice! In this a
politician imitates the devil, as the devil imitates a canon;
wheresoever he comes to do mischief, he comes with his
backside towards you.

Enter the FRENCH [AMBASSADOR].

FRENCH AMBASSADOR: The proofs are evident.   20

FLAMINEO: Proof! 'Twas corruption. O gold, what a god
art thou! And O man, what a devil art thou to be tempted
by that cursed mineral! Yon diversivolent lawyer, mark
him! Knaves turn informers, as maggots turn to flies,
you may catch gudgeons with either. A cardinal! I
would he would hear me: there's nothing so holy but
money will corrupt and putrify it, like victual under the
line.

Enter ENGLISH AMBASSADOR.

25. *Gudgeons:* figuratively, dupes.

You are happy in England, my lord; here they sell
30 justice with those weights they press men to death with.
O horrible salary!

ENGLISH AMBASSADOR: Fie, fie, Flamineo.

FLAMINEO: Bells ne'er ring well, till they are at their full
pitch; and I hope yon cardinal shall never have the grace
to pray well till he come to the scaffold.

[*Exeunt* AMBASSADORS.]

If they were racked now to know the confederacy: but
your noblemen are privileged from the rack; and well
may, for a little thing would pull some of them a-pieces
afore they came to their arraignment. Religion, oh, how
40 it is commeddled with policy! The first blood shed in the
world happened about religion. Would I were a Jew!

MARCELLO: Oh, there are too many!

FLAMINEO: You are deceived; there are not Jews enough,
priests enough, nor gentlemen enough.

MARCELLO: How?

FLAMINEO: I'll prove it; for if there were Jews enough, so
many Christians would not turn usurers; if priests
enough, one should not have six benefices; and if
gentlemen enough, so many early mushrooms, whose
50 best growth sprang from a dunghill, should not aspire
to gentility. Farewell: let others live by begging: be
thou one of them; practise the art of Wolner in England,
to swallow all's given thee: and yet let one purgation
make thee as hungry again as fellows that work in a
saw-pit. I'll go hear the screech-owl.

[*Exit.*]

LODOVICO: This was Brachiano's pander; and 'tis strange
That in such open, and apparent guilt
Of his adulterous sister, he dare utter
So scandalous a passion. I must wind him.

Enter FLAMINEO.

60 FLAMINEO: How dares this banished count return to Rome,

34. *Pitch*: height.   49. *Mushrooms*: upstarts.
59. *Wind*: get wind of.

His pardon not yet purchased? I have heard
The deceased duchess gave him pension,
And that he came along from Padua
I'th'train of the young prince. There's somewhat in't:
Physicians, that cure poisons, still do work
With counter-poisons.

MARCELLO: Mark this strange encounter.

FLAMINEO: The god of melancholy turn thy gall to
poison,
And let the stigmatic wrinkles in thy face,
Like to the boisterous waves in a rough tide,
One still overtake another.

LODOVICO: I do thank thee,   70
And I do wish ingeniously for thy sake,
The dog-days all year long.

FLAMINEO: How croaks the raven?
Is our good duchess dead?

LODOVICO: Dead.

FLAMINEO: O fate!
Misfortune comes like the coroner's business
Huddle upon huddle.

LODOVICO: Shalt thou and I join housekeeping?

FLAMINEO: Yes, content:
Let's be unsociably sociable.

LODOVICO: Sit some three days together, and discourse.

FLAMINEO: Only with making faces;
Lie in our clothes.   80

LODOVICO: With faggots for our pillows.

FLAMINEO: And be lousy.

LODOVICO: In taffeta linings, that's genteel melancholy;
Sleep all day.

FLAMINEO: Yes; and like your melancholic hare,
Feed after midnight.

Enter ANTONELLI [*and* GASPARO].

61. *Purchased:* obtained, not necessarily for money.
68. *Stigmatic:* marked by nature.
71. *Ingeniously:* used interchangeably with 'ingenuously'.

We are observed: see how yon couple grieve.

LODOVICO: What a strange creature is a laughing
fool!
As if man were created to no use
But only to show his teeth.

FLAMINEO: I'll tell thee what,
It would do well instead of looking-glasses,
90 To set one's face each morning by a saucer
Of a witch's congealed blood.

LODOVICO: Precious girn, rogue!
We'll never part.

FLAMINEO: Never, till the beggary of courtiers,
The discontent of churchmen, want of soldiers,
And all the creatures that hang manacled,
Worse than strappadoed, on the lowest felly
Of fortune's wheel, be taught, in our two lives.
To scorn that world which life of means deprives.

ANTONELLI: My lord, I bring good news. The Pope, on's
death-bed,
100 At th'earnest suit of the great Duke of Florence,
Hath signed your pardon, and restored unto you –

LODOVICO: I thank you for your news. Look up again,
Flamineo, see my pardon.

FLAMINEO: Why do you laugh?
There was no such condition in our covenant.

LODOVICO: Why?

FLAMINEO: You shall not seem a happier man than I:
You know our vow, sir; if you will be merry,
Do it i'th'like posture, as if some great man
Sat while his enemy were executed:
110 Though it be very lechery unto thee,
Do't with a crabbed politician's face.

LODOVICO: Your sister is a damnable whore.

90. *Saucer*: receptacle used in blood letting.
91. *Girn*: (i) snarl (grin), (ii) snare, wile.
96. *Strappadoed*: hung by hands tied behind back. *Felly*: section of
wheel-rim.

FLAMINEO: Ha?

LODOVICO: Look you, I spake that laughing.

FLAMINEO: Dost ever think to speak again?

LODOVICO: Do you hear?
  Wilt sell me forty ounces of her blood
  To water a mandrake?

FLAMINEO: Poor lord, you did vow
  To live a lousy creature.

LODOVICO: Yes.

FLAMINEO: Like one
  That had for ever forfeited the daylight,
  By being in debt.

LODOVICO: Ha, Ha!

FLAMINEO: I do not greatly wonder you do break,   120
  Your lordship learned't long since. But I'll tell you.

LODOVICO: What?

FLAMINEO: And't shall stick by you.

LODOVICO: I long for it.

FLAMINEO: This laughter scurvily becomes your face:
  If you will not be melancholy, be angry.
    Strikes him.
  See, now I laugh too.

MARCELLO: You are to blame: I'll force you hence.

LODOVICO: Unhand me.
    Exeunt MARCELLO *and* FLAMINEO.
  That e'er I should be forced to right myself,
  Upon a pander!

ANTONELLI: My lord.

LODOVICO: H'had been as good met with his fist a
  thunderbolt.   130

GASPARO: How this shows!

LODOVICO: Ud's death! How did my sword miss
  him?
  These rogues that are most weary of their lives
  Still 'scape the greatest dangers.
  A pox upon him; all his reputation,

      120. *Break:* (i) break your oath, (ii) go bankrupt.

Nay, all the goodness of his family,
Is not worth half this earthquake:
I learn'd it of no fencer to shake thus:
Come, I'll forget him, and go drink some wine.
    Exeunt.

[ACT FOUR]

*

[SCENE ONE]

Enter FRANCISCO *and* MONTICELSO.

MONTICELSO: Come, come, my lord, untie your folded thoughts,
    And let them dangle loose, as a bride's hair.
    Your sister's poisoned.

FRANCISCO: Far be it from my thoughts
    To seek revenge.

MONTICELSO: What, are you turned all marble?

FRANCISCO: Shall I defy him, and impose a war,
    Most burthensome on my poor subjects' necks,
    Which at my will I have not power to end?
    You know, for all the murders, rapes, and thefts,
    Committed in the horrid lust of war,
    He that unjustly caused it first proceed,   10
    Shall find it in his grave, and in his seed.

MONTICELSO: That's not the course I'd wish you; pray observe me.
    We see that undermining more prevails
    Than doth the cannon. Bear your wrongs concealed,
    And, patient as the tortoise, let this camel
    Stalk o'er your back unbruised: sleep with the lion,
    And let this brood of secure foolish mice
    Play with your nostrils, till the time be ripe
    For th'bloody audit, and the fatal gripe:
    Aim like a cunning fowler, close one eye,   20
    That you the better may your game espy.

FRANCISCO: Free me, my innocence, from treacherous acts!
    I know there's thunder yonder; and I'll stand,
    Like a safe valley, which low bends the knee
    To some aspiring mountain: since I know
    Treason, like spiders weaving nets for flies,

By her foul work is found, and in it dies. –
To pass away these thoughts, my honoured lord,
It is reported you possess a book,
30   Wherein you have quoted, by intelligence,
The names of all notorious offenders
Lurking about the city.

MONTICELSO: Sir, I do;
And some there are which call it my black book.
Well may the title hold; for though it teach not
The art of conjuring, yet in it lurk
The names of many devils.

FRANCISCO: Pray let's see it.

MONTICELSO: I'll fetch it to your lordship.
  Exit.

FRANCISCO: Monticelso,
I will not trust thee, but in all my plots
I'll rest as jealous as a town besieged.
40   Thou canst not reach what I intend to act:
Your flax soon kindles, soon is out again,
But gold slow heats, and long will hot remain.
  Enter MONTICELSO, *presents* FRANCISCO *with a book.*

MONTICELSO: 'Tis here, my lord.

FRANCISCO: First, your intelligencers, pray let's see.

MONTICELSO: Their number rises strangely;
And some of them
You'd take for honest men.
Next are panders.
These are your pirates; and these following leaves
50   For base rogues that undo young gentlemen
By taking up commodities; for politic bankrupts;
For fellows that are bawds to their own wives,
Only to put off horses, and slight jewels,
Clocks, defaced plate, and such commodities,
At birth of their first children.

FRANCISCO: Are there such?

MONTICELSO: These are for impudent bawds

39. *Jealous:* watchful.

That go in men's apparel; for usurers
That share with scriveners for their good reportage:
For lawyers that will antedate their writs:
And some divines you might find folded there,   60
But that I slip them o'er for conscience' sake.
Here is a general catalogue of knaves:
A man might study all the prisons o'er,
Yet never attain this knowledge.

FRANCISCO: Murderers?
Fold down the leaf, I pray;
Good my lord, let me borrow this strange doctrine.

MONTICELSO: Pray use't my lord.

FRANCISCO: I do assure your lordship,
You are a worthy member of the State,
And have done infinite good in your discovery
Of these offenders.

MONTICELSO: Somewhat, sir.

FRANCISCO: O God!   70
Better than tribute of wolves paid in England;
'Twill hang their skins o'th'hedge.

MONTICELSO: I must make bold
To leave your lordship.

FRANCISCO: Dearly, sir, I thank you:
If any ask for me at court, report
You have left me in the company of knaves.

   Exit MONTICELSO.

I gather now by this, some cunning fellow
That's my lord's officer, one that lately skipped
From a clerk's desk up to a justice' chair,
Hath made this knavish summons, and intends,
As th' Irish rebels wont were to sell heads,   80
So to make prize of these. And thus it happens:
Your poor rogues pay for't, which have not the means
To present bribe in fist; the rest o'th'band
Are razed out of the knaves' record; or else
My lord he winks at them with easy will;
His man grows rich, the knaves are the knaves still.

But to the use I'll make of it; it shall serve
To point me out a list of murderers,
Agents for any villainy. Did I want
90 Ten leash of courtesans, it would furnish me;
Nay, laundress three armies. That in so little paper
Should lie th'undoing of so many men!
'Tis not so big as twenty declarations.
See the corrupted use some make of books:
Divinity, wrested by some factious blood,
Draws swords, swells battles, and o'erthrows all good.
To fashion my revenge more seriously,
Let me remember my dead sister's face:
Call for her picture? No, I'll close mine eyes,
100 And in a melancholic thought I'll frame
Her figure 'fore me.

    Enter ISABELLA's *Ghost.*

                Now I ha' 't – how strong
Imagination works! How she can frame
Things which are not! Methinks she stands afore me.
And by the quick idea of my mind,
Were my skill pregnant, I could draw her picture.
Thought, as a subtle juggler, makes us deem
Things supernatural, which have cause
Common as sickness. 'Tis my melancholy.
How cam'st thou by thy death? – how idle am I
110 To question mine own idleness! – Did ever
Man dream awake till now? – remove this object;
Out of my brain with't: what have I to do
With tombs, or death-beds, funerals, or tears,
That have to meditate upon revenge?

    [*Exit Ghost.*]

So, now 'tis ended, like an old wife's story.
Statesmen think often they see stranger sights

90. *Leash:* sporting term meaning 'set of three'.
93. *Declarations:* public proclamations.
106. *Juggler:* magician.
110. *Idleness:* folly.

Than madmen. Come, to this weighty business.
My tragedy must have some idle mirth in't,
Else it will never pass. I am in love,
In love with Corombona; and my suit   120
Thus halts to her in verse. –
   He writes.
I have done it rarely: Oh, the fate of princes!
I am so used to frequent flattery,
That, being alone, I now flatter myself:
But it will serve; 'tis sealed.
   [*Enter servant.*]
                         Bear this
To the House of Convertites, and watch your leisure
To give it to the hands of Corombona,
Or to the Matron, when some followers
Of Brachiano may be by. Away!
   Exit servant.
He that deals all by strength, his wit is shallow;   130
When a man's head goes through, each limb will follow.
The engine for my business, bold Count Lodowick;
'Tis gold must such an instrument procure,
With empty fist no man doth falcons lure.
Brachiano, I am now fit for thy encounter:
Like the wild Irish, I'll ne'er think thee dead
Till I can play at football with thy head,
Flectere si nequeo superos, Acheronta movebo.
   Exit.

[SCENE TWO]

   Enter the MATRON, *and* FLAMINEO.
MATRON: Should it be known the duke hath such recourse
   To your imprisoned sister, I were like
   T'incur much damage by it.
FLAMINEO: Not a scruple.
      3. *Scruple:* a minute quantity.

The Pope lies on his death-bed, and their heads
Are troubled now with other business
Than guarding of a lady.

Enter SERVANT.

SERVANT: Yonder's Flamineo in conference
With the Matrona. – [*To the* MATRON] Let me speak with
you:
I would entreat you to deliver for me
10   This letter to the fair Vittoria.

MATRON: I shall, sir.

Enter BRACHIANO.

SERVANT: With all care and secrecy;
Hereafter you shall know me, and receive
Thanks for this courtesy.

Exit.

FLAMINEO: How now? What's that?

MATRON: A letter.

FLAMINEO: To my sister? I'll see't delivered.

Exit MATRON.

BRACHIANO: What's that you read, Flamineo?

FLAMINEO: Look.

BRACHIANO: Ha! 'To the most unfortunate, his best
respected Vittoria'.
Who was the messenger?

FLAMINEO: I know not.

BRACHIANO: No! Who sent it?

FLAMINEO: Ud's foot! You speak as if a man
Should know what fowl is coffined in a baked meat
20   Afore you cut it up.

BRACHIANO: I'll open it, were't her heart. What's here
subscribed –
Florence? This juggling is gross and palpable.
I have found out the conveyance. Read it, read it.

FLAMINEO [*reads the letter*]: *Your tears I'll turn to triumphs,*
be but mine;

19. *Coffin:* common term for 'pie-crust'.
23. *Conveyance:* (i) device, (ii) means of communication.

Your prop is fallen: I pity that a vine,
Which princes heretofore have longed to gather,
Wanting supporters, now should fade and wither.
Wine, i' faith, my lord, with lees would serve his turn.
Your sad imprisonment I'll soon uncharm,
And with a princely uncontrolléd arm   30
Lead you to Florence, where my love and care
Shall hang your wishes in my silver hair.
A halter on his strange equivocation!
Nor for my years return me the sad willow;
Who prefer blossoms before fruit that's mellow?
Rotten, on my knowledge, with lying too long i'th'bed-
straw.
And all the lines of age this line convinces;
The gods never wax old, no more do princes.
A pox on't, tear it; let's have no more atheists, for God's
sake.

BRACHIANO: Ud's death, I'll cut her into atomies,   40
And let th'irregular north wind sweep her up,
And blow her int'his nostrils: where's this whore?
FLAMINEO: That? What do you call her?
BRACHIANO: Oh, I could be mad!
Prevent the cursed disease she'll bring me to,
And tear my hair off. Where's this changeable stuff?
FLAMINEO: O'er head and ears in water, I assure you;
She is not for your wearing.
BRACHIANO: In, you pander!
FLAMINEO: What, me, my lord? Am I your dog?
BRACHIANO: A bloodhound: do you brave, do you
stand me?
FLAMINEO: Stand you? Let those that have diseases run; 50
I need no plasters.
BRACHIANO: Would you be kicked?

36. *Bedstraw:* straw for ripening fruit.
39. *Atheists:* unbelievers, or wicked persons generally.
45. *Changeable stuff:* fickle woman.
49. *Stand:* defy (cf. 'face' in line 66 below).

FLAMINEO: Would you have your neck broke?
I tell you duke, I am not in Russia;
My shins must be kept whole.

BRACHIANO: Do you know me?

FLAMINEO: Oh my lord, methodically!
As in this world there are degrees of evils,
So in this world there are degrees of devils.
You're a great duke, I your poor secretary.
I do look now for a Spanish fig, or an Italian sallet,
    daily.

BRACHIANO: Pander, ply your convoy, and leave your
60   prating.

FLAMINEO: All your kindness to me, is like that miserable
courtesy of Polyphemus to Ulysses; you reserve me to be
devoured last: you would dig turves out of my grave to
feed your larks; that would be music to you. Come, I'll
lead you to her.

BRACHIANO: Do you face me?

FLAMINEO: Oh, sir, I would not go before a politic
enemy with my back towards him, though there were
behind me a whirlpool.

   Enter VITTORIA *to* BRACHIANO *and* FLAMINEO.

BRACHIANO: Can you read, mistress? look upon that
70   letter:
There are no characters, nor hieroglyphics.
You need no comment; I am grown your receiver.
God's precious! you shall be a brave great lady,
A stately and advancéd whore.

VITTORIA: Say, sir?

BRACHIANO: Come, come let's see your cabinet, discover
Your treasury of love-letters. Death and furies!
I'll see them all.

    56. *Methodically:* everything is under control.
    60. *Ply your convoy:* do your business.
    71. *Characters:* magical signs or emblems.
    72. *Receiver:* pimp.
    73. *God's precious:* God's blood.

VITTORIA: Sir, upon my soul,
  I have not any. Whence was this directed?
BRACHIANO: Confusion on your politic ignorance!
  You are reclaimed, are you? I'll give you the bells, 80
  [*Gives her letter.*] And let you fly to the devil.
FLAMINEO: Ware hawk, my lord.
VITTORIA: Florence! This is some treacherous plot, my lord;
  To me he ne'er was lovely, I protest,
  So much as in my sleep.
BRACHIANO: Right! They are plots.
  Your beauty! Oh, ten thousand curses on 't!
  How long have I beheld the devil in crystal!
  Thou hast led me, like an heathen sacrifice,
  With music, and with fatal yokes of flowers,
  To my eternal ruin. Woman to man
  Is either a god, or a wolf.
VITTORIA: My lord –
BRACHIANO: Away! 90
  We'll be as differing as two adamants,
  The one shall shun the other. What? Dost weep?
  Procure but ten of thy dissembling trade,
  Ye'd furnish all the Irish funerals
  With howling past wild Irish.
FLAMINEO: Fie, my lord!
BRACHIANO: That hand, that curséd hand, which I have
    wearied
  With doting kisses! – Oh, my sweetest duchess,
  How lovely art thou now! [*To* VITTORIA.] Thy loose
    thoughts
  Scatter like quicksilver: I was bewitched;
  For all the world speaks ill of thee.
VITTORIA: No matter; 100
  I'll live so now, I'll make that world recant,
  And change her speeches. You did name your duchess.

  80. *Reclaimed:* (i) brought back from evil, (ii) recalled or tamed (of
a hawk, in falconry).
  91. *Adamants:* magnets.

BRACHIANO: Whose death God pardon!

VITTORIA: Whose death God revenge
On thee, most godless duke!

FLAMINEO: Now for two whirlwinds.

VITTORIA: What have I gained by thee, but infamy?
Thou hast stained the spotless honour of my house,
And frighted thence noble society:
Like those which sick o'th'palsy and retain
Ill-scenting foxes 'bout them, are still shunned
110 By those of choicer nostrils. What do you call this house?
Is this your palace? Did not the judge style it
A house of penitent whores? Who sent me to it?
Who hath the honour to advance Vittoria
To this incontinent college? Is't not you?
Is't not your high preferment? Go, go, brag
How many ladies you have undone, like me.
Fare you well, sir; let me hear no more of you.
I had a limb corrupted to an ulcer,
But I have cut it off; and now I'll go
120 Weeping to heaven on crutches. For your gifts,
I will return them all, and I do wish
That I could make you full executor
To all my sins. O that I could toss myself
Into a grave as quickly! for all thou art worth
I'll not shed one tear more – I'll burst first.
    She throws herself upon a bed.

BRACHIANO: I have drunk Lethe: Vittoria!
My dearest happiness! Vittoria!
What do you ail, my love? Why do you weep?

VITTORIA: Yes, I now weep poniards, do you see?

BRACHIANO: Are not those matchless eyes mine?

130 VITTORIA: I had rather
They were not matches.

BRACHIANO: Is not this lip mine?

VITTORIA: Yes; thus to bite it off, rather than give it thee.

FLAMINEO: Turn to my lord, good sister.

---

129. *Poniards:* daggers.   131. *Not matches:* not a pair.

VITTORIA: Hence, you pander!

FLAMINEO: Pander! Am I the author of your sin?

VITTORIA: Yes; he's a base thief that a thief lets in.

FLAMINEO: We're blown up, my lord –

BRACHIANO: Wilt thou hear me?
Once to be jealous of thee, is t'express
That I will love thee everlastingly,
And never more be jealous.

VITTORIA: O thou fool,
Whose greatness hath by much o'ergrown thy wit: 140
What dar'st thou do, that I not dare to suffer,
Excepting to be still thy whore? For that,
In the sea's bottom sooner thou shalt make
A bonfire.

FLAMINEO: Oh, no oaths, for God's sake!

BRACHIANO: Will you hear me?

VITTORIA: Never.

FLAMINEO: What a damned imposthume is a woman's
    will!
Can nothing break it? Fie, fie, my lord,
    Aside to BRACHIANO.
Women are caught as you take tortoises,
She must be turned on her back. – Sister, by this hand
I am on your side. – Come, come, you have wronged 150
    her;
What a strange credulous man were you, my lord,
To think the Duke of Florence would love her!
– Will any mercer take another's ware
When once 'tis toused and sullied? – And yet, sister,
How scurvily this forwardness becomes you!
– Young leverets stand not long, and women's anger
Should, like their flight, procure a little sport;
A full cry for a quarter of an hour,
And then be put to th'dead quat.

146. *Imposthume:* festering swelling.
157. *Leverets:* young hares. *Stand:* hold out (hunting term).
159. *Quat:* squat (hunting term).

BRACHIANO: Shall these eyes,
160   Which have so long time dwelt upon your face,
Be now put out?

FLAMINEO: No cruel landlady i'th'world,
Which lends forth groats to broom-men, and takes use
For them, would do't.
  Aside to BRACHIANO.
Hand her, my lord, and kiss her: be not like
A ferret, to let go your hold with blowing.

BRACHIANO: Let us renew right hands.

VITTORIA: Hence!

BRACHIANO: Never shall rage, or the forgetful wine,
Make me commit like fault.

FLAMINEO [*aside to* BRACHIANO]: Now you are i'th'way
170   on't, follow't hard.

BRACHIANO: Be thou at peace with me, let all the world
Threaten the cannon.

FLAMINEO: Mark his penitence;
Best natures do commit the grossest faults,
When they're given o'er to jealousy, as best wine,
Dying, makes strongest vinegar. I'll tell you:
The sea's more rough and raging than calm rivers,
But not so sweet, nor wholesome. A quiet woman
Is a still water under a great bridge;
A man may shoot her safely.

VITTORIA: O ye dissembling men!

180 FLAMINEO: We sucked that, sister,
From women's breasts, in our first infancy.

VITTORIA: To add misery to misery!

BRACHIANO: Sweetest!

VITTORIA: Am I not low enough?
Ay, ay, your good heart gathers like a snowball,
Now your affection's cold.

FLAMINEO: Ud's foot, it shall melt
To a heart again, or all the wine in Rome
Shall run o'th'lees for't.

162. *Use:* interest.   168. *Forgetful:* inducing forgetfulness.

VITTORIA: Your dog or hawk should be rewarded better
    Than I have been. I'll speak not one word more.
FLAMINEO: Stop her mouth   190
    With a sweet kiss, my lord. So,
    Now the tide's turned, the vessel's come about.
    He's a sweet armful. Oh, we curled-haired men
    Are still most kind to women! This is well.
BRACHIANO: That you should chide thus!
FLAMINEO: Oh, sir, your little chimneys
    Do ever cast most smoke! I sweat for you.
    Couple together with as deep a silence,
    As did the Grecians in their wooden horse.
    My lord, supply your promises with deeds;
    You know that painted meat no hunger feeds.   200
BRACHIANO: Stay, ungrateful Rome –
FLAMINEO: Rome! It deserves to be called Barbary,
    For our villainous usage.
BRACHIANO: Soft; the same project which the Duke of
        Florence,
    Whether in love or gullery I know not –
    Laid down for her escape, will I pursue.
FLAMINEO: And no time fitter than this night, my lord.
    The Pope being dead, and all the cardinals entered
    The conclave, for th'electing a new Pope;
    The city in a great confusion;   210
    We may attire her in a page's suit;
    Lay her post-horse, take shipping, and amain
    For Padua.
BRACHIANO: I'll instantly steal forth the Prince Giovanni,
    And make for Padua. You two with your old mother,
    And young Marcello that attends on Florence,
    If you can work him to it, follow me:
    I will advance you all; for you, Vittoria,
    Think of a duchess' title.
FLAMINEO: Lo you, sister!

194. *Still:* always.   205. *Gullery:* as a trap.
212. *Amain:* at once.

220 Stay, my lord; I'll tell you a tale. The crocodile, which
lives in the River Nilus, hath a worm breeds i'th'teeth
of it, which puts it to extreme anguish: a little bird, no
bigger than a wren, is barber-surgeon to this crocodile;
flies into the jaws of't, picks out the worm, and brings
present remedy. The fish, glad of ease, but ungrateful to
her that did it, that the bird may not talk largely of her
abroad for non-payment, closeth her chaps, intending to
swallow her, and so put her to perpetual silence. But
nature, loathing such ingratitude, hath armed this bird

230 with a quill or prick on the head, top o'th'which wounds
the crocodile i'th'mouth, forceth her open her bloody
prison, and away flies the pretty tooth-picker from her
cruel patient.

BRACHIANO: Your application is, I have not rewarded
The service you have done me.

FLAMINEO: No, my lord.
You, sister, are the crocodile: you are blemished in your
fame, my lord cures it; and though the comparison hold
not in every particle, yet observe, remember, what good
the bird with the prick i'th'head hath done you, and

240 scorn ingratitude.
[*Aside*] It may appear to some ridiculous
Thus to talk knave and madman, and sometimes
Come in with a dried sentence, stuffed with sage:
But this allows my varying of shapes;
Knaves do grow great by being great men's apes.
  Exeunt.

[SCENE THREE]

Enter LODOVICO, GASPARO, *and six Ambassadors.*
At another door [FRANCISCO,] *the Duke of Florence.*
FRANCISCO: So, my lord, I commend your diligence –
Guard well the conclave; and, as the order is,

243. *Sentence:* aphorism.

Let none have conference with the cardinals.

LODOVICO: I shall, my lord. Room for the ambassadors.

GASPARO: They're wondrous brave today: why do they wear
These several habits?

LODOVICO: Oh, sir, they're knights
Of several orders:
That lord i'th'black cloak, with the silver cross,
Is Knight of Rhodes; the next, Knight of St Michael;
That, of the Golden Fleece; the Frenchman, there,   10
Knight of the Holy Ghost; my Lord of Savoy,
Knight of th'Annunciation; the Englishman
Is Knight of th'honoured Garter, dedicated
Unto their saint, St George. I could describe to you
Their several institutions, with the laws
Annexed to their orders; but that time
Permits not such discovery.

FRANCISCO: Where's Count Lodowick?

LODOVICO: Here, my lord.

FRANCISCO: 'Tis o'th'point of dinner time;
Marshal the cardinals' service.

LODOVICO: Sir, I shall.
    [*Enter* SERVANTS, *with several dishes covered.*]
Stand, let me search your dish. Who's this for?   20

SERVANT: For my Lord Cardinal Monticelso.

LODOVICO: Whose this?

SERVANT: For my Lord Cardinal of Bourbon.

FRENCH AMBASSADOR: Why doth he search the dishes? to observe
What meat is dressed?

ENGLISH AMBASSADOR: No, sir, but to prevent
Lest any letters should be conveyed in,
To bribe or to solicit the advancement
Of any cardinal. When first they enter,
'Tis lawful for the ambassadors of princes
To enter with them, and to make their suit   30
For any man their prince affecteth best;

But after, till a general election,
No man may speak with them.

LODOVICO: You that attend on the lord cardinals,
Open the window, and receive their viands.

CONCLAVIST [*appearing at window*]: You must return the
service: the lord cardinals
Are busied 'bout electing of the Pope;
They have given o'er scrutiny, and are fallen
To admiration.

LODOVICO: Away, away.

40 FRANCISCO: I'll lay a thousand ducats you hear news
Of a Pope presently. Hark; sure he's elected;
Behold my Lord of Arragon appears
On the church battlements.

          Cardinal [*of* ARRAGON] *on the terrace.*

ARRAGON: *Denuntio vobis gaudium magnum: Reverendissimus*
Cardinalis Lorenzo de Monticelso electus est in sedem aposto-
licam, et elegit sibi nomen Paulum Quartum.

OMNES: *Vivat Sanctus Pater Paulus Quartus!*

          [*Enter* SERVANT.]

SERVANT: Vittoria, my lord –

FRANCISCO: Well, what of her?

SERVANT: Is fled the city –

FRANCISCO: Ha!

SERVANT: With Duke Brachiano.

FRANCISCO: Fled! Where's the Prince Giovanni?

50 SERVANT: Gone with his father.

FRANCISCO: Let the Matrona of the Convertites
Be apprehended. Fled? O damnable!

          [*Exit* SERVANT.]

[*Aside*] How fortunate are my wishes! Why, 'twas this
I only laboured: I did send the letter
T'instruct him what to do. Thy fame, fond duke,
I first have poisoned; directed thee the way
To marry a whore; what can be worse? This follows:
The hand must act to drown the passionate tongue,

          55. *Fond:* infatuated, foolish.

I scorn to wear a sword and prate of wrong.
Enter MONTICELSO *in State.*
MONTICELSO: *Concedimus vobis Apostolicam benedictionem, et* 60
remissionem peccatorum.
   [FRANCISCO *whispers to him.*]
My lord reports Vittoria Corombona
Is stolen from forth the House of Convertites
By Brachiano, and they're fled the city.
Now, though this be the first day of our seat,
We cannot better please the Divine Power,
Than to sequester from the Holy Church
These cursèd persons. Make it therefore known,
We do denounce excommunication
Against them both: all that are theirs in Rome   70
We likewise banish. Set on.
   Exeunt [all but FRANCISCO *and* LODOVICO].
FRANCISCO: Come, dear Lodovico;
   You have ta'en the sacrament to prosecute
   Th'intended murder?
LODOVICO: With all constancy.
   But sir, I wonder you'll engage yourself
   In person, being a great prince.
FRANCISCO: Divert me not.
   Most of his court are of my faction,
   And some are of my counsel. Noble friend,
   Our danger shall be like in this design: 80
   Give leave part of the glory may be mine.
   Exit FRANCISCO.
   Enter MONTICELSO.
MONTICELSO: Why did the Duke of Florence with such
   care
   Labour your pardon? Say.
LODOVICO: Italian beggars will resolve you that,
   Who, begging of an alms, bid those they beg of,
   Do good for their own sakes; or't may be,
   He spreads his bounty with a sowing hand,

                65. *Seat:* technical term for Papal throne.

Like kings, who many times give out of measure,
Not for desert so much, as for their pleasure.

MONTICELSO: I know you're cunning. Come, what devil
90   was that
That you were raising?

LODOVICO: Devil, my lord?

MONTICELSO: I ask you,
How doth the duke employ you, that his bonnet,
Fell with such compliment unto his knee,
When he departed from you?

LODOVICO: Why, my lord,
He told me of a resty Barbary horse
Which he would fain have brought to the career,
The 'sault, and the ring galliard: now, my lord,
I have a rare French rider.

MONTICELSO: Take you heed,
Lest the jade break your neck. Do you put me off
100 With your wild horse-tricks? Sirrah, you do lie.
Oh, thou'rt a foul black cloud, and thou dost threat
A violent storm!

LODOVICO: Storms are i'th'air, my lord;
I am too low to storm.

MONTICELSO: Wretched creature!
I know that thou art fashion'd for all ill,
Like dogs, that once get blood, they'll ever kill.
About some murder, was't not?

LODOVICO: I'll not tell you:
And yet I care not greatly if I do;
Marry, with this preparation. Holy father,
I come not to you as an intelligencer,
110 But as a penitent sinner: what I utter

90. *Cunning:* (i) crafty, (ii) having magical powers.

96-7. *Career ... 'sault ... ring galliard:* standard equestrian exercises.

100. *Horse-tricks:* (i) equestrian exercises, (ii) horse-play, improprieties.

109. *Intelligencer:* informer.

Is in confession merely; which, you know,
Must never be revealed.
MONTICELSO: You have o'erta'en me.
LODOVICO: Sir, I did love Brachiano's duchess dearly,
Or rather I pursued her with hot lust,
Though she ne'er knew on't. She was poisoned;
Upon my soul she was: for which I have sworn
T'avenge her murder.
MONTICELSO: To the Duke of Florence?
LODOVICO: To him I have.
MONTICELSO: Miserable creature!
If thou persist in this, 'tis damnable.
Dost thou imagine, thou canst slide on blood,   120
And not be tainted with a shameful fall?
Or, like the black and melancholic yew-tree,
Dost think to root thyself in dead men's graves,
And yet to prosper? Instruction to thee
Comes like sweet showers to over-hardened ground;
They wet, but pierce not deep. And so I leave thee,
With all the furies hanging 'bout thy neck,
Till by thy penitence thou remove this evil,
In conjuring from thy breast that cruel devil.
    Exit.
LODOVICO: I'll give it o'er; he says 'tis damnable: 130
Besides I did expect his suffrage,
By reason of Camillo's death.
    Enter SERVANT *and* FRANCISCO.
FRANCISCO: Do you know that count?
SERVANT: Yes, my lord.
FRANCISCO: Bear him these thousand ducats to his
    lodging.
Tell him the Pope hath sent them. Happily
That will confirm more than all the rest.
    Exit.
SERVANT: Sir.
LODOVICO: To me, sir?

    121. *Tainted:* (i) sullied, injured, (ii) attainted, proved guilty.

SERVANT: His Holiness hath sent you a thousand crowns,
    And wills you, if you travel, to make him
140   Your patron for intelligence.
    [*Exit* SERVANT.]
LODOVICO: His creature ever to be commanded. –
    Why now 'tis come about. He rail'd upon me;
    And yet these crowns were told out, and laid ready,
    Before he knew my voyage. Oh, the art,
    The modest form of greatness! That do sit,
    Like brides at wedding-dinners, with their looks turned
    From the least wanton jests, their puling stomach
    Sick of the modesty, when their thoughts are loose,
    Even acting of those hot and lustful sports
150   Are to ensue about midnight: such his cunning!
    He sounds my depth thus with a golden plummet.
    I am doubly armed now. Now to th'act of blood.
    There's but three furies found in spacious hell,
    But in a great man's breast three thousand dwell.
    [*Exit.*]

[ACT FIVE]

*

[SCENE ONE]

A passage over the stage of BRACHIANO, FLAMINEO,
MARCELLO, HORTENSIO, [VITTORIA] COROMBONA,
CORNELIA, ZANCHE, *and others.* [FLAMINEO *and*
HORTENSIO *remain.*]

FLAMINEO: In all the weary minutes of my life,
Day ne'er broke up till now. This marriage
Confirms me happy.

HORTENSIO: 'Tis a good assurance
Saw you not yet the Moor that's come to court?

FLAMINEO: Yes, and conferred with him i'th'duke's
closet.
I have not seen a goodlier personage,
Nor ever talk'd with man better experienced
In State affairs, or rudiments of war.
He hath, by report, served the Venetian
In Candy these twice seven years, and been chief   10
In many a bold design.

HORTENSIO: What are those two
That bear him company?

FLAMINEO: Two noblemen of Hungary, that, living in the
emperor's service as commanders, eight years since,
contrary to the expectation of all the court, entered into
religion, into the strict Order of Capuchins; but, being
not well settled in their undertaking, they left their
Order, and returned to court; for which, being after
troubled in conscience, they vowed their service against
the enemies of Christ, went to Malta, were there   20
knighted, and in their return back, at this great solemnity, they are resolved for ever to forsake the world, and
settle themselves here in a house of Capuchins in Padua.

8. *Rudiments:* principles, rather than first steps.
10. *Candy:* Crete.

HORTENSIO: 'Tis strange.

FLAMINEO: One thing makes it so: they have vowed for
ever to wear, next their bare bodies, those coats of mail
they served in.

HORTENSIO: Hard penance! Is the Moor a Christian?

FLAMINEO: He is.

30 HORTENSIO: Why proffers he his service to our duke?

FLAMINEO: Because he understands there's like to grow
Some wars between us and the Duke of Florence,
In which he hopes employment.
I never saw one in a stern bold look
Wear more command, nor in a lofty phrase
Express more knowing, or more deep contempt
Of our slight airy courtiers. He talks
As if he had travelled all the princes' courts
Of Christendom: in all things strives t'express
40 That all that should dispute with him may know
Glories, like glow-worms, afar off shine bright,
But looked to near, have neither heat nor light.
The duke!

 Enter BRACHIANO, [FRANCISCO, *Duke of*] *Florence*
 disguised like MULINASSAR, LODOVICO, ANTONELLI
 [*and*] GASPARO, *bearing their swords and helmets*, [CARLO
 and PEDRO].

BRACHIANO: You are nobly welcome. We have heard at
full
Your honourable service 'gainst the Turk.
To you, brave Mulinassar, we assign
A competent pension: and are inly sorry,
The vows of those two worthy gentlemen
Make them incapable of our proffered bounty.
50 Your wish is you may leave your warlike swords
For monuments in our chapel: I accept it,
As a great honour done me, and must crave
Your leave to furnish out our duchess' revels.
Only one thing, as the last vanity
You e'er shall view, deny me not to stay

To see a barriers prepared tonight:
You shall have private standings. It hath pleased
The great ambassadors of several princes,
In their return from Rome to their own countries
To grace our marriage, and to honour me   60
With such a kind of sport.

FRANCISCO: I shall persuade them
  To stay, my lord.

BRACHIANO: Set on there to the presence.
    Exeunt BRACHIANO, FLAMINEO, *and* [HOR-
    TENSIO].

LODOVICO: Noble my lord, most fortunately welcome;
    The conspirators here embrace.
  You have our vows, sealed with the sacrament,
  To second your attempts.

GASPARO: And all things ready;
  He could not have invented his own ruin,
  Had he despaired, with more propriety.

LODOVICO: You would not take my way.

FRANCISCO: 'Tis better ordered.

LODOVICO: T'have poisoned his prayer-book, or a pair of
    beads
  The pommel of his saddle, his looking-glass,   70
  Or th'handle of his racket, – Oh, that, that!
  That while he had been bandying at tennis,
  He might have sworn himself to hell, and struck
  His soul into the hazard! Oh my lord!
  I would have our plot be ingenious,
  And have it hereafter recorded for example,
  Rather than borrow example.

FRANCISCO: There's no way
  More speeding than this thought on.

LODOVICO: On, then.

FRANCISCO: And yet methinks that this revenge is poor,
  Because it steals upon him like a thief: 80

    56. *Barriers:* see note to I. ii. 30.
    62. *Presence:* presence-chamber.   69. *Pair:* set.

To have ta'en him by the casque in a pitched field,
Led him to Florence –

LODOVICO: It had been rare: and there
Have crowned him with a wreath of stinking garlic,
T'have shown the sharpness of his government,
And rankness of his lust. Flamineo comes.

Exeunt [all except FRANCISCO].

Enter FLAMINEO, MARCELLO, *and* ZANCHE.

MARCELLO: Why doth this devil haunt you? Say.

FLAMINEO: I know not:
For by this light I do not conjure for her.
'Tis not so great a cunning as men think
To raise the devil; for here's one up already;
90   The greatest cunning were to lay him down.

MARCELLO: She is your shame.

FLAMINEO: I prithee pardon her.
In faith, you see, women are like to burrs,
Where their affection throws them, there they'll stick.

ZANCHE: That is my countryman, a goodly person;
When he's at leisure, I'll discourse with him
In our own language.

FLAMINEO: I beseech you do.

Exit ZANCHE.

How is't, brave soldier? Oh, that I had seen
Some of your iron days! I pray relate
Some of your service to us.

100 FRANCISCO: 'Tis a ridiculous thing for a man to be his
own chronicle: I did never wash my mouth with mine
own praise for fear of getting a stinking breath.

MARCELLO: You're too stoical. The duke will expect other
discourse from you.

FRANCISCO: I shall never flatter him: I have studied man
too much to do that. What difference is between the duke
and I? No more than between two bricks, all made of one
clay: only't may be one is placed on the top of a turret,
the other in the bottom of a well, by mere chance. If I

88. *Cunning:* magic.

were placed as high as the duke, I should stick as fast, 110
make as fair a show, and bear out weather equally.

FLAMINEO: If this soldier had a patent to beg in churches,
then he would tell them stories.

MARCELLO: I have been a soldier too.

FRANCISCO: How have you thrived?

MARCELLO: Faith, poorly.

FRANCISCO: That's the misery of peace: only outsides are
then respected. As ships seem very great upon the river,
which show very little upon the seas, so some men
i'th'court seem Colossuses in a chamber, who, if they 12c
came into the field, would appear pitiful pygmies.

FLAMINEO: Give me a fair room yet hung with arras,
and some great cardinal to lug me by th'ears, as his
endearéd minion.

FRANCISCO: And thou mayest do the devil knows what
villainy.

FLAMINEO: And safely.

FRANCISCO: Right: you shall see in the country, in
harvest-time, pigeons, though they destroy never so
much corn, the farmer dare not present the fowling- 130
piece to them: why? Because they belong to the lord of
the manor; whilst your poor sparrows, that belong to the
Lord of Heaven, they go to the pot for't.

FLAMINEO: I will now give you some politic instruction.
The duke says he will give you pension; that's but bare
promise; get it under his hand. For I have known men
that have come from serving against the Turk, for three
or four months they have had pension to buy them new
wooden legs, and fresh plasters; but after, 'twas not to
be had. And this miserable courtesy shows as if a tor- 140
mentor should give hot cordial drinks to one three-
quarters dead o'th'rack, only to fetch the miserable soul
again to endure more dog-days.

Enter HORTENSIO, *a young Lord*, ZANCHE, *and two
more.*

122. *Arras:* tapestries.

How now, gallants? What, are they ready for the barriers?

YOUNG LORD: Yes: the lords are putting on their armour.

[*Exit* FRANCISCO.]

HORTENSIO: What's he?

FLAMINEO: A new upstart; one that swears like a falconer,
and will lie in the duke's ear day by day, like a maker of
almanacs: and yet I knew him, since he came to th'court,

150   smell worse of sweat than an under tennis-court keeper.

HORTENSIO: Look you, yonder's your sweet mistress.

FLAMINEO: Thou art my sworn brother: I'll tell thee,
I do love that Moor, that witch, very constrainedly.
She knows some of my villainy. I do love her just as a
man holds a wolf by the ears; but for fear of [her] turning
upon me, and pulling out my throat, I would let her go
to the devil.

HORTENSIO: I hear she claims marriage of thee.

FLAMINEO: 'Faith, I made to her some such dark promise;

160   and, in seeking to fly from't, I run on, like a frighted dog
with a bottle at's tail, that fain would bite it off, and yet
dares not look behind him. Now, my precious gipsy.

ZANCHE: Ay, your love to me rather cools than heats.

FLAMINEO: Marry, I am the sounder lover; we have many
wenches about the town heat too fast.

HORTENSIO: What do you think of these perfumed
gallants, then?

FLAMINEO: Their satin cannot save them: I am confident
They have a certain spice of the disease;

170   For they that sleep with dogs shall rise with fleas.

ZANCHE: Believe it! A little painting and gay clothes make
you loathe me.

FLAMINEO: How, love a lady for painting or gay apparel?
I'll unkennel one example more for thee. Aesop had a
foolish dog that let go the flesh to catch the shadow;
I would have courtiers be better diners.

ZANCHE: You remember your oaths?

FLAMINEO: Lovers' oaths are like mariners' prayers,
uttered in extremity; but when the tempest is o'er, and

that the vessel leaves tumbling, they fall from protesting 180
to drinking. And yet, amongst gentlemen, protesting
and drinking go together, and agree as well as shoe-
makers and Westphalia bacon: they are both drawers
on; for drink draws on protestation, and protestation
draws on more drink. Is not this discourse better now
than the morality of your sunburnt gentleman?

    Enter CORNELIA.

CORNELIA: Is this your perch, you haggard? Fly to
th'stews.

    [*Strikes* ZANCHE.]

FLAMINEO: You should be clapped by th'heels now:
strike i'th'court! 190

    [*Exit* CORNELIA.]

ZANCHE: She's good for nothing, but to make her
    maids
Catch cold a-nights: they dare not use a bedstaff,
For fear of her light fingers.

MARCELLO: You're a strumpet,
An impudent one.

    [*Kicks* ZANCHE.]

FLAMINEO: Why do you kick her, say?
Do you think that she's like a walnut tree?
Must she be cudgelled ere she bear good fruit?

MARCELLO: She brags that you shall marry her.

FLAMINEO: What then?

MARCELLO: I had rather she were pitched upon a stake
In some new-seeded garden, to affright
Her fellow crows thence.

FLAMINEO: You're a boy, a fool, 200
Be guardian to your hound; I am of age.

MARCELLO: If I take her near you I'll cut her throat.

FLAMINEO: With a fan of feathers?

MARCELLO: And, for you, I'll whip
This folly from you.

    180. *Tumbling: double entendre.*
    187. *Haggard:* female hawk, whore. 188. *Stews:* brothels.

FLAMINEO: Are you choleric?
I'll purge't with rhubarb.

HORTENSIO: Oh, your brother!

FLAMINEO: Hang him!
He wrongs me most that ought t'offend me least:
I do suspect my mother played foul play,
When she conceived thee.

MARCELLO: Now by all my hopes,
Like the two slaughtered sons of Oedipus,
210 The very flames of our affection
Shall turn two ways. Those words I'll make thee answer
With thy heart-blood.

FLAMINEO: Do, like the geese in the progress;
You know where you shall find me.

MARCELLO: Very good.

[*Exit* FLAMINEO.]
An thou be'st a noble friend, bear him my sword,
And bid him fit the length on't.

YOUNG LORD: Sir, I shall.

[*Exeunt all but* ZANCHE.]

ZANCHE: He comes. Hence petty thought of my disgrace –
Enter FRANCISCO [*disguised as* MULINASSAR].
I ne'er loved my complexion till now,
'Cause I may boldly say, without a blush,
I love you.

220 FRANCISCO: Your love is untimely sown; there's a spring
at Michaelmas, but 'tis but a faint one: I am sunk in
years, and I have vowed never to marry.

ZANCHE: Alas! Poor maids get more lovers than husbands:
yet you may mistake my wealth. For, as when ambassadors are sent to congratulate princes, there's commonly sent along with them a rich present, so that
though the prince like not the ambassador's person nor
words, yet he likes well of the presentment; so I may
come to you in the same manner, and be better loved for
230 my dowry than my virtue.

FRANCISCO: I'll think on the motion.

ZANCHE: Do; I'll now detain you no longer. At your
  better leisure, I'll tell you things shall startle your blood:
  Nor blame me that this passion I reveal;
  Lovers die inward that their flames conceal.
FRANCISCO: Of all intelligence this may prove the best:
  Sure I shall draw strange fowl from this foul nest.
  [*Exeunt.*]

[SCENE TWO]

Enter MARCELLO *and* CORNELIA.
CORNELIA: I hear a whispering all about the court,
  You are to fight: who is your opposite?
  What is the quarrel?
MARCELLO: 'Tis an idle rumour.
CORNELIA: Will you dissemble? Sure you do not well
  To fright me thus: you never look thus pale,
  But when you are most angry. I do charge you,
  Upon my blessing – nay, I'll call the duke,
  And he shall school you.
MARCELLO: Publish not a fear,
  Which would convert to laughter: 'tis not so.
  Was not this crucifix my father's?
CORNELIA: Yes.   10
MARCELLO: I have heard you say, giving my brother suck
  He took the crucifix between his hands,
    Enter FLAMINEO.
  And broke a limb off.
CORNELIA: Yes, but 'tis mended.
FLAMINEO: I have brought your weapon back.
    FLAMINEO *runs* MARCELLO *through*.
CORNELIA: Ha! Oh, my horror!
MARCELLO: You have brought it home, indeed.
CORNELIA: Help! Oh, he's murdered!
FLAMINEO: Do you turn your gall up? I'll to sanctuary,
  And send a surgeon to you.
    [*Exit.*]

Enter CARLO, HORTENSIO, PEDRO.

HORTENSIO: How? O'th'ground!

MARCELLO: Oh mother, now remember what I told
Of breaking off the crucifix: farewell –
20   There are some sins which heaven doth duly punish
In a whole family. This it is to rise
By all dishonest means. Let all men know,
That tree shall long time keep a steady foot,
Whose branches spread no wider than the root.
    [*Dies.*]

CORNELIA: Oh, my perpetual sorrow!

HORTENSIO: Virtuous Marcello
He's dead. Pray leave him, lady: come, you shall.

CORNELIA: Alas! He is not dead; he's in a trance. Why
here's nobody shall get anything by his death. Let me
call him again, for God's sake!

30 CARLO: I would you were deceived.

CORNELIA: Oh you abuse me, you abuse me, you abuse
me! how many have gone away thus, for lack of ten-
dance! Rear up's head, rear up's head; his bleeding
inward will kill him.

HORTENSIO: You see he is departed.

CORNELIA: Let me come to him; give me him as he is, if
he be turned to earth; let me but give him one hearty
kiss, and you shall put us both into one coffin. Fetch a
looking-glass: see if his breath will not stain it; or pull
40   out some feathers from my pillow, and lay them to his
lips. Will you lose him for a little painstaking?

HORTENSIO: Your kindest office is to pray for him.

CORNELIA: Alas! I would not pray for him yet. He may
live to lay me i'th'ground, and pray for me, if you'll let
me come to him.

    Enter BRACHIANO, *all armed, save the beaver, with*
    FLAMINEO [FRANCISCO *disguised as* MULINASSAR,
    LODOVICO *disguised, and a Page*].

BRACHIANO: Was this your handiwork?

45. S.D. *Beaver:* face-piece of helmet.

FLAMINEO: It was my misfortune.

CORNELIA: He lies, he lies! he did not kill him: these have
  killed him, that would not let him be better looked to.

BRACHIANO: Have comfort, my grieved mother.　　　　　50

CORNELIA: Oh, you screech-owl!

HORTENSIO: Forbear, good madam.

CORNELIA: Let me go, let me go.

　　She runs to FLAMINEO *with her knife drawn, and coming
　　to him lets it fall.*

  The God of Heaven forgive thee! Dost not wonder
  I pray for thee? I'll tell thee what's the reason,
  I have scarce breath to number twenty minutes;
  I'd not spend that in cursing. Fare thee well –
  Half of thyself lies there; and may'st thou live
  To fill an hour-glass with his mouldered ashes,
  To tell how thou shouldst spend the time to come　　60
  In blest repentance!

BRACHIANO:　　　　　Mother, pray tell me
  How came he by his death? What was the quarrel?

CORNELIA: Indeed, my younger boy presumed too much
  Upon his manhood, gave him bitter words,
  Drew his sword first; and so, I know not how,
  For I was out of my wits, he fell with's head
  Just in my bosom.

PAGE: This is not true, madam.

CORNELIA:　　　　　I pray thee, peace.
  One arrow's grazed already; it were vain
  T'lose this, for that will ne'er be found again.　　70

BRACHIANO: Go, bear the body to Cornelia's lodging:
  And we command that none acquaint our duchess
  With this sad accident. For you, Flamineo,
  Hark you, I will not grant your pardon.

FLAMINEO:　　　　　　　　　No?

BRACHIANO: Only a lease of your life; and that shall last
  But for one day: thou shalt be forced each evening
  To renew it, or be hanged.

　　　　69. *Grazed:* 'grassed' (lost in the grass).

FLAMINEO: At your pleasure.

> LODOVICO *sprinkles* BRACHIANO'*s beaver with a poison.*

Your will is law now, I'll not meddle with it.

BRACHIANO: You once did brave me in your sister's
lodging:

80   I'll now keep you in awe for't. Where's our beaver?

FRANCISCO [*aside*]: He calls for his destruction. Noble
youth

I pity thy sad fate! Now to the barriers.

This shall his passage to the black lake further;

The last good deed he did, he pardoned murder.

> *Exeunt.*

[SCENE THREE]

> *Charges and shouts. They fight at barriers: first single pairs,
> then three to three.*
>
> *Enter* BRACHIANO *and* FLAMINEO, *with others (in-
> cluding* VITTORIA, GIOVANNI, *and* FRANCISCO
> *disguised as* MULINASSAR).

BRACHIANO: An armourer! Ud's death, an armourer!

FLAMINEO: Armourer! Where's the armourer?

BRACHIANO: Tear off my beaver.

FLAMINEO: Are you hurt, my lord?

BRACHIANO: Oh my brain's on fire!

> *Enter* ARMOURER.

                                The helmet is poisoned.

ARMOURER: My lord, upon my soul –

BRACHIANO: Away with him to torture.

> *Exit* ARMOURER, *guarded.*

There are some great ones that have hand in this,

And near about me.

VITTORIA: Oh, my loved lord! Poisoned!

FLAMINEO: Remove the bar. Here's unfortunate revels!

8. *Bar:* barrier (or possibly a fastening in Brachiano's helmet).

Call the physicians.
> *Enter two* PHYSICIANS.

A plague upon you!
We have too much of your cunning here already: 10
I fear the ambassadors are likewise poisoned.

BRACHIANO: Oh, I am gone already, the infection
Flies to the brain and heart. O thou strong heart!
There's such a covenant 'tween the world and it,
They're loath to break.

GIOVANNI: Oh, my most loved father!

BRACHIANO: Remove the boy away –
Where's this good woman? Had I infinite worlds,
They were too little for thee: must I leave thee?
What say you, screech-owls, is the venom mortal?

PHYSICIANS: Most deadly.

BRACHIANO: Most corrupted politic hangman,   20
You kill without book; but your art to save
Fails you as oft as great men's needy friends.
I that have given life to offending slaves
And wretched murderers, have I not power
To lengthen mine own a twelvemonth?
[*To* VITTORIA] Do not kiss me, for I shall poison thee.
This unction is sent from the great Duke of Florence.

FRANCISCO: Sir, be of comfort.

BRACHIANO: O thou soft natural death, that art joint-twin
To sweetest slumber! No rough-bearded comet   30
Stares on thy mild departure; the dull owl
Beats not against thy casement; the hoarse wolf
Scents not thy carrion. Pity winds thy corse,
Whilst horror waits on princes.

VITTORIA: I am lost for ever.

BRACHIANO: How miserable a thing it is to die
'Mongst women howling!
> [*Enter* LODOVICO *and* GASPARO, *as Capuchins.*]

What are those?

FLAMINEO: Franciscans:
They have brought the extreme unction.

BRACHIANO: On pain of death, let no man name death
to me;
40   It is a word infinitely terrible.
Withdraw into our cabinet.
     Exeunt [all] but FRANCISCO *and* FLAMINEO.

FLAMINEO: To see what solitariness is about dying
princes! As heretofore they have unpeopled towns,
divorced friends, and made great houses unhospitable;
so now, O justice! Where are their flatterers now?
Flatterers are but the shadows of princes' bodies – the
least thick cloud makes them invisible.

FRANCISCO: There's great moan made for him.

FLAMINEO: 'Faith, for some few hours salt-water will run
50   most plentifully in every office o'th'court; but believe it,
most of them do but weep over their stepmothers' graves.

FRANCISCO: How mean you?

FLAMINEO: Why, they dissemble; as some men do that
live within compass o'th'verge.

FRANCISCO: Come, you have thrived well under him.

FLAMINEO: 'Faith, like a wolf in a woman's breast; I have
been fed with poultry: but for money, understand me,
I had as good a will to cozen him as e'er an officer of them
all; but I had not cunning enough to do it.

60 FRANCISCO: What didst thou think of him? 'faith, speak
freely.

FLAMINEO: He was a kind of statesman, that would sooner
have reckoned how many cannon-bullets he had discharged against a town, to count his expense that way,
than how many of his valiant and deserving subjects he
lost before it.

FRANCISCO: Oh, speak well of the duke.
     Enter LODOVICO [*disguised as before*].

FLAMINEO: I have done.
Wilt hear some of my court-wisdom? To reprehend
70   princes is dangerous; and to over-commend some of
them is palpable lying.

----

56. *Wolf*: ulcer.

FRANCISCO: How is it with the duke?

LODOVICO: Most deadly ill.
He's fall'n into a strange distraction:
He talks of battles and monopolies,
Levying of taxes; and from that descends
To the most brain-sick language. His mind fastens
On twenty several objects, which confound
Deep sense with folly. Such a fearful end
May teach some men that bear too lofty crest,
Though they live happiest yet they die not best.   80
He hath conferred the whole state of the dukedom
Upon your sister, till the prince arrive
At mature age.

FLAMINEO: There's some good luck in that yet.

FRANCISCO: See, here he comes.

> Enter BRACHIANO, *presented in a bed*, VITTORIA *and*
> *others* [*including* GASPARO, *disguised as before*].

There's death in's face already.

VITTORIA: Oh, my good lord!

BRACHIANO: Away, you have abused me:
These speeches are several kinds of distractions, and in the
action should appear so.
You have conveyed coin forth our territories,
Bought and sold offices, oppressed the poor,
And I ne'er dreamt on't. Make up your accounts,
I'll now be mine own steward.

FLAMINEO: Sir, have patience.

BRACHIANO: Indeed I am to blame: 90
For did you ever hear the dusky raven
Chide blackness? Or was't ever known the devil
Railed against cloven creatures?

VITTORIA: Oh, my lord!

BRACHIANO: Let me have some quails to supper.

FLAMINEO: Sir, you shall.

BRACHIANO: No, some fried dog-fish; your quails feed
on poison.
That old dog-fox, that politician, Florence!

I'll forswear hunting, and turn dog-killer.
Rare! I'll be friends with him; for mark you sir, one dog
Still sets another a-barking. Peace, peace,
Yonder's a fine slave come in now.

FLAMINEO: Where?

BRACHIANO: Why, there,
In a blue bonnet, and a pair of breeches
With a great cod-piece: ha, ha, ha!
Look you, his cod-piece is stuck full of pins,
With pearls o'th'head of them. Do not you know him?

FLAMINEO: No, my lord.

BRACHIANO: Why, 'tis the devil.
I know him by a great rose he wears on's shoe,
To hide his cloven foot. I'll dispute with him;
He's a rare linguist.

VITTORIA: My lord, here's nothing.

BRACHIANO: Nothing! Rare! Nothing! When I want
money,
Our treasury is empty, there is nothing:
I'll not be used thus.

VITTORIA: Oh lie still, my lord!

BRACHIANO: See, see, Flamineo that killed his brother,
Is dancing on the ropes there, and he carries
A money-bag in each hand, to keep him even,
For fear of breaking's neck: and there's a lawyer,
In a gown whipped with velvet, stares and gapes
When the money will fall. How the rogue cuts capers!
It should have been in a halter.
'Tis there; what's she?

FLAMINEO: Vittoria, my lord.

BRACHIANO: Ha, ha, ha! Her hair is sprinkled with orris
powder,
That makes her look as if she had sinned in the pastry.
What's he?

FLAMINEO: A divine, my lord.

117. *Whipped:* elaborately trimmed.
122. *Pastry:* place where pastry is made.

BRACHIANO: He will be drunk; avoid him: th'argument is
fearful when churchmen stagger in't.
Look you, six grey rats that have lost their tails
Crawl up the pillow; send for a rat-catcher:
I'll do a miracle, I'll free the court
From all foul vermin. Where's Flamineo?   130

FLAMINEO: I do not like that he names me so often,
Especially on's death-bed; 'tis a sign
I shall not live long. See, he's near his end.

> BRACHIANO *seems here near his end;* LODOVICO *and*
> GASPARO, *in the habit of Capuchins, present him in his bed*
> *with a crucifix and hallowed candle.*

LODOVICO: Pray, give us leave. *Attende, domine Brachiane.*

FLAMINEO: See, see, how firmly he doth fix his eye
Upon the crucifix.

VITTORIA: Oh, hold it constant!
It settles his wild spirits; and so his eyes
Melt into tears.

LODOVICO [*by the crucifix*]: *Domine Brachiane, solebas in bello*
tutus esse tuo clypeo; nunc hunc clypeum hosti tuo opponas 140
infernali.

GASPARO [*by the hallowed taper*]: *Olim hasta valuisti in bello;*
nunc hanc sacram hastam vibrabis contra hostem animarum.

LODOVICO: *Attende, Domine Brachiane, si nunc quoque probas*
ea, quae acta sunt inter nos, flecte caput in dextrum.

GASPARO: *Esto securus, Domine Brachiane; cogita, quantum*
habeas meritorum; denique memineris meam animam pro tua
oppignoratam si quid esset periculi.

LODOVICO: *Si nunc quoque probas ea, quae acta sunt inter nos,*
flecte caput in laevum.   150
He is departing: pray stand all apart,
And let us only whisper in his ears
Some private meditations, which our order
Permits you not to hear.

> *Here, the rest being departed,* LODOVICO *and* GASPARO
> *discover themselves.*

GASPARO: Brachiano.

LODOVICO: Devil Brachiano, thou art damned.

GASPARO: Perpetually.

LODOVICO: A slave condemned and given up to the gallows,

Is thy great lord and master.

GASPARO: True; for thou

Art given up to the devil.

LODOVICO: Oh, you slave!

You that were held the famous politician,

Whose art was poison.

160 GASPARO: And whose conscience, murder.

LODOVICO: That would have broke your wife's neck down the stairs,

Ere she was poisoned.

GASPARO: That had your villainous sallets.

LODOVICO: And fine embroidered bottles, and perfumes,

Equally mortal with a winter plague.

GASPARO: Now there's mercury –

LODOVICO: And copperas –

GASPARO: And quicksilver –

LODOVICO: With other devilish 'pothecary stuff,

A-melting in your politic brains: dost hear?

GASPARO: This is Count Lodovico.

LODOVICO: This, Gasparo:

And thou shalt die like a poor rogue.

GASPARO: And stink

Like a dead fly-blown dog.

170 LODOVICO: And be forgotten

Before thy funeral sermon.

BRACHIANO: Vittoria!

Vittoria!

LODOVICO: Oh, the cursed devil

Comes to himself again! We are undone.

160. *Conscience:* deepest thought.
165. *Mercury:* wild mercury plant. *Copperas:* sulphate of copper.
Quicksilver: mercury.

GASPARO: Strangle him in private.
> *Enter* VITTORIA *and the Attendants.*
What! Will you call him again
To live in treble torments? For charity,
For Christian charity, avoid the chamber.
> [VITTORIA *and the rest retire.*]
LODOVICO: You would prate, sir? This is a true-love knot
Sent from the Duke of Florence.
> BRACHIANO *is strangled.*
GASPARO: What, is it done?   180
LODOVICO: The snuff is out. No woman-keeper i'th'world,
Though she had practised seven year at the pest-house,
Could have done't quaintlier. My lords, he's dead.
> [VITTORIA *and the others come forward.*]
OMNES: Rest to his soul!
VITTORIA: Oh me! this place is hell.
> *Exit* VITTORIA [*and all except* LODOVICO, FRAN-
> CISCO *and* FLAMINEO].
FRANCISCO: How heavily she takes it!
FLAMINEO: Oh, yes, yes;
Had women navigable rivers in their eyes,
They would dispend them all. Surely I wonder
Why we should wish more rivers to the city,
When they sell water so good cheap. I'll tell thee,
These are but moonish shades of griefs or fears;   190
There's nothing sooner dry than women's tears.
Why, here's an end of all my harvest, he has given me
    nothing.
Court promises! let wise men count them curst;
For while you live he that scores best pays worst.
FRANCISCO: Sure this was Florence' doing.
FLAMINEO: Very likely:
Those are found weighty strokes which come from th'hand,
But those are killing strokes which come from th'head.
Oh, the rare tricks of a Machiavillian!
He doth not come like a gross plodding slave,

181. *Snuff:* candle-end.   190. *Moonish:* changeable.

200 And buffet you to death; no, my quaint knave,
He tickles you to death, makes you die laughing,
As if you had swallowed down a pound of saffron.
You see the feat, 'tis practised in a trice;
To teach court honesty it jumps on ice.

FRANCISCO: Now have the people liberty to talk,
And descant on his vices.

FLAMINEO: Misery of princes,
That must of force be censured by their slaves!
Not only blamed for doing things are ill,
But for not doing all that all men will:
210 One were better be a thresher.
Ud's death, I would fain speak with this duke yet.

FRANCISCO: Now he's dead?

FLAMINEO: I cannot conjure; but if prayers or oaths
Will get to th'speech of him, though forty devils
Wait on him in his livery of flames,
I'll speak to him, and shake him by the hand,
Though I be blasted.
     Exit.

FRANCISCO: Excellent Lodovico!
What? Did you terrify him at the last gasp?

LODOVICO: Yes, and so idly, that the duke had like
T'have terrified us.

FRANCISCO: How?
     Enter [ZANCHE] *the Moor*.

220 LODOVICO: You shall hear that hereafter.
See, yon's the infernal, that would make up sport.
Now to the revelation of that secret
She promised when she fell in love with you.

FRANCISCO: You're passionately met in this sad world.

ZANCHE: I would have you look up, sir; these court tears
Claim not your tribute to them: let those weep,
That guiltily partake in the sad cause.
I knew last night, by a sad dream I had,
Some mischief would ensue: yet, to say truth,
My dream most concerned you.

LODOVICO: Shall's fall a-dreaming? 230
FRANCISCO: Yes, and for fashion sake I'll dream with her:
ZANCHE: Methought, sir, you came stealing to my bed:
FRANCISCO: Wilt thou believe me, sweeting? By this
    light,
  I was a-dreamt on thee too; for methought
  I saw thee naked.
ZANCHE: Fie, sir! as I told you,
  Methought you lay down by me.
FRANCISCO: So dreamt I;
  And lest thou shouldst take cold, I covered thee
  With this Irish mantle.
ZANCHE: Verily I did dream
  You were somewhat bold with me: but to come to't –
LODOVICO: How! how! I hope you will not go to't here. 240
FRANCISCO: Nay, you must hear my dream out.
ZANCHE: Well, sir, forth.
FRANCISCO: When I threw the mantle o'er thee, thou
    didst laugh
  Exceedingly, methought.
ZANCHE: Laugh!
FRANCISCO: And criedst out,
  The hair did tickle thee.
ZANCHE: There was a dream indeed.
LODOVICO: Mark her, I prithee – she simpers like the suds
  A collier hath been washed in.
ZANCHE: Come, sir; good fortune tends you. I did tell you
  I would reveal a secret: – Isabella,
  The Duke of Florence' sister, was empoisoned
  By a fumed picture; and Camillo's neck   250
  Was broke by damned Flamineo, the mischance
  Laid on a vaulting-horse.
FRANCISCO: Most strange!
ZANCHE: Most true.
LODOVICO: The bed of snakes is broke.
ZANCHE: I sadly do confess, I had a hand
  In the black deed.

FRANCISCO: Thou kept'st their counsel.
ZANCHE: Right;
For which, urged with contrition, I intend
This night to rob Vittoria.
LODOVICO: Excellent penitence!
Usurers dream on't while they sleep out sermons.
ZANCHE: To further our escape, I have entreated
260 Leave to retire me, till the funeral,
Unto a friend i'th'country: that excuse
Will further our escape. In coin and jewels
I shall at least make good unto your use
An hundred thousand crowns.
FRANCISCO: Oh noble wench!
LODOVICO: Those crowns we'll share.
ZANCHE: It is a dowry,
Methinks, should make that sun-burnt proverb false,
And wash the Aethiop white.
FRANCISCO: It shall; – away!
ZANCHE: Be ready for our flight.
FRANCISCO: An hour 'fore day.
    Exit [ZANCHE] *the Moor.*
O strange discovery! Why, till now we knew not
270 The circumstance of either of their deaths.
    [*Re-*]*enter* [ZANCHE] *the Moor.*
ZANCHE: You'll wait about midnight in the chapel?
FRANCISCO: There.
    [*Exit* ZANCHE.]
LODOVICO: Why, now our action's justified.
FRANCISCO: Tush for justice!
What harms it justice? We now, like the partridge
Purge the disease with laurel; for the fame
Shall crown the enterprise, and quit the shame.
    Exeunt.

[SCENE FOUR]

Enter FLAMINEO *and* GASPARO, *at one door; another way,* GIOVANNI, *attended.*

GASPARO: The young duke: did you e'er see a sweeter prince?

FLAMINEO: I have known a poor woman's bastard better favoured – this is behind him. Now, to his face – all comparisons were hateful. Wise was the courtly peacock, that, being a great minion, and being compared for beauty by some dottrels that stood by to the kingly eagle, said the eagle was a far fairer bird than herself, not in respect of her feathers, but in respect of her long talons: his will grow out in time. – My gracious lord.   10

GIOVANNI: I pray leave me sir.

FLAMINEO: Your Grace must be merry; 'tis I have cause to mourn; for wot you what said the little boy that rode behind his father on horseback?

GIOVANNI: Why, what said he?

FLAMINEO: When you are dead, father, said he, I hope then I shall ride in the saddle. Oh 'tis a brave thing for a man to sit by himself; he may stretch himself in the stirrups, look about, and see the whole compass of the hemisphere. You're now, my lord, i'th'saddle.   20

GIOVANNI: Study your prayers sir, and be penitent:
'Twere fit you'd think on what hath former been;
I have heard grief named the eldest child of sin.

Exit GIOVANNI (*and all except* FLAMINEO).

FLAMINEO: Study my prayers! He threatens me divinely! I am falling to pieces already. I care not, though, like Anacharsis, I were pounded to death in a mortar: and yet that death were fitter for usurers, gold and themselves to be beaten together, to make a most cordial cullis for the devil.

7. *Dottrels*: simpletons (a species of plover considered to be easy game).

29. *Cullis*: broth.

30 He hath his uncle's villainous look already,
In decimo-sexto. [*Enter* COURTIER.] Now, sir, what are
you?

COURTIER: It is the pleasure, sir, of the young duke,
That you forbear the presence, and all rooms
That owe him reverence.

FLAMINEO: So, the wolf and the raven are very pretty
fools when they are young. Is it your office, sir, to keep
me out?

COURTIER: So the duke wills.

FLAMINEO: Verily, master courtier, extremity is not to be
40 used in all offices: say that a gentlewoman were taken out
of her bed about midnight, and committed to Castle
Angelo, to the tower yonder, with nothing about her
but her smock, would it not show a cruel part in the
gentleman-porter to lay claim to her upper garment, pull
it o'er her head and ears, and put her in naked?

COURTIER: Very good: you are merry.
Exit.

FLAMINEO: Doth he make a court-ejectment of me? A
flaming firebrand casts more smoke without a chimney
than within't. I'll smoor some of them.

[*Enter* FRANCISCO *disguised as* MULINASSAR.]
50 How now? Thou art sad.

FRANCISCO: I met even now with the most piteous sight.

FLAMINEO: Thou meet'st another here, a pitiful
Degraded courtier.

FRANCISCO: Your reverend mother
Is grown a very old woman in two hours.
I found them winding of Marcello's corse;
And there is such a solemn melody,
'Tween doleful songs, tears, and sad elegies;
Such as old grandames, watching by the dead,
Were wont t'outwear the nights with, that, believe me,

31. *Decimo-sexto:* literally one sixteenth; technical name for small
book-size.
33. *Presence:* presence-chambers.   49. *Smoor:* smother.

I had no eyes to guide me forth the room,   60
They were so o'ercharged with water.

FLAMINEO: I will see them.

FRANCISCO: 'Twere much uncharity in you; for your sight
Will add unto their tears.

FLAMINEO: I will see them:
They are behind the traverse; I'll discover
Their superstitious howling.

> [*He draws the traverse.*] CORNELIA, [ZANCHE] *the
> Moor, and three other Ladies discovered winding* MAR-
> CELLO's *corse. A song.*

CORNELIA: This rosemary is withered; pray, get fresh.
I would have these herbs grow up in his grave,
When I am dead and rotten. Reach the bays,
I'll tie a garland here about his head;
'Twill keep my boy from lightning. This sheet   70
I have kept this twenty year, and every day
Hallowed it with my prayers, – I did not think
He should have wore it.

ZANCHE: Look you; who are yonder?

CORNELIA: O reach me the flowers.

ZANCHE: Her ladyship's foolish.

WOMAN: Alas, her grief
Hath turned her child again!

CORNELIA: You're very welcome:
[*To* FLAMINEO] There's rosemary for you, and rue for
you,
Heart's-ease for you; I pray make much of it,
I have left more for myself.

FRANCISCO: Lady, who's this?

CORNELIA: You are, I take it, the grave-maker.

FLAMINEO: So.   80

ZANCHE: 'Tis Flamineo.

CORNELIA: Will you make me such a fool? Here's a white
hand:

> CORNELIA *doth this in several forms of distraction.*

65. S.D. *Traverse:* curtain across inner stage.

243

Can blood so soon be washed out? let me see;
When screech-owls croak upon the chimney-tops,
And the strange cricket i'th'oven sings and hops,
When yellow spots do on your hands appear,
Be certain then you of a corse shall hear.
Out upon't, how 'tis speckled! H' 'as handled a toad sure.
Cowslip water is good for the memory:
90   Pray, buy me three ounces of't.

FLAMINEO: I would I were from hence.

CORNELIA: Do you hear, sir?
I'll give you a saying which my grandmother
Was wont, when she heard the bell toll, to sing o'er
Unto her lute.

FLAMINEO: Do, an you will, do.

CORNELIA: *Call for the robin redbreast, and the wren,*
Since o'er shady groves they hover,
And with leaves and flowers do cover
The friendless bodies of unburiéd men.
Call unto his funeral dole
100   *The ant, the fieldmouse, and the mole,*
To rear him hillocks that shall keep him warm,
And – when gay tombs are robbed – sustain no harm;
But keep the wolf far thence, that's foe to men,
For with his nails he'll dig them up again.
They would not bury him 'cause he died in a quarrel;
But I have an answer for them:
Let holy Church receive him duly,
Since he paid the church-tithes truly.
His wealth is summed, and this is all his store,
110   This poor men get, and great men get no more.
Now the wares are gone, we may shut up shop.
Bless you all, good people.

          Exeunt CORNELIA, ZANCHE, *and Ladies.*

FLAMINEO: I have a strange thing in me, to th'which
I cannot give a name, without it be
Compassion. I pray leave me.

          Exit FRANCISCO.

This night I'll know the utmost of my fate;
I'll be resolved what my rich sister means
T'assign me for my service. I have lived
Riotously ill, like some that live in court,
And sometimes when my face was full of smiles,   120
Have felt the maze of conscience in my breast.
Oft gay and honoured robes those tortures try:
We think caged birds sing, when indeed they cry.

> *Enter* BRACHIANO's *Ghost, in his leather cassock and
> breeches, boots, a cowl; in his hand a pot of lily flowers, with
> a skull in't.*

Ha! I can stand thee: nearer, nearer yet.
What a mockery hath death made of thee!
Thou look'st sad.
In what place art thou? In yon starry gallery?
Or in the cursed dungeon? No? Not speak?
Pray, sir, resolve me, what religion's best
For a man to die in? Or is it in your knowledge   130
To answer me how long I have to live?
That's the most necessary question.
Not answer? Are you still like some great men
That only walk like shadows up and down,
And to no purpose; say –

> *The Ghost throws earth upon him, and shows him the skull.*

What's that? O fatal! He throws earth upon me.
A dead man's skull beneath the roots of flowers.
I pray speak sir: our Italian churchmen
Make us believe dead men hold conference
With their familiars, and many times   140
Will come to bed to them, and eat with them.

> *Exit Ghost.*

He's gone; and see, the skull and earth are vanished.
This is beyond melancholy.
I do dare my fate
To do its worst. Now to my sister's lodging,
And sum up all these horrors: the disgrace
The prince threw on me; next the piteous sight

Of my dead brother; and my mother's dotage;
And last this terrible vision: all these
150   Shall with Vittoria's bounty turn to good,
Or I will drown this weapon in her blood.
    Exit.

[SCENE FIVE]

Enter FRANCISCO, LODOVICO, *and* HORTENSIO
(*overhearing them*).

LODOVICO: My lord, upon my soul you shall no further;
  You have most ridiculously engaged yourself
  Too far already. For my part, I have paid
  All my debts: so, if I should chance to fall,
  My creditors fall not with me; and I vow,
  To quite all in this bold assembly,
  To the meanest follower. My lord, leave the city,
  Or I'll forswear the murder.
    [*Exit.*]
FRANCISCO: Farewell, Lodovico:
  If thou dost perish in this glorious act,
10   I'll rear unto thy memory that fame,
  Shall in the ashes keep alive thy name.
    [*Exit.*]
HORTENSIO: There's some black deed on foot. I'll
  presently
  Down to the citadel, and raise some force.
  These strong court-factions, that do brook no checks,
  In the career oft break the riders' necks.
    [*Exit.*]

    6. *Quite:* requite.   15. *Career:* short, high-speed gallop.

[SCENE SIX]

Enter VITTORIA *with a book in her hand;* ZANCHE;
FLAMINEO *following them.*

FLAMINEO: What, are you at your prayers? Give o'er.

VITTORIA: How, ruffin?

FLAMINEO: I come to you 'bout worldly business.
  Sit down, sit down. Nay stay, blowze, you may hear it:
  The doors are fast enough.

VITTORIA: Ha! Are you drunk?

FLAMINEO: Yes, yes, with wormwood water; you shall taste
  Some of it presently.

VITTORIA: What intends the fury?

FLAMINEO: You are my lord's executrix; and I claim
  Reward for my long service.

VITTORIA: For your service!

FLAMINEO: Come therefore, here is pen and ink, set down
  What you will give me.   10
  She writes.

VITTORIA: There.

FLAMINEO: Ha! Have you done already?
  'Tis a most short conveyance.

VITTORIA: I will read it: –
  'I give that portion to thee, and no other,
  Which Cain groaned under, having slain his brother.'

FLAMINEO: A most courtly patent to beg by.

VITTORIA: You are a villain!

FLAMINEO: Is't come to this? They say affrights cure
  agues:
  Thou hast a devil in thee; I will try
  If I can scare him from thee. Nay, sit still:
  My lord hath left me yet two case of jewels,   20
  Shall make me scorn your bounty; you shall see them.
  Exit.

1. *Ruffin:* devil.   3. *Blowze:* fat, red-faced wench.

VITTORIA: Sure he's distracted.

ZANCHE: Oh, he's desperate!
  For your own safety give him gentle language.
    [Re-]enter [FLAMINEO] *with two case of pistols.*

FLAMINEO: Look, these are better far at a dead lift,
  Than all your jewel house.

VITTORIA: And yet, methinks,
  These stones have no fair lustre, they are ill set.

FLAMINEO: I'll turn the right side towards you: you shall see
  How they will sparkle.

VITTORIA: Turn this horror from me!
  What do you want? What would you have me do?

30   Is not all mine yours? Have I any children?

FLAMINEO: Pray thee good woman, do not trouble me
  With this vain worldly business; say your prayers:
  I made a vow to my deceaséd lord,
  Neither yourself nor I should outlive him
  The numbering of four hours.

VITTORIA: Did he enjoin it?

FLAMINEO: He did, and 'twas a deadly jealousy,
  Lest any should enjoy thee after him,
  That urged him vow me to it. For my death,
  I did propound it voluntarily, knowing,

40   If he could not be safe in his own court,
  Being a great duke, what hope then for us?

VITTORIA: This is your melancholy, and despair.

FLAMINEO: Away:
  Fool [that] thou art, to think that politicians
  Do use to kill the effects of injuries
  And let the cause live. Shall we groan in irons
  Or be a shameful and a weighty burthen
  To a public scaffold? This is my resolve:
  I would not live at any man's entreaty,
  Nor die at any's bidding.

VITTORIA: Will you hear me?

23. S.D. *case:* pair.   24. *dead lift:* emergency.

FLAMINEO: My life hath done service to other men,   50
  My death shall serve mine own turn: make you ready.
VITTORIA: Do you mean to die indeed?
FLAMINEO: With as much pleasure,
  As e'er my father gat me.
VITTORIA [to ZANCHE]: Are the doors locked?
ZANCHE: Yes, madam.

VITTORIA: Are you grown an atheist? will you turn your
    body,
  Which is the goodly palace of the soul,
  To the soul's slaughter-house? O the cursèd devil,
  Which doth present us with all other sins
  Thrice candied o'er, despair with gall and stibium,   60
  Yet we carouse it off. [Aside to ZANCHE] Cry out for
    help!
  Makes us forsake that which was made for man,
  The world, to sink to that was made for devils,
  Eternal darkness!
ZANCHE: Help, help!
FLAMINEO: I'll stop your throat
  With winter plums, –
VITTORIA: I pray thee yet remember,
  Millions are now in graves, which at last day
  Like mandrakes shall rise shrieking.
FLAMINEO: Leave your prating,
  For these are but grammatical laments,
  Feminine arguments: and they move me,
  As some in pulpits move their auditory,   70
  More with their exclamation than sense
  Of reason, or sound doctrine.
ZANCHE [aside]: Gentle madam,
  Seem to consent, only persuade him teach
  The way to death; let him die first.
VITTORIA: 'Tis good, I apprehend it. –
  To kill one's self is meat that we must take
  Like pills, not chew't, but quickly swallow it;

60. *Stibium:* antimony

The smart o'th'wound, or weakness of the hand,
May else bring treble torments.

80 FLAMINEO: I have held it
A wretched and most miserable life,
Which is not able to die.

VITTORIA: O but frailty!
Yet I am now resolved: farewell, affliction!
Behold, Brachiano, I that while you lived
Did make a flaming altar of my heart
To sacrifice unto you, now am ready
To sacrifice heart and all. Farewell, Zanche.

ZANCHE: How, madam! Do you think that I'll outlive you;
Especially when my best self, Flamineo,
Goes the same voyage?

90 FLAMINEO: O most loved Moor!

ZANCHE: Only, by all my love, let me entreat you,
Since it is most necessary one of us
Do violence on ourselves, let you or I
Be her sad taster, teach her how to die.

FLAMINEO: Thou dost instruct me nobly; take these
pistols,
Because my hand is stained with blood already:
Two of these you shall level at my breast,
The other 'gainst your own, and so we'll die
Most equally contented: but first swear

100   Not to outlive me.

VITTORIA and ZANCHE: Most religiously.

FLAMINEO: Then here's an end of me; farewell, daylight.
And O contemptible physic! That dost take
So long a study, only to preserve
So short a life, I take my leave of thee.
    Showing the pistols.
These are two cupping-glasses, that shall draw
All my infected blood out. Are you ready?

BOTH: Ready.

FLAMINEO: Whither shall I go now? O Lucian, thy

106. *Cupping-glasses:* surgical vessels used in blood-letting.

ridiculous purgatory! To find Alexander the Great 110
cobbling shoes, Pompey tagging points, and Julius
Caesar making hair-buttons, Hannibal selling blacking,
and Augustus crying garlic, Charlemagne selling lists by
the dozen, and King Pepin crying apples in a cart drawn
with one horse!
Whether I resolve to fire, earth, water, air,
Or all the elements by scruples, I know not,
Nor greatly care. – Shoot. Shoot!
Of all deaths, the violent death is best;
For from ourselves it steals ourselves so fast, 120
The pain, once apprehended, is quite past.
   They shoot and run to him and tread upon him.
VITTORIA: What, are you dropped?
FLAMINEO: I am mixed with earth already: as you are
   noble,
Perform your vows, and bravely follow me.
VITTORIA: Whither? To hell?
ZANCHE: To most assured damnation?
VITTORIA: Oh, thou most curséd devil!
ZANCHE: Thou art caught –
VITTORIA: In thine own engine. I tread the fire out
   That would have been my ruin.
FLAMINEO: Will you be perjured? What a religious oath
   was Styx, that the gods never durst swear by, and 130
   violate! Oh, that we had such an oath to minister, and to
   be so well kept in our courts of justice!
VITTORIA: Think whither thou art going.
ZANCHE: And remember
   What villainies thou hast acted.
VITTORIA: This thy death
   Shall make me, like a blazing ominous star,
   Look up and tremble.

111. *Tagging points:* fixing metal ends to laces used for fastenin
garments.
113. *Lists:* strips of cloth.
117. *Scruples:* minute portions.

FLAMINEO: Oh, I am caught with a spring!

VITTORIA: You see the fox comes many times short
    home;
    'Tis here proved true.

FLAMINEO: Killed with a couple of braches!

VITTORIA: No fitter offering for the infernal furies,
140   Than one in whom they reigned while he was living.

FLAMINEO: Oh, the way's dark and horrid! I cannot see:
    Shall I have no company?

VITTORIA: Oh yes, thy sins
    Do run before thee to fetch fire from hell,
    To light thee thither.

FLAMINEO: Oh, I smell soot,
    Most stinking soot! The chimney is afire:
    My liver's parboiled, like Scotch holy-bread;
    There's a plumber laying pipes in my guts, it scalds.
    Wilt thou outlive me?

ZANCHE: Yes, and drive a stake
    Through thy body; for we'll give it out,
150   Thou didst this violence upon thyself.

FLAMINEO: Oh, cunning devils! now I have tried your love,
    And doubled all your reaches: I am not wounded.

      FLAMINEO *riseth.*

    The pistols held no bullets; 'twas a plot
    To prove your kindness to me; and I live
    To punish your ingratitude. I knew,
    One time or other, you would find a way
    To give me a strong potion. O men,
    That lie upon your death-beds, and are haunted
    With howling wives! Ne'er trust them; they'll re-marry
160   Ere the worm pierce your winding-sheet, ere the spider
    Make a thin curtain for your epitaphs.
    How cunning you were to discharge! Do you practise

136. *Spring:* snare.
137. *Comes . . . home:* does not return.
138. *With:* by. *Braches:* bitches.
154. *Kindness:* natural feeling.

at the Artillery yard? Trust a woman? Never, never;
Brachiano be my precedent. We lay our souls to pawn
to the devil for a little pleasure, and a woman makes the
bill of sale. That ever man should marry! For one
Hypermnestra that saved her lord and husband, forty-
nine of her sisters cut their husbands' throats all in one
night. There was a shoal of virtuous horse-leeches!
Here are two other instruments.

> *Enter* LODOVICO, GASPARO *[disguised as Capuchins]*
> *[with]* PEDRO, CARLO.

VITTORIA: Help! help!   170
FLAMINEO: What noise is that? Ha! False keys i'th'court!
LODOVICO: We have brought you a mask.
FLAMINEO: A matachin it seems
  By your drawn swords. Churchmen turned revellers!
GASPARO: Isabella! Isabella!
LODOVICO: Do you know us now?
  [Throwing off disguises.]
FLAMINEO: Lodovico and Gasparo!
LODOVICO: Yes; and that Moor the duke gave pension to
  Was the great Duke of Florence.
VITTORIA: Oh, we are lost!
FLAMINEO: You shall not take justice from forth my
  hands,
  Oh, let me kill her. – I'll cut my safety
  Through your coats of steel. Fate's a spaniel,   180
  We cannot beat it from us. What remains now?
  Let all that do ill, take this precedent:
  Man may his fate foresee, but not prevent;
  And of all axioms this shall win the prize:
  'Tis better to be fortunate than wise.
GASPARO: Bind him to the pillar.
VITTORIA: Oh, your gentle pity!
  I have seen a blackbird that would sooner fly
  To a man's bosom, than to stay the gripe
  Of the fierce sparrow-hawk.

      169. *Horse-leeches:* blood-suckers.

GASPARO: Your hope deceives you.

VITTORIA: If Florence be i'th'court, would he would
190   kill me.

GASPARO: Fool! Princes give rewards with their own
    hands,
But death or punishment by the hands of others.

LODOVICO: Sirrah, you once did strike me; I'll strike you
Into the centre.

FLAMINEO: Thou'lt do it like a hangman, a base hangman,
Not like a noble fellow, for thou see'st
I cannot strike again.

LODOVICO: Dost laugh?

FLAMINEO: Wouldst have me die as I was born, in
    whining?

GASPARO: Recommend yourself to heaven.

FLAMINEO: No, I will carry mine own commendations
200   thither.

LODOVICO: Oh, could I kill you forty times a day,
And use't four years together, 'twere too little.
Naught grieves but that you are too few to feed
The famine of our vengeance. What dost think on?

FLAMINEO: Nothing; of nothing: leave thy idle ques-
    tions, –
I am i'th'way to study a long silence:
To prate were idle. – I remember nothing.
There's nothing of so infinite vexation
As man's own thoughts.

LODOVICO: O thou glorious strumpet!
210 Could I divide thy breath from this pure air
When't leaves thy body, I would suck it up,
And breathe't upon some dunghill.

VITTORIA: You, my death's-man!
Methinks thou dost not look horrid enough,
Thou hast too good a face to be a hangman:
If thou be, do thy office in right form;
Fall down upon thy knees, and ask forgiveness.

194. *Centre:* heart.

LODOVICO: Oh, thou hast been a most prodigious
 comet!
But I'll cut off your train. Kill the Moor first.
VITTORIA: You shall not kill her first; behold my breast:
I will be waited on in death; my servant   220
Shall never go before me.
GASPARO: Are you so brave?
VITTORIA: Yes, I shall welcome death,
As princes do some great ambassadors;
I'll meet thy weapon half-way.
LODOVICO: Thou dost tremble:
Methinks, fear should dissolve thee into air.
VITTORIA: Oh, thou art deceived, I am too true a woman!
Conceit can never kill me. I'll tell thee what,
I will not in my death shed one base tear,
Or if look pale, for want of blood, not fear.
GASPARO: Thou art my task, black fury.
ZANCHE: I have blood 230
As red as either of theirs: wilt drink some?
'Tis good for the falling-sickness. I am proud
Death cannot alter my complexion,
For I shall ne'er look pale.
LODOVICO: Strike, strike,
With a joint motion.
 [*They strike.*]
VITTORIA: 'Twas a manly blow;
The next thou giv'st, murder some sucking infant;
And then thou wilt be famous.
FLAMINEO: Oh, what blade is't?
A Toledo, or an English fox?
I ever thought a cutler should distinguish
The cause of my death, rather than a doctor. 240
Search my wound deeper; tent it with the steel
That made it.

    227. *Conceit*: (i) apprehension, (ii) vanity.
    238. *Fox*: kind of sword-blade.
    241. *Tent*: (i) probe, (ii) bind.

VITTORIA: Oh, my greatest sin lay in my blood!
Now my blood pays for't.

FLAMINEO: Th'art a noble sister!
I love thee now; if woeman do breed man,
She ought to teach him manhood. Fare thee well.
Know, many glorious women that are famed
For masculine virtue, have been vicious,
Only a happier silence did betide them:
250   She hath no faults, who hath the art to hide them.

VITTORIA: My soul like to a ship in a black storm,
Is driven, I know not whither.

FLAMINEO: Then cast anchor.
Prosperity doth bewitch men, seeming clear;
But seas do laugh, show white, when rocks are near.
We cease to grieve, cease to be fortune's slaves,
Nay, cease to die by dying. Art thou gone?
And thou so near the bottom? false report,
Which says that women vie with the nine Muses,
For nine tough durable lives! I do not look
260   Who went before, nor who shall follow me;
No, at myself I will begin and end.
While we look up to heaven, we confound
Knowledge with knowledge. Oh, I am in a mist!

VITTORIA: Oh, happy they that never saw the court,
Nor ever knew great men but by report!

          VITTORIA *dies*.

FLAMINEO: I recover like a spent taper, for a flash,
And instantly go out.
Let all that belong to great men remember th'old wives'
tradition, to be like the lions i'th'Tower on Candlemas-
270   day; to mourn if the sun shine, for fear of the pitiful
remainder of winter to come.
'Tis well yet there's some goodness in my death;
My life was a black charnel. I have caught
An everlasting cold; I have lost my voice

243-4. *Blood . . . blood:* (i) passion, (ii) life-blood.
270. *Candlemas-day:* 2 February.

Most irrecoverably. Farewell, glorious villains.
This busy trade of life appears most vain,
Since rest breeds rest, where all seek pain by pain.
Let no harsh flattering bells resound my knell;
Strike, thunder, and strike loud, to my farewell!
    Dies.

    Enter AMBASSADORS *and* GIOVANNI [*with soldiers*].

ENGLISH AMBASSADOR: This way, this way! break ope 280
  the doors! this way!
LODOVICO: Ha, are we betrayed?
  Why then let's constantly die all together;
  And having finished this most noble deed,
  Defy the worst of fate, not fear to bleed.
ENGLISH AMBASSADOR: Keep back the prince – shoot!
  Shoot!
    [*Soldiers shoot* LODOVICO.]
LODOVICO: Oh, I am wounded!
  I fear I shall be ta'en.
GIOVANNI: You bloody villains,
  By what authority have you committed
  This massacre?
LODOVICO: By thine.
GIOVANNI: Mine!
LODOVICO: Yes; thy uncle,   290
  Which is a part of thee, enjoined us to't:
  Thou know'st me, I am sure; I am Count Lodowick;
  And thy most noble uncle in disguise
  Was last night in thy court.
GIOVANNI: Ha!
LODOVICO: Yes, that Moor
  Thy father chose his pensioner.
GIOVANNI: He turned murderer!
  Away with them to prison, and to torture:
  All that have hands in this shall taste our justice,
  As I hope heaven.
LODOVICO: I do glory yet,
  That I can call this act mine own. For my part,

300   The rack, the gallows, and the torturing wheel,
        Shall be but sound sleeps to me: here's my rest;
        I limned this night-piece and it was my best.
   GIOVANNI: Remove the bodies. – See, my honoured lord,
        What use you ought make of their punishment.
        Let guilty men remember, their black deeds
        Do lean on crutches made of slender reeds.
        [*Exeunt.*]

*

Instead of an epilogue, only this of Martial supplies me:

Haec fuerint nobis praemia, si placui.

For the action of the play, 'twas generally well, and I dare
affirm, with the joint testimony of some of their own
quality (for the true imitation of life, without striving to
make nature a monster), the best that ever became them:
whereof as I make a general acknowledgement, so in
particular I must remember the well-approved industry of
my friend Master Perkins, and confess the worth of his
10 action did crown both the beginning and end.

THE

CHANGELING:

As it was Acted (with great Applause)
at the Privat house in D r u r y Ļ L a n e,
and *Salisbury Court.*

Written by $\left\{\begin{array}{c}THOMAS\ MIDLETON,\\ \text{and}\\ WILLIAM\ ROWLEY.\end{array}\right\}$ Gent'.

Never Printed before.

L O N D O N,

Printed for H u m p h r e y M o s e l e y, and are to
be sold at his shop at the sign of the *Princes-Arms*
in St *Pauls* Church-yard, 1 6 5 3.

DRAMATIS PERSONAE

*

VERMANDERO, Father to Beatrice.
TOMAZO DE PIRACQUO, a Noble Lord.
ALONZO DE PIRACQUO, his Brother, Suitor to Beatrice.
ALSEMERO, a Nobleman, afterwards married to Beatrice.
JASPERINO, his friend.
ALIBIUS, a jealous Doctor.
LOLLIO, his man.
PEDRO, Friend to Antonio.
ANTONIO, the Changeling.
FRANCISCUS, the Counterfeit Madman.
DE FLORES, Servant to Vermandero.
                    Madmen, Servants.
BEATRICE-JOANNA, Daughter to Vermandero.
DIAPHANTA, her Waiting-woman.
ISABELLA, Wife to Alibius.

*The Action takes place in the Spanish seaport of
Alicante.*

ACT ONE

*

[SCENE ONE]

Enter ALSEMERO.

[ALSEMERO]: 'Twas in the temple where I first beheld her,
  And now again the same; what omen yet
  Follows of that? None but imaginary;
  Why should my hopes or fate be timorous?
  The place is holy, so is my intent:
  I love her beauties to the holy purpose,
  And that, methinks, admits comparison
  With man's first creation, the place blest,
  And is his right home back, if he achieve it.
  The Church hath first begun our interview,   10
  And that's the place must join us into one,
  So there's beginning and perfection too.
    Enter JASPERINO.
JASPERINO: Oh sir, are you here? Come, the wind's fair
  with you,
  Y'are like to have a swift and pleasant passage.
ALSEMERO: Sure y'are deceived, friend, 'tis contrary
  In my best judgement.
JASPERINO: What, for Malta?
  If you could buy a gale amongst the witches,
  They could not serve you such a lucky pennyworth
  As comes a'God's name.
ALSEMERO: Even now I observed
  The temple's vane to turn full in my face;   20
  I know 'tis against me.
JASPERINO: Against you?
  Then you know not where you are.
ALSEMERO: Not well indeed.
JASPERINO: Are you not well, sir?

        6. *Holy purpose:* marriage.
        19. *A'God's name: gratis.*

ALSEMERO: Yes, Jasperino,
– Unless there be some hidden malady
Within me, that I understand not.

JASPERINO: And that
I begin to doubt, sir; I never knew
Your inclinations to travels at a pause
With any cause to hinder it, till now.
Ashore, you were wont to call your servants up

30   And help to trap your horses for the speed;
At sea, I have seen you weigh the anchor with'em,
Hoist sails for fear to lose the foremost breath,
Be in continual prayers for fair winds, –
And have you changed your orisons?

ALSEMERO: No, friend,
I keep the same church, same devotion.

JASPERINO: Lover I'm sure y'are none, the Stoic
Was found in you long ago; your mother
Nor best friends, who have set snares of beauty – ay,
And choice ones too – could never trap you that way.
What might be the cause?

40 ALSEMERO: Lord, how violent
Thou art; I was but meditating of
Somewhat I heard within the temple.

JASPERINO: Is this violence? 'Tis but idleness
Compared with your haste yesterday.

ALSEMERO: I'm all this while a-going, man.

     Enter SERVANTS.

JASPERINO: Backwards I think, sir. Look, your servants.

I. SERVANT: The seamen call; shall we board your trunks?

ALSEMERO: No, not today.

JASPERINO: 'Tis the critical day it seems, and the sign in

50   Aquarius.

II. SERVANT [*aside*]: We must not to sea today; this smoke
will bring forth fire.

        26. *Doubt:* fear.
        30. *Trap . . . speed:* hasten arrangements.
        49. *Critical:* propitious.

ALSEMERO: Keep all on shore; I do not know the end
(Which needs I must do) of an affair in hand
Ere I can go to sea.

I. SERVANT: Well, your pleasure.

II. SERVANT [*aside*]: Let him e'en take his leisure too; we
are safer on land.

Exeunt SERVANTS.

Enter BEATRICE, DIAPHANTA, *and Servants.* [ALSE-
MERO *greets and kisses* BEATRICE.]

JASPERINO [*aside*]: How now! The laws of the Medes are
changed, sure. Salute a woman? He kisses too – won- 60
derful! Where learnt he this? And does it perfectly too –
in my conscience, he ne'er rehearsed it before. Nay, go
on, this will be stranger and better news at Valencia
than if he had ransomed half Greece from the Turk.

BEATRICE: You are a scholar, sir.

ALSEMERO: A weak one, lady.

BEATRICE: Which of the sciences is this love you speak of?

ALSEMERO: From your tongue I take it to be music.

BEATRICE: You are skilful in't, can sing at first sight.

ALSEMERO: And I have showed you all my skill at once.
I want more words to express me further   70
And must be forced to repetition:
I love you dearly.

BEATRICE: Be better advised, sir:
Our eyes are sentinels unto our judgements
And should give certain judgement what they see;
But they are rash sometimes, and tell us wonders
Of common things, which when our judgements find,
They can then check the eyes, and call them blind.

ALSEMERO: But I am further, lady; yesterday
Was mine eyes' employment, and hither now
They brought my judgement, where are both agreed.   80
Both houses then consenting, 'tis agreed;
Only there wants the confirmation
By the hand royal, that's your part, lady.

62. *In my conscience*: upon my word. A stock phrase.

BEATRICE: Oh, there's one above me, sir. [*Aside*] For five
    days past
    To be recalled! Sure, mine eyes were mistaken,
    This was the man was meant me; that he should come
    So near his time, and miss it!
JASPERINO [*aside*]: We might have come by the carriers
    from Valencia, I see, and saved all our sea-provision; we

90   are at farthest, sure. Methinks I should do something too.
    I meant to be a venturer in this voyage.
    Yonder's another vessel, I'll board her,
    If she be lawful prize, down goes her top-sail.
    [*Greets* DIAPHANTA.]
    Enter DE FLORES.
DE FLORES: Lady, your father –
BEATRICE: Is in health, I hope.
DE FLORES: Your eye shall instantly instruct you, lady.
    He's coming hitherward.
BEATRICE: What needed then
    Your duteous preface? I had rather
    He had come unexpected; you must 'stall

100   A good presence with unnecessary blabbing. –
    And how welcome for your part you are
    I'm sure you know.
DE FLORES [*aside*]: Wilt never mend, this scorn,
    One side nor other? Must I be enjoined
    To follow still whilst she flies from me? Well,
    Fates do your worst, I'll please myself with sight
    Of her, at all opportunities,
    If but to spite her anger; I know she had
    Rather see me dead than living, and yet

110   She knows no cause for't, but a peevish will.
ALSEMERO: You seem'd displeased, lady, on the sudden.
BEATRICE: Your pardon sir, 'tis my infirmity,
    Nor can I other reason render you
    Than his or hers, or some particular thing

90. *At farthest:* wildly off course.
99. *'Stall:* forestall.

They must abandon as a deadly poison,
Which to a thousand other tastes were wholesome;
Such to mine eyes is that same fellow there,
The same that report speaks of the basilisk.

ALSEMERO: This is a frequent frailty in our nature;
    There's scarce a man amongst a thousand sound,   120
    But hath his imperfection: one distastes
    The scent of roses, which to infinites
    Most pleasing is, and odoriferous;
    One oil, the enemy of poison;
    Another wine, the cheerer of the heart
    And lively refresher of the countenance.
    Indeed this fault, if so it be, is general;
    There's scarce a thing but is both loved and loathed, –
    Myself, I must confess, have the same frailty.

BEATRICE: And what may be your poison, sir? I am bold
    with you.   130

ALSEMERO: What might be your desire perhaps, a cherry.

BEATRICE: I am no enemy to any creature
    My memory has, but yon gentleman.

ALSEMERO: He does ill to tempt your sight, if he knew it.

BEATRICE: He cannot be ignorant of that, sir,
    I have not spared to tell him so; and I want
    To help myself, since he's a gentleman
    In good respect with my father, and follows him.

ALSEMERO: He's out of his place then, now.
    [*They talk apart.*]

JASPERINO: I'm a mad wag, wench.   140

DIAPHANTA: So methinks; but for your comfort I can
    tell you, we have a doctor in the city that undertakes the
    cure of such.

JASPERINO: Tush, I know what physic is best for the
    state of mine own body.

DIAPHANTA: 'Tis scarce a well-governed state, I believe.

JASPERINO: I could show thee such a thing with an

118. *Basilisk:* mythical beast which killed with its glance.
136. *Want:* lack means.

ingredient that we two would compound together, and
if it did not tame the maddest blood i'th'town for two
150 hours after, I'll ne'er profess physic again.

DIAPHANTA: A little poppy sir, were good to cause you
sleep.

JASPERINO: Poppy? I'll give thee a pop i'th'lips for that
first, and begin there: [*Kisses her.*] poppy is one simple
indeed, and cuckoo what-you-call't another: I'll discover
no more now, another time I'll show thee all.

BEATRICE: My father, sir.

    Enter VERMANDERO *and Servants.*

VERMANDERO: Oh Joanna, I came to meet thee, –
Your devotion's ended?

BEATRICE: For this time, sir.
160 [*Aside*] I shall change my saint, I fear me; I find
A giddy turning in me. [*To* VERMANDERO] Sir, this
    while
I am beholding to this gentleman
Who left his own way to keep me company,
And in discourse I find him much desirous
To see your castle: he hath deserved it, sir,
If ye please to grant it.

VERMANDERO: With all my heart, sir.
Yet there's an article between, I must know
Your country; we use not to give survey
Of our chief strengths to strangers; our citadels
170 Are placed conspicuous to outward view
On promonts' tops; but within are secrets.

ALSEMERO: A Valencian sir.

VERMANDERO: A Valencian?
That's native, sir; of what name, I beseech you?

ALSEMERO: Alsemero, sir.

VERMANDERO: Alsemero? Not the son
Of John de Alsemero?

154. *Simple:* medicinal herb.   155. *Cuckoo:* wake-robin, wild arum;
euphemism for male sexual organ.
167. *Article between:* condition to be settled.

ALSEMERO: The same, sir.

VERMANDERO: My best love bids you welcome.

BEATRICE [*aside*]: He was wont
To call me so, and then he speaks a most
Unfeignéd truth.

VERMANDERO: Oh sir, I knew your father;
We two were in acquaintance long ago,
Before our chins were worth Iulan down,   180
And so continued till the stamp of time
Had coined us into silver: well, he's gone, –
A good soldier went with him.

ALSEMERO: You went together in that, sir.

VERMANDERO: No, by Saint Jacques, I came behind him.
Yet I have done somewhat too; an unhappy day
Swallowed him at last at Gibraltar
In fight with those rebellious Hollanders,
Was it not so?

ALSEMERO: Whose death I had revenged
Or followed him in fate, had not the late league   190
Prevented me.

VERMANDERO: Ay, ay, 'twas time to breathe:
Oh Joanna, I should ha'told thee news,
I saw Piracquo lately.

BEATRICE [*aside*]: That's ill news.

VERMANDERO: He's hot preparing for this day of
triumph,
Thou must be a bride within this sevennight.

ALSEMERO [*aside*]: Ha!

BEATRICE: Nay, good sir, be not so violent, with speed
I cannot render satisfaction
Unto the dear companion of my soul,
Virginity, whom I thus long have lived with,   200
And part with it so rude and suddenly;
Can such friends divide, never to meet again,
Without a solemn farewell?

VERMANDERO: Tush, tush, there's a toy.

ALSEMERO [*aside*]: I must now part, and never meet again

With any joy on earth. [*To* VERMANDERO] Sir, your
    pardon,
My affairs call on me.

VERMANDERO: How, sir? By no means;
Not changed so soon, I hope? You must see my castle
And her best entertainment, ere we part;
I shall think myself unkindly used else.

210   Come, come, let's on; I had good hope your stay
Had been a while with us in Alicant;
I might have bid you to my daughter's wedding.

ALSEMERO [*aside*]: He means to feast me, and poisons me
    beforehand.
[*To* VERMANDERO] I should be dearly glad to be there,
    sir,
Did my occasions suit as I could wish.

BEATRICE: I shall be sorry if you be not there
When it is done, sir – but not so suddenly.

VERMANDERO: I tell you sir, the gentleman's complete,
A courtier and a gallant, enriched

220   With many fair and noble ornaments;
I would not change him for a son-in-law
For any he in Spain, the proudest he, –
And we have great ones, that you know.

ALSEMERO: He's much
Bound to you, sir.

VERMANDERO: He shall be bound to me
As fast as this tie can hold him; I'll want
My will else.

BEATRICE [*aside*]: I shall want mine if you do it.

VERMANDERO: But come, by the way I'll tell you more of
    him.

ALSEMERO [*aside*]: How shall I dare to venture in his
    castle,

230   When he discharges murderers at the gate?
But I must on, for back I cannot go.

                227. *Want:* fail to have.
                230. *Murderers:* small cannon.

BEATRICE [*aside*]: Not this serpent gone yet?
　　[*Drops glove.*]
VERMANDERO: 　　　　　　Look girl, thy glove's fall'n;
　　Stay, stay, – De Flores, help a little.
　　[*Exeunt* VERMANDERO, ALSEMERO, JASPERINO,
　　and Servants.]
DE FLORES [*offering glove*]: 　　　　　　Here, lady.
BEATRICE: Mischief on your officious forwardness!
　　Who bade you stoop? They touch my hand no more:
　　There, for t'other's sake I part with this;
　　[*Takes off and throws down second glove.*]
　　Take 'em and draw thine own skin off with 'em.
　　Exeunt [*all but* DE FLORES].
DE FLORES: Here's a favour come – with a mischief! Now
　　I know
　　She had rather wear my pelt tanned in a pair
　　Of dancing pumps, than I should thrust my fingers　　240
　　Into her sockets here; I know she hates me,
　　Yet cannot choose but love her;
　　No matter; if but to vex her, I'll haunt her still,
　　Though I get nothing else, I'll have my will.
　　Exit.

[SCENE TWO]

Enter ALIBIUS *and* LOLLIO.
ALIBIUS: Lollio, I must trust thee with a secret,
　　But thou must keep it.
LOLLIO: I was ever close to a secret, sir.
ALIBIUS: The diligence that I have found in thee,
　　The care and industry already past,
　　Assures me of thy good continuance.
　　Lollio, I have a wife.
LOLLIO: Fie sir, .'tis too late to keep her secret, she's
　　known to be married all the town and country over.
ALIBIUS: Thou goest too fast, my Lollio; that knowledge　10

I allow no man can be barred it;
But there is a knowledge which is nearer,
Deeper and sweeter, Lollio.

LOLLIO: Well sir, let us handle that between you and I.

ALIBIUS: 'Tis that I go about, man; Lollio,
My wife is young.

LOLLIO: So much the worse to be kept secret, sir.

ALIBIUS: Why now thou meet'st the substance of the
point:
I am old, Lollio.

20 LOLLIO: No sir, 'tis I am old Lollio.

ALIBIUS: Yet why may not this concord and sympathize?
Old trees and young plants often grow together,
Well enough agreeing.

LOLLIO: Ay sir, but the old trees raise themselves higher
and broader than the young plants.

ALIBIUS: Shrewd application! There's the fear, man;
I would wear my ring on my own finger;
Whilst it is borrowed it is none of mine,
But his that useth it.

30 LOLLIO: You must keep it on still, then; if it but lie by,
one or other will be thrusting into it.

ALIBIUS: Thou conceiv'st me, Lollio; here thy watchful
eye
Must have employment; I cannot always be
At home.

LOLLIO: I dare swear you cannot.

ALIBIUS: I must look out.

LOLLIO: I know't, you must look out, 'tis every man's
case.

ALIBIUS: Here I do say must thy employment be,
To watch her treadings, and in my absence
40 Supply my place.

LOLLIO: I'll do my best, sir, yet surely I cannot see who
you should have cause to be jealous of.

ALIBIUS: Thy reason for that, Lollio? 'Tis a comfortable
question.

LOLLIO: We have but two sorts of people in the house,
and both under the whip – that's fools and madmen; the
one has not wit enough to be knaves, and the other not
knavery enough to be fools.

ALIBIUS: Ay, those are all my patients, Lollio.
I do profess the cure of either sort:
My trade, my living 'tis, I thrive by it;   50
But here's the care that mixes with my thrift:
The daily visitants, that come to see
My brainsick patients, I would not have
To see my wife: gallants I do observe
Of quick enticing eyes, rich in habits,
Of stature and proportion very comely. –
These are most shrewd temptations, Lollio.

LOLLIO: They may be easily answered, sir; if they come to
see the fools and madmen, you and I may serve the turn,
and let my mistress alone – she's of neither sort.   60

ALIBIUS: 'Tis a good ward; indeed, come they to see
Our madmen or our fools, let 'em see no more
Than what they come for; by that consequent
They must not see her; I'm sure she's no fool.

LOLLIO: And I'm sure she's no madman.

ALIBIUS: Hold that buckler fast, Lollio; my trust
Is on thee, and I account it firm and strong.
What hour is't, Lollio?

LOLLIO: Towards belly-hour, sir.

ALIBIUS: Dinner time? Thou mean'st twelve o'clock.   70

LOLLIO: Yes sir, for every part has his hour; we wake at
six and look about us, that's eye-hour; at seven we
should pray, that's knee-hour; at eight walk, that's leg-
hour; at nine gather flowers and pluck a rose, that's
nose-hour; at ten we drink, that's mouth-hour; at eleven
lay about us for victuals, that's hand-hour; at twelve go
to dinner, that's belly-hour.

ALIBIUS: Profoundly, Lollio! It will be long

51. *Thrift:* thriving, profit.   55. *Habits:* dress.
61. *Ward:* defence, answer.   74. *Pluck a rose:* urinate.

Ere all thy scholars learn this lesson, and
80   I did look to have a new one entered; – stay,
I think my expectation is come home.

Enter PEDRO, *and* ANTONIO *like an Idiot.*

PEDRO: Save you, sir; my business speaks itself,
This sight takes off the labour of my tongue.

ALIBIUS: Ay, ay, sir;
'Tis plain enough, you mean him for my patient.

PEDRO: And if your pains prove but commodious, to give
but some little strength to his sick and weak part of
nature in him, these [*Giving him money*] are but patterns
to show you of the whole pieces that will follow to you,
90   beside the charge of diet, washing and other necessaries
fully defrayed.

ALIBIUS: Believe it sir, there shall no care be wanting.

LOLLIO: Sir, an officer in this place may deserve something; the trouble will pass through my hands.

PEDRO: 'Tis fit something should come to your hands
then, sir.

[*Gives him money.*]

LOLLIO: Yes sir, 'tis I must keep him sweet, and read to
him. What is his name?

PEDRO: His name is Antonio; marry, we use but half to
100   him, only Tony.

LOLLIO: Tony, Tony, 'tis enough, and a very good name
for a fool; what's your name, Tony?

ANTONIO: He, he, he! Well, I thank you, cousin; he,
he, he!

LOLLIO: Good boy! Hold up your head: he can laugh, I
perceive by that he is no beast.

PEDRO: Well, sir,
If you can raise him but to any height,
Any degree of wit, might he attain,
110   As I might say, to creep but on all four
Towards the chair of wit, or walk on crutches,
'Twould add an honour to your worthy pains,
And a great family might pray for you,

To which he should be heir, had he discretion
To claim and guide his own; assure you, sir,
He is a gentleman.

LOLLIO: Nay, there's nobody doubted that; at first sight I
knew him for a gentleman, he looks no other yet.

PEDRO: Let him have good attendance and sweet lodging.

LOLLIO: As good as my mistress lies in, sir; and as you   120
allow us time and means, we can raise him to the higher
degree of discretion.

PEDRO: Nay, there shall no cost want, sir.

LOLLIO: He will hardly be stretched up to the wit of a
magnifico.

PEDRO: Oh no, that's not to be expected, far shorter will
be enough.

LOLLIO: I'll warrant you [I'll] make him fit to bear office
in five weeks; I'll undertake to wind him up to the wit of
constable.   130

PEDRO: If it be lower than that it might serve turn.

LOLLIO: No, fie, to level him with a headborough, beadle,
or watchman were but little better than he is; constable
I'll able him: if he do come to be a justice afterwards,
let him thank the keeper. Or I'll go further with you;
say I do bring him up to my own pitch, say I make him
as wise as myself.

PEDRO: Why, there I would have it.

LOLLIO: Well, go to; either I'll be as arrant a fool as he,
or he shall be as wise as I, and then I think 'twill serve   140
his turn.

PEDRO: Nay, I do like thy wit passing well.

LOLLIO: Yes, you may, yet if I had not been a fool, I had
had more wit than I have too; remember what state you
find me in.

PEDRO: I will, and so leave you: your best cares, I beseech
you.

ALIBIUS: Take you none with you, leave 'em all with us.
    Exit PEDRO.

125. *Magnifico:* Grandee.

ANTONIO: Oh, my cousin's gone, cousin, cousin oh!

150 LOLLIO: Peace, peace, Tony, you must not cry, child, you must be whipped if you do; your cousin is here still, I am your cousin, Tony.

ANTONIO: He, he, then I'll not cry, if thou be'st my cousin, he, he, he.

LOLLIO: I were best try his wit a little, that I may know what form to place him in.

ALIBIUS: Ay do, Lollio, do.

LOLLIO: I must ask him easy questions at first; – Tony, how many true fingers has a tailor on his right hand?

160 ANTONIO: As many as on his left, cousin.

LOLLIO: Good; and how many on both?

ANTONIO: Two less than a deuce, cousin.

LOLLIO: Very well answered. I come to you again, cousin Tony: how many fools goes to a wise man?

ANTONIO: Forty in a day sometimes, cousin.

LOLLIO: Forty in a day? How prove you that?

ANTONIO: All that fall out amongst themselves and go to a lawyer to be made friends.

LOLLIO: A parlous fool! He must sit in the fourth form at
170 least, I perceive that. I come again, Tony: how many knaves make an honest man?

ANTONIO: I know not that, cousin.

LOLLIO: No, the question is too hard for you: I'll tell you, cousin; there's three knaves may make an honest man, – a sergeant, a jailor and a beadle; the sergeant catches him, the jailor holds him, and the beadle lashes him; and if he be not honest then, the hangman must cure him.

ANTONIO: Ha, ha, ha, that's fine sport, cousin!

180 ALIBIUS: This was too deep a question for the fool, Lollio.

LOLLIO: Yes, this might have served yourself, tho' I say't; once more and you shall go play, Tony.

164. *Goes to:* (i) constitute (Lollio's sense), (ii) visit (Antonio's sense).　169. *Parlous:* shrewd.

ANTONIO: Ay, play at push-pin, cousin, ha, he!

LOLLIO: So thou shalt; say how many fools are here —

ANTONIO: Two, cousin, thou and I.

LOLLIO: Nay, y'are too forward there, Tony; mark my question: how many fools and knaves are here? — A fool before a knave, a fool behind a knave, between every two fools a knave. — How many fools, how many 190 knaves?

ANTONIO: I never learnt so far, cousin.

ALIBIUS: Thou putt'st too hard questions to him, Lollio.

LOLLIO: I'll make him understand it easily; cousin, stand there.

ANTONIO: Ay, cousin.

LOLLIO: Master, stand you next the fool.

ALIBIUS: Well, Lollio?

LOLLIO: Here's my place: mark now, Tony, there a fool before a knave.   200

ANTONIO: That's I, cousin.

LOLLIO: Here's a fool behind a knave, that's I; and between us two fools, there's a knave, that's my master; 'tis but we three, that's all.

ANTONIO: We three, we three, cousin!

Madmen within.

I. WITHIN: Put's head i'th' pillory, the bread's too little.

II. WITHIN: Fly, fly, and he catches the swallow.

III. WITHIN: Give her more onion, or the devil put the rope about her crag.

LOLLIO: You may hear what time of day it is, the chimes 210 of Bedlam goes.

ALIBIUS: Peace, peace, or the wire comes!

III. WITHIN: Cat-whore, cat-whore, her permasant, her permasant!

ALIBIUS: Peace, I say! Their hour's come, they must be fed, Lollio.

209. *Crag:* neck.
212. *Wire:* whip.
213. *Her:* stage-Welsh for 'my'. *Permasant:* Parmesan (cheese).

LOLLIO: There's no hope of recovery of that Welsh madman, was undone by a mouse that spoiled him a permasant; lost his wits for't.

220 ALIBIUS: Go to your charge, Lollio, I'll to mine.

LOLLIO: Go you to your madmen's ward, let me alone with your fools.

ALIBIUS: And remember my last charge, Lollio.

Exit.

LOLLIO: Of which your patients do you think I am? Come, Tony, you must amongst your school-fellows now; there's pretty scholars amongst 'em, I can tell you; there's some of 'em at *stultus, stulta, stultum*.

ANTONIO: I would see the madmen, cousin, if they would not bite me.

230 LOLLIO: No, they shall not bite thee, Tony.

ANTONIO: They bite when they are at dinner, do they not, coz?

LOLLIO: They bite at dinner indeed, Tony. Well, I hope to get credit by thee; I like thee the best of all the scholars that ever I brought up, and thou shalt prove a wise man, or I'll prove a fool myself.

Exeunt.

227. *Stultus:* Latin; foolish.

ACT TWO

*

[SCENE ONE]

Enter BEATRICE *and* JASPERINO *severally.*

BEATRICE: Oh sir, I'm ready now for that fair service
  Which makes the name of friend sit glorious on you.
  Good angels and this conduct be your guide, –
    [*Gives him a paper.*]
  Fitness of time and place is there set down, sir.
JASPERINO: The joy I shall return rewards my service.
  Exit.
BEATRICE: How wise is Alsemero in his friend!
  It is a sign he makes his choice with judgement.
  Then I appear in nothing more approved,
  Than making choice of him;
  For 'tis a principle, he that can choose   10
  That bosom well, who of his thoughts partakes,
  Proves most discreet in every choice he makes.
  Methinks I love now with the eyes of judgement,
  And see the way to merit, clearly see it.
  A true deserver like a diamond sparkles,
  In darkness you may see him, that's in absence,
  Which is the greatest darkness falls on love;
  Yet is he best discernéd then
  With intellectual eyesight; what's Piracquo
  My father spends his breath for? And his blessing   20
  Is only mine as I regard his name,
  Else it goes from me, and turns head against me,
  Transformed into a curse. Some speedy way
  Must be remembered; he's so forward too,
  So urgent that way, scarce allows me breath
  To speak to my new comforts.
    Enter DE FLORES.
DE FLORES [*aside*]:   Yonder's she.
  Whatever ails me, now o'late especially,

I can as well be hanged as refrain seeing her;
Some twenty times a day, nay, not so little,
30 Do I force errands, frame ways and excuses
To come into her sight, and I have small reason for't,
And less encouragement; for she baits me still
Every time worse than other, does profess herself
The cruellest enemy to my face in town,
At no hand can abide the sight of me,
As if danger, or ill luck hung in my looks.
I must confess my face is bad enough,
But I know far worse has better fortune,
And not endured alone, but doted on;
40 And yet such pick-haired faces, chins like witches',
Here and there five hairs, whispering in a corner,
As if they grew in fear one of another,
Wrinkles like troughs, where swine deformity swills
The tears of perjury that lie there like wash
Fallen from the slimy and dishonest eye, –
Yet such a one plucked sweets without restraint,
And has the grace of beauty to his sweet.
Though my hard fate has thrust me out to servitude,
I tumbled into th'world a gentleman. –
50 She turns her blessed eye upon me now,
And I'll endure all storms before I part with't.
BEATRICE [*aside*]: Again!
This ominous ill-faced fellow more disturbs me
Than all my other passions.
DE FLORES [*aside*]:   Now't begins again;
I'll stand this storm of hail though the stones pelt me.
BEATRICE: Thy business? What's thy business?
DE FLORES [*aside*]:   Soft and fair,
I cannot part so soon now.
BEATRICE [*aside*]:   The villain's fixed –
[*To* DE FLORES] Thou standing toad-pool!
DE FLORES [*aside*]:   The shower falls amain now.

---

35. *At no hand:* by no means.

BEATRICE: Who sent thee? What's thy errand? Leave my
  sight.

DE FLORES: My lord your father charged me to deliver   60
  A message to you.

BEATRICE: What, another since?
  Do't and be hanged then, let me be rid of thee.

DE FLORES: True service merits mercy.

BEATRICE: What's thy message?

DE FLORES: Let beauty settle but in patience,
  You shall hear all.

BEATRICE: A dallying, trifling torment!

DE FLORES: Signor Alonzo de Piracquo, lady,
  Sole brother to Tomazo de Piracquo –

BEATRICE: Slave, when wilt make an end?

DE FLORES [aside]:   Too soon I shall.

BEATRICE: What all this while of him?

DE FLORES: The said Alonzo,
  With the foresaid Tomazo –

BEATRICE: Yet again?   70

DE FLORES: Is new alighted.

BEATRICE: Vengeance strike the news!
  Thou thing most loathed, what cause was there in this
  To bring thee to my sight?

DE FLORES: My lord your father
  Charged me to seek you out.

BEATRICE: Is there no other
  To send his errand by?

DE FLORES: It seems 'tis my luck
  To be i'th'way still.

BEATRICE: Get thee from me!

DE FLORES: So; –
  [Aside] Why, am not I an ass, to devise ways
  Thus to be railed at? I must see her still.
  I shall have a mad qualm within this hour again,
  I know't; and like a common Garden-bull,   80
  I do but take breath to be lugged again.

        81. *Lugged*: baited.

What this may bode I know not; I'll despair the less,
Because there's daily precedents of bad faces
Belov'd beyond all reason; these foul chops
May come into favour one day, 'mongst his fellows:
Wrangling has proved the mistress of good pastime;
As children cry themselves asleep, I ha' seen
Women have chid themselves abed to men.

  Exit DE FLORES.

BEATRICE: I never see this fellow, but I think
90 Of some harm towards me, danger's in my mind still,
I scarce leave trembling of an hour after.
The next good mood I find my father in,
I'll get him quite discarded; – oh, I was
Lost in this small disturbance, and forgot
Affliction's fiercer torrent, that now comes
To bear down all my comforts.

  Enter VERMANDERO, ALONZO, TOMAZO.

VERMANDERO: Y'are both welcome,
But an especial one belongs to you, sir,
To whose most noble name our love presents
The addition of a son, our son Alonzo.

100 ALONZO: The treasury of honour cannot bring forth
A title I should more rejoice in, sir.

VERMANDERO: You have improved it well; daughter, prepare,
The day will steal upon thee suddenly.

BEATRICE [*aside*]: Howe'er, I will be sure to keep the night,
If it should come so near me.

  [BEATRICE *and* VERMANDERO *talk apart*.]

TOMAZO: Alonzo.
ALONZO: Brother?
TOMAZO: In troth I see small welcome in her eye.
ALONZO: Fie, you are too severe a censurer
Of love in all points, there's no bringing on you.
If lovers should mark everything a fault,

  91. *Of*: off. 104. *Keep*: ward off, guard against.

Affection would be like an ill-set book 110
Whose faults might prove as big as half the volume.

BEATRICE: That's all I do entreat.

VERMANDERO: It is but reasonable:
I'll see what my son says to't: son Alonzo,
Here's a motion made but to reprieve
A maidenhead three days longer; the request
Is not far out of reason, for indeed
The former time is pinching.

ALONZO: Though my joys
Be set back so much time as I could wish
They had been forward, yet since she desires it,
The time is set as pleasing as before, 120
I find no gladness wanting.

VERMANDERO: May I ever meet it in that point still:
Y'are nobly welcome, sirs.

    Exeunt VERMANDERO *and* BEATRICE.

TOMAZO: So; did you mark the dullness of her parting
    now?

ALONZO: What dullness? Thou art so exceptious still.

TOMAZO: Why, let it go then, I am but a fool
To mark your harms so heedfully.

ALONZO: Where's the oversight?

TOMAZO: Come, your faith's cozened in her, strongly
    cozened:
Unsettle your affection with all speed
Wisdom can bring it to, your peace is ruined else. 130
Think what a torment 'tis to marry one
Whose heart is leapt into another's bosom:
If ever pleasure she receive from thee,
It comes not in thy name, or of thy gift;
She lies but with another in thine arms,
He the half-father unto all thy children
In the conception; if he get'em not,
She helps to get'em for him, in his passions, and how
    dangerous

128. *Cozened:* cheated.
283

And shameful her restraint may go in time to,
140　It is not to be thought on without sufferings.

ALONZO: You speak as if she loved some other, then.

TOMAZO: Do you apprehend so slowly?

ALONZO:　　　　　　　　　　　　　　　Nay, an that
Be your fear only, I am safe enough.
Preserve your friendship and your counsel, brother,
For times of more distress; I should depart
An enemy, a dangerous, deadly one
To any but thyself, that should but think
She knew the meaning of inconstancy,
Much less the use and practice; yet w'are friends.
150　Pray let no more be urged; I can endure
Much, till I meet an injury to her,
Then I am not myself. Farewell, sweet brother,
How much w'are bound to heaven to depart lovingly.
　　Exit.

TOMAZO: Why, here is love's tame madness, thus a man
Quickly steals into his vexation.
　　Exit.

[SCENE TWO]

Enter DIAPHANTA *and* ALSEMERO.

DIAPHANTA: The place is my charge, you have kept your
　　hour,
And the reward of a just meeting bless you.
I hear my lady coming; complete gentlemen,
I dare not be too busy with my praises,
Th'are dangerous things to deal with.
　　Exit.

ALSEMERO:　　　　　　　　　　　　This goes well;
These women are the ladies' cabinets,
Things of most precious trust are lock[ed] into'em.
　　Enter BEATRICE.

BEATRICE: I have within mine eye all my desires;
Requests that holy prayers ascend heaven for,

And brings'em down to furnish our defects,   10
Come not more sweet to our necessities
Than thou unto my wishes.
ALSEMERO: W'are so like
In our expressions, lady, that unless I borrow
The same words, I shall never find their equals.
  [*They embrace.*]
BEATRICE: How happy were this meeting, this embrace,
If it were free from envy! This poor kiss,
It has an enemy, a hateful one,
That wishes poison to't: how well were I now
If there were none such name known as Piracquo,
Nor no such tie as the command of parents.   20
I should be but too much blessed.
ALSEMERO: One good service
Would strike off both your fears, and I'll go near it too,
Since you are so distressed; remove the cause,
The command ceases, so there's two fears blown out
With one and the same blast.
BEATRICE: Pray let me find you, sir.
What might that service be, so strangely happy?
ALSEMERO: The honourablest piece 'bout man, valour.
I'll send a challenge to Piracquo instantly.
BEATRICE: How? Call you that extinguishing of fear,
When 'tis the only way to keep it flaming?   30
Are not you ventured in the action
That's all my joys and comforts? Pray, no more, sir.
Say you prevailed, you're danger's and not mine then;
The law would claim you from me, or obscurity
Be made the grave to bury you alive.
I'm glad these thoughts come forth; oh keep not one
Of this condition, sir; here was a course
Found to bring sorrow on her way to death:
The tears would ne'er ha'dried till dust had choked'em.
Blood-guiltiness becomes a fouler visage, –   40
[*Aside*] And now I think on one, – I was to blame,

10. *Furnish ... defects:* supply what we lack.

285

I ha'marred so good a market with my scorn;
'T had been done questionless; the ugliest creature
Creation framed for some use, yet to see
I could not mark so much where it should be!

ALSEMERO: Lady –

BEATRICE [*aside*]: Why, men of art make much of poison,
Keep one to expel another; where was my art?

ALSEMERO: Lady, you hear not me.

BEATRICE: I do especially, sir;
50 The present times are not so sure of our side
As those hereafter may be; we must use'em then
As thrifty folks their wealth, sparingly now,
Till the time opens.

ALSEMERO: You teach wisdom, lady.

BEATRICE: Within there, – Diaphanta!

    Enter DIAPHANTA.

DIAPHANTA: Do you call, madam?

BEATRICE: Perfect your service and conduct this gentle-
    man
The private way you brought him.

DIAPHANTA: I shall, madam.

ALSEMERO: My love's as firm as love e'er built upon.

    Exeunt DIAPHANTA *and* ALSEMERO.
    Enter DE FLORES.

DE FLORES [*aside*]: I have watched this meeting, and do
    wonder much
What shall become of t'other; I'm sure both
60 Cannot be served unless she transgress; happily
Then I'll put in for one: for if a woman
Fly from one point, from him she makes a husband,
She spreads and mounts then like arithmetic,
One, ten, a hundred, a thousand, ten thousand,
Proves in time sutler to an army royal.
– Now do I look to be most richly railed at,
Yet I must see her.

BEATRICE [*aside*]:   Why, put case I loathed him

65. *Sutler:* purveyor of provisions.

As much as youth and beauty hates a sepulchre,
Must I needs show it? Cannot I keep that secret
And serve my turn upon him? See, he's here.   70
– De Flores.
DE FLORES [*aside*]: Ha, I shall run mad with joy!
She called me fairly by my name, De Flores,
And neither rogue nor rascal.
BEATRICE: What ha' you done
To your face a-late? Y'ave met with some good
  physician;
Y'ave pruned yourself methinks, you were not wont
To look so amorously.
DE FLORES: Not I. –
[*Aside*] 'Tis the same physnomy to a hair and pimple,
Which she called scurvy scarce an hour ago:
How is this?
BEATRICE: Come hither; nearer, man.   80
DE FLORES [*aside*]: I'm up to the chin in heaven!
BEATRICE: Turn, let me see;
Faugh, 'tis but the heat of the liver, I perceive't.
I thought it had been worse.
DE FLORES [*aside*]:   Her fingers touched me!
She smells all amber.
BEATRICE: I'll make a water for you shall cleanse this
Within a fortnight.
DE FLORES: With your own hands, lady?
BEATRICE: Yes, mine own, sir, in a work of cure
I'll trust no other.
DE FLORES [*aside*]: 'Tis half an act of pleasure
To hear her talk thus to me.
BEATRICE: When we are used
To a hard face, 'tis not so unpleasing;   90
It mends still in opinion, hourly mends,
I see it by experience.
DE FLORES [*aside*]:   I was blest
To light upon this minute; I'll make use on't.

88. *Act of pleasure:* sexual act.

BEATRICE: Hardness becomes the visage of a man well;
   It argues service, resolution, manhood,
   If cause were of employment.
DE FLORES: 'Twould be soon seen,
   If e'er your ladyship had cause to use it.
   I would but wish the honour of a service
   So happy as that mounts to.
BEATRICE: We shall try you –
   Oh my De Flores!
100 DE FLORES [*aside*]:   How's that?
   She calls me hers already, *my* De Flores!
   – You were about to sigh out somewhat, madam.
BEATRICE: No, was I? I forgot, – Oh!
DE FLORES: There 'tis again,
   The very fellow on't.
BEATRICE: You are too quick, sir.
DE FLORES: There's no excuse for't, now I heard it twice,
   madam;
   That sigh would fain have utterance, take pity on't,
   And lend it a free word; 'las, how it labours
   For liberty! I hear the murmur yet
   Beat at your bosom.
BEATRICE: Would creation –
DE FLORES: Ay, well said, that's it.
110 BEATRICE: Had formed me man.
DE FLORES: Nay, that's not it.
BEATRICE: Oh, 'tis the soul of freedom!
   I should not then be forced to marry one
   I hate beyond all depths; I should have power
   Then to oppose my loathings, nay, remove 'em
   For ever from my sight.
DE FLORES: Oh blest occasion! –
   Without change to your sex, you have your wishes.
   Claim so much man in me.
BEATRICE: In thee, De Flores?
   There's small cause for that.
DE FLORES: Put it not from me,

It's a service that I kneel for to you.   120
   [*Kneels.*]
BEATRICE: You are too violent to mean faithfully;
   There's horror in my service, blood and danger,
   Can those be things to sue for?
DE FLORES: If you knew
   How sweet it were to me to be employed
   In any act of yours, you would say then
   I failed, and used not reverence enough
   When I receive the charge on't.
BEATRICE [*aside*]:   This is much, methinks;
   Belike his wants are greedy, and to such
   Gold tastes like angels' food. [*To* DE FLORES] – Rise.
DE FLORES: I'll have the work first.
BEATRICE [*aside*]:   Possible his need   130
   Is strong upon him; [*Giving him money.*] – there's to
      encourage thee:
   As thou art forward and thy service dangerous,
   Thy reward shall be precious.
DE FLORES: That I have thought on;
   I have assured myself of that beforehand,
   And know it will be precious, – the thought ravishes!
BEATRICE: Then take him to thy fury.
DE FLORES: I thirst for him.
BEATRICE: Alonzo de Piracquo.
DE FLORES: His end's upon him,
   He shall be seen no more.
      [*Rises.*]
BEATRICE: How lovely now
   Dost thou appear to me! Never was man
   Dearlier rewarded.
DE FLORES: I do think of that.   140
BEATRICE: Be wondrous careful in the execution.
DE FLORES: Why, are not both our lives upon the cast?
BEATRICE: Then I throw all my fears upon thy service.
DE FLORES: They ne'er shall rise to hurt you.

142. *Upon the cast:* of the dice.

BEATRICE: When the deed's done,
  I'll furnish thee with all things for thy flight;
  Thou may'st live bravely in another country.
DE FLORES: Ay, ay, we'll talk of that hereafter.
BEATRICE [*aside*]:   I shall rid myself
  Of two inveterate loathings at one time,
  Piracquo, and his dog-face.
     Exit.
DE FLORES: Oh my blood!
150 Methinks I feel her in mine arms already,
  Her wanton fingers combing out this beard,
  And being pleased, praising this bad face.
  Hunger and pleasure – they'll commend sometimes
  Slovenly dishes, and feed heartily on 'em,
  Nay, which is stranger, refuse daintier for 'em.
  Some women are odd feeders. – I'm too loud.
  Here comes the man goes supperless to bed,
  Yet shall not rise tomorrow to his dinner.
     Enter ALONZO.
ALONZO: De Flores.
DE FLORES: My kind, honourable lord?
ALONZO: I am glad I ha'met with thee.
DE FLORES: Sir.
160 ALONZO: Thou canst show me
  The full strength of the castle?
DE FLORES: That I can, sir.
ALONZO: I much desire it.
DE FLORES: And if the ways and straits
  Of some of the passages be not too tedious for you,
  I will assure you, worth your time and sight, my lord.
ALONZO: Push, that shall be no hindrance.
DE FLORES: I'm your servant then:
  'Tis now near dinner-time; 'gainst your lordship's rising
  I'll have the keys about me.
ALONZO: Thanks, kind De Flores.
DE FLORES [*aside*]: He's safely thrust upon me beyond hopes.
     Exeunt.

[ACT THREE]

*

[SCENE ONE]

Enter ALONZO *and* DE FLORES.
In the Act-time DE FLORES *hides a naked Rapier.*

DE FLORES: Yes, here are all the keys; I was afraid, my
   lord,
   I'd wanted for the postern, this is it.
   I've all, I've all, my lord: this for the sconce.

ALONZO: 'Tis a most spacious and impregnable fort.

DE FLORES: You'll tell me more, my lord: this descent
   Is somewhat narrow, we shall never pass
   Well with our weapons, they'll but trouble us.

ALONZO: Thou say'st true.

DE FLORES: Pray let me help your lordship.

ALONZO: 'Tis done. Thanks, kind De Flores.

DE FLORES: Here are hooks, my lord,
   To hang such things on purpose.
      [*He hangs up the swords.*]

ALONZO: Lead, I'll follow thee. 10
   Exeunt at one door and enter at the other.

[SCENE TWO]

DE FLORES: All this is nothing; you shall see anon
   A place you little dream on.

ALONZO: I am glad
   I have this leisure; all your master's house
   Imagine I ha'taken a gondola.

DE FLORES: All but myself, sir, [*Aside*] which makes up
   my safety.

   S.D. *Act-time:* Interval between acts.
   2. *Postern:* rear-door.   3. *Sconce:* small fortress.

– My lord, I'll place you at a casement here
Will show you the full strength of all the castle.
Look, spend your eye awhile upon that object.

ALONZO: Here's rich variety, De Flores.

DE FLORES: Yes, sir.

ALONZO: Goodly munition.

10 DE FLORES: Ay, there's ordnance, sir,
No bastard metal, will ring you a peal like bells
At great men's funerals; keep your eye straight, my lord,
Take special notice of that sconce before you,
There you may dwell awhile.
      [*Takes hidden rapier.*]

ALONZO: I am upon't.

DE FLORES: And so am I.
      [*Stabs him.*]

ALONZO: De Flores! Oh, De Flores,
Whose malice hast thou put on?

DE FLORES: Do you question
A work of secrecy? I must silence you.
      [*Stabs him.*]

ALONZO: Oh, oh, oh.

DE FLORES: I must silence you.
      [*Stabs him.*]
So, here's an undertaking well accomplished.

20 This vault serves to good use now. – Ha, what's that
Threw sparkles in my eye? Oh, 'tis a diamond
He wears upon his finger: it was well found,
This will approve the work. What, so fast on?
Not part in death? I'll take a speedy course then,
Finger and all shall off. [*Cuts off finger.*] So, now I'll clear
The passages from all suspect or fear.
      Exit with Body.

23. *Approve:* prove.

[SCENE THREE]

Enter ISABELLA *and* LOLLIO.

ISABELLA: Why, sirrah? Whence have you commission
To fetter the doors against me?
If you keep me in a cage, pray whistle to me,
Let me be doing something.

LOLLIO: You shall be doing, if it please you; I'll whistle
to you if you'll pipe after.

ISABELLA: Is it your master's pleasure or your own,
To keep me in this pinfold?

LOLLIO: 'Tis for my master's pleasure, lest being taken in
another man's corn, you might be pounded in another 10
place.

ISABELLA: 'Tis very well, and he'll prove very wise.

LOLLIO: He says you have company enough in the house,
if you please to be sociable, of all sorts of people.

ISABELLA: Of all sorts? Why, here's none but fools and
madmen.

LOLLIO: Very well: and where will you find any other,
if you should go abroad? There's my master and I to
boot too.

ISABELLA: Of either sort one, a madman and a fool.

LOLLIO: I would ev'n participate of both then, if I were as 20
you; I know y'are half mad already, – be half foolish too.

ISABELLA: Y'are a brave saucy rascal! Come on, sir,
Afford me then the pleasure of your bedlam;
You were commending once today to me
Your last-come lunatic, what a proper
Body there was, without brains to guide it,
And what a pitiful delight appeared
In that defect, as if your wisdom had found
A mirth in madness; pray sir, let me partake   30
If there be such a pleasure.

LOLLIO: If I do not show you the handsomest, discreetest

6. *Pipe after:* follow my lead.
24. *Bedlam:* madhouse.   26. *Proper:* handsome.

madman, one that I may call the understanding madman,
then say I am a fool.

ISABELLA: Well, a match, I will say so.

LOLLIO: When you have a taste of the madman, you shall,
if you please, see Fools' College, o'th'side; I seldom lock
there, 'tis but shooting a bolt or two, and you are
amongst'em.

Exit. Enter presently.

40 Come on sir, let me see how handsomely you'll behave
yourself now.

Enter FRANCISCUS.

FRANCISCUS: How sweetly she looks! Oh, but there's a
wrinkle in her brow as deep as philosophy. Anacreon,
drink to my mistress' health, I'll pledge it; stay, stay,
there's a spider in the cup. No, 'tis but a grape-stone,
swallow it, fear nothing, poet; so, so, lift higher.

ISABELLA: Alack, alack, 'tis too full of pity
To be laughed at; how fell he mad? Canst thou tell?

LOLLIO: For love, mistress; he was a pretty poet too, and
50 that set him forwards first; the muses then forsook him,
he ran mad for a chambermaid, yet she was but a dwarf
neither.

FRANCISCUS: Hail, bright Titania!
Why stand'st thou idle on these flow'ry banks?
Oberon is dancing with his Dryades;
I'll gather daisies, primrose, violets,
And bind them in a verse of poesy.

LOLLIO: Not too near; you see your danger.
[*Shows whip.*]

FRANCISCUS: Oh hold thy hand, great Diomed,
60 Thou feed'st thy horses well, they shall obey thee;
Get up, Bucephalus kneels.
[*Kneels.*]

LOLLIO: You see how I awe my flock; a shepherd has not
his dog at more obedience.

ISABELLA: His conscience is unquiet, sure that was
The cause of this. A proper gentleman.

FRANCISCUS: Come hither, Esculapius; hide the poison.

LOLLIO: Well, 'tis hid.

    [*Lowers whip.*]

FRANCISCUS [*rising*]: Didst thou never hear of one Tiresias,

  A famous poet?

LOLLIO: Yes, that kept tame wild-geese. 70

FRANCISCUS: That's he; I am the man.

LOLLIO: No!

FRANCISCUS: Yes; but make no words on't, I was a man Seven years ago.

LOLLIO: A stripling I think you might.

FRANCISCUS: Now I'm a woman, all feminine.

LOLLIO: I would I might see that.

FRANCISCUS: Juno struck me blind.

LOLLIO: I'll ne'er believe that; for a woman, they say, has an eye more than a man. 80

FRANCISCUS: I say she struck me blind.

LOLLIO: And Luna made you mad; you have two trades to beg with.

FRANCISCUS: Luna is now big-bellied, and there's room

  For both of us to ride with Hecate;

  I'll drag thee up into her silver sphere,

  And there we'll kick the dog and beat the bush,

  That barks against the witches of the night;

  The swift lycanthropi that walks the round,

  We'll tear their wolvish skins, and save the sheep. 90

    [*Tries to seize* LOLLIO.]

LOLLIO: Is't come to this? Nay, then my poison comes forth again, mad slave; indeed, abuse your keeper!

    [*Showing whip.*]

ISABELLA: I prithee hence with him, now he grows dangerous.

FRANCISCUS sing[*s*]:

      Sweet love, pity me,

      Give me leave to lie with thee.

LOLLIO: No, I'll see you wiser first: to your own kennel.

FRANCISCUS: No noise, she sleeps, draw all the curtains round,
  Let no soft sound molest the pretty soul
  But love, and love creeps in at a mouse-hole.

100 LOLLIO: I would you would get into your hole.
  Exit FRANCISCUS.
  Now mistress, I will bring you another sort, you shall be fooled another while. Tony, come hither Tony, look who's yonder, Tony.
  Enter ANTONIO.

ANTONIO: Cousin, is it not my aunt?

LOLLIO: Yes, 'tis one of'em, Tony.

ANTONIO: He, he, how do you, uncle?

LOLLIO: Fear him not, mistress, 'tis a gentle nigget; you may play with him, as safely with him as with his bauble.

110 ISABELLA: How long hast thou been a fool?

ANTONIO: Ever since I came hither, cousin.

ISABELLA: Cousin? I'm none of thy cousins, fool.

LOLLIO: Oh mistress, fools have always so much wit as to claim their kindred.

MADMAN *within*: Bounce, bounce, he falls, he falls!

ISABELLA: Hark you, your scholars in the upper room Are out of order.

LOLLIO: Must I come amongst you there? Keep you the fool, mistress; I'll go up and play left-handed Orlando
120   amongst the madmen.
  Exit.

ISABELLA: Well, sir.

ANTONIO: 'Tis opportuneful now, sweet lady! Nay,
  Cast no amazing eye upon this change.

ISABELLA: Ha!

ANTONIO: This shape of folly shrouds your dearest love,
  The truest servant to your powerful beauties,
  Whose magic had this force thus to transform me.

104. *Aunt:* whore.
107. *Nigget:* idiot, fool.

296

ISABELLA: You are a fine fool indeed!

ANTONIO: Oh, 'tis not strange:
  Love has an intellect that runs through all
  The scrutinous sciences, and like   130
  A cunning poet, catches a quantity
  Of every knowledge, yet brings all home
  Into one mystery, into one secret
  That he proceeds in.

ISABELLA: Y'are a parlous fool.

ANTONIO: No danger in me: I bring nought but Love,
  And his soft-wounding shafts to strike you with:
  Try but one arrow; if it hurt you,
  I'll stand you twenty back in recompense.
    [Kisses her.]

ISABELLA: A forward fool too!

ANTONIO: This was love's teaching:
  A thousand ways he fashioned out my way,   140
  And this I found the safest and the nearest
  To tread the Galaxia to my star.

ISABELLA: Profound, withal! Certain you dreamed of
    this;
  Love never taught it waking.

ANTONIO: Take no acquaintance
  Of these outward follies; there is within
  A gentleman that loves you.

ISABELLA: When I see him,
  I'll speak with him; so in the meantime, keep
  Your habit, it becomes you well enough.
  As you are a gentleman, I'll not discover you;
  That's all the favour that you must expect: 150
  When you are weary, you may leave the school,
  For all this while you have but played the fool.
    Enter LOLLIO.

ANTONIO: And must again. – He, he, I thank you, cousin;
  I'll be your valentine tomorrow morning.

LOLLIO: How do you like the fool, mistress?

142. *Galaxia:* Milky Way.

ISABELLA: Passing well, sir.

LOLLIO: Is he not witty pretty well, for a fool?

ISABELLA: If he hold on as he begins, he is like
To come to something.

160 LOLLIO: Ay, thank a good tutor. You may put him to't;
he begins to answer pretty hard questions. – Tony, how
many is five times six?

ANTONIO: Five times six, is six times five.

LOLLIO: What arithmetician could have answered better?
How many is one hundred and seven?

ANTONIO: One hundred and seven, is seven hundred and
one, cousin.

LOLLIO: This is no wit to speak on; will you be rid of the
fool now?

170 ISABELLA: By no means, let him stay a little.

MADMAN *within*: Catch there, catch the last couple in hell!

LOLLIO: Again? Must I come amongst you? Would my
master were come home! I am not able to govern both
these wards together.

    Exit.

ANTONIO: Why should a minute of love's hour be lost?

ISABELLA: Fie, out again! I had rather you kept
Your other posture: you become not your tongue
When you speak from your clothes.

ANTONIO: How can he freeze,
Lives near so sweet a warmth? Shall I alone

180 Walk through the orchard of the Hesperides,
And cowardly not dare to pull an apple?
This with the red cheeks I must venture for.

    [*Tries to kiss her.*]

    Enter LOLLIO *above.*

ISABELLA: Take heed, there's giants keep'em.

LOLLIO [*aside*]: How now, fool, are you good at that? Have
you read Lipsius? He's past *Ars Amandi*; I believe I must
put harder questions to him, I perceive that –

ISABELLA: You are bold without fear too.

ANTONIO: What should I fear,

Having all joys about me? Do you smile,
And love shall play the wanton on your lip,
Meet and retire, retire and meet again: 190
Look you but cheerfully, and in your eyes
I shall behold mine own deformity
And dress myself up fairer; I know this shape
Becomes me not, but in those bright mirrors
I shall array me handsomely.

LOLLIO: Cuckoo, cuckoo!

    Exit.

    [Enter] Madmen above, some as birds, others as beasts.

ANTONIO: What are these?

ISABELLA: Of fear enough to part us;
Yet are they but our schools of lunatics,
That act their fantasies in any shapes
Suiting their present thoughts; if sad, they cry;   200
If mirth be their conceit, they laugh again.
Sometimes they imitate the beasts and birds,
Singing, or howling, braying, barking, all
As their wild fancies prompt'em.

    [Exeunt Madmen above.]

    Enter LOLLIO.

ANTONIO: These are no fears.

ISABELLA: But here's a large one, my man.

ANTONIO: Ha, he, that's fine sport indeed, cousin.

LOLLIO: I would my master were come home, 'tis too
much for one shepherd to govern two of these flocks;
nor can I believe that one churchman can instruct two
benefices at once; there will be some incurable mad of   210
the one side, and very fools on the other. Come, Tony.

ANTONIO: Prithee cousin, let me stay here still.

LOLLIO: No, you must to your book now, you have play'd
sufficiently.

ISABELLA: Your fool is grown wondrous witty.

LOLLIO: Well, I'll say nothing; but I do not think but he
will put you down one of these days.

    Exeunt LOLLIO *and* ANTONIO.

ISABELLA: Here the restrainéd current might make
    breach,
    Spite of the watchful bankers; would a woman stray,
220   She need not gad abroad to seek her sin,
    It would be brought home one ways or other:
    The needle's point will to the fixéd north,
    Such drawing arctics women's beauties are.
    Enter LOLLIO.

LOLLIO: How dost thou, sweet rogue?

ISABELLA: How now?

LOLLIO: Come, there are degrees, one fool may be better
than another.

ISABELLA: What's the matter?

LOLLIO: Nay, if thou giv'st thy mind to fool's-flesh, have
at thee!
    [*Tries to kiss her.*]

230 ISABELLA: You bold slave, you!

LOLLIO: I could follow now as t'other fool did, –
    'What should I fear,
    Having all joys about me? Do you but smile,
    And love shall play the wanton on your lip,
    Meet and retire, retire and meet again:
    Look you but cheerfully, and in your eyes
    I shall behold my own deformity
    And dress myself up fairer; I know this shape
    Becomes me not –' And so, as it follows; but is not this
240   the more foolish way? Come, sweet rogue, kiss me, my
little Lacedemonian. Let me feel how thy pulses beat;
thou hast a thing about thee would do a man pleasure, –
I'll lay my hand on't.

ISABELLA: Sirrah, no more! I see you have discovered
    This love's knight-errant, who hath made adventure
    For purchase of my love. Be silent, mute,
    Mute as a statue, or his injunction
    For me enjoying, shall be to cut thy throat:

219. *Bankers:* labourers who make banks of earth.

I'll do it, though for no other purpose,
And be sure he'll not refuse it.   250
LOLLIO: My share, that's all; I'll have my fool's part with
you.
ISABELLA: No more! Your master.
   Enter ALIBIUS.
ALIBIUS: Sweet, how dost thou?
ISABELLA: Your bounden servant, sir.
ALIBIUS: Fie, fie, sweetheart,
No more of that.
ISABELLA: You were best lock me up.
ALIBIUS: In my arms and bosom, my sweet Isabella,
I'll lock thee up most nearly. Lollio,
We have employment, we have task in hand;
At noble Vermandero's, our castle-captain,
There is a nuptial to be solemnized –   260
Beatrice-Joanna, his fair daughter, bride, –
For which the gentleman hath bespoke our pains:
A mixture of our madmen and our fools
To finish, as it were and make the fag
Of all the revels, the third night from the first;
Only an unexpected passage over,
To make a frightful pleasure, that is all,
But not the all I aim at; could we so act it,
To teach it in a wild, distracted measure,
Though out of form and figure, breaking time's head, 270
– It were no matter, 'twould be healed again
In one age or other, if not in this, –
This, this, Lollio; there's a good reward begun,
And will beget a bounty, be it known.
LOLLIO: This is easy, sir, I'll warrant you: you have
about you fools and madmen that can dance very well;
and 'tis no wonder, your best dancers are not the wisest
men; the reason is, with often jumping they jolt their
brains down into their feet, that their wits lie more in
their heels than in their heads.   280

       269. *Measure:* dance.

ALIBIUS: Honest Lollio, thou giv'st me a good reason,
   And a comfort in it.
ISABELLA: Y'ave a fine trade on't,
   Madmen and fools are a staple commodity.
ALIBIUS: Oh wife, we must eat, wear clothes, and live;
   Just at the lawyer's haven we arrive,
   By madmen and by fools we both do thrive.
     Exeunt.

[SCENE FOUR]

    Enter VERMANDERO, ALSEMERO, JASPERINO *and*
    BEATRICE.
VERMANDERO: Valencia speaks so nobly of you, sir,
   I wish I had a daughter now for you.
ALSEMERO: The fellow of this creature were a partner
   For a king's love.
VERMANDERO: I had her fellow once, sir,
   But heaven has married her to joys eternal;
   'Twere sin to wish her in this vale again. –
   Come sir, your friend and you shall see the pleasures
   Which my health chiefly joys in.
ALSEMERO: I hear the beauty of this seat largely.
VERMANDERO: It falls much short of that.
    Exeunt. BEATRICE *remains.*
10 BEATRICE: So, here's one step
   Into my father's favour; time will fix him.
   I have got him now the liberty of the house:
   So wisdom by degrees works out her freedom;
   And if that eye be darkened that offends me, –
   I wait but that eclipse, – this gentleman
   Shall soon shine glorious in my father's liking
   Through the refulgent virtue of my love.
    Enter DE FLORES.

285–6: Bawcutt cites an anecdote from a popular jest-book, about
a lawyer who leaves all his money to Bedlam because he wanted to
give it back to madmen, from whom he had got it.

DE FLORES [*aside*]: My thoughts are at a banquet; for the deed,

I feel no weight in't, 'tis but light and cheap

For the sweet recompense that I set down for't.   20

BEATRICE: De Flores.

DE FLORES: Lady.

BEATRICE: Thy looks promise cheerfully.

DE FLORES: All things are answerable, – time, circumstance,

Your wishes and my service.

BEATRICE: Is it done then?

DE FLORES: Piracquo is no more.

BEATRICE: My joys start at mine eyes; our sweet'st delights

Are evermore born weeping.

DE FLORES: I've a token for you.

BEATRICE: For me?

DE FLORES: But it was sent somewhat unwillingly, –

I could not get the ring without the finger.

   [*Shows her* ALONZO's *finger*.]

BEATRICE: Bless me! What hast thou done?

DE FLORES: Why, is that more

Than killing the whole man? I cut his heart-strings.   30

A greedy hand thrust in a dish at court,

In a mistake, hath had as much as this.

BEATRICE: 'Tis the first token my father made me send him.

DE FLORES: And I made him send it back again

For his last token; I was loath to leave it,

And I'm sure dead men have no use of jewels.

He was as loath to part with't, for it stuck

As if the flesh and it were both one substance.

BEATRICE: At the stag's fall the keeper has his fees:

'Tis soon applied, – all dead men's fees are yours, sir;   40

I pray, bury the finger, but the stone

You may make use on shortly; the true value,

Take't of my truth, is near three hundred ducats.

DE FLORES: 'Twill hardly buy a capcase for one's con-
    science, though,
  To keep it from the worm, as fine as 'tis.
  Well, being my fees, I'll take it;
  Great men have taught me that, or else my merit
  Would scorn the way on't.

BEATRICE: It might justly, sir:
  Why, thou mistak'st, De Flores, 'tis not given
  In state of recompense.

50 DE FLORES: No, I hope so, lady,
  You should soon witness my contempt to't then.

BEATRICE: Prithee, thou look'st as if thou wert offended.

DE FLORES: That were strange, lady; 'tis not possible
  My service should draw such a cause from you.
  Offended? Could you think so? That were much
  For one of my performance, and so warm
  Yet in my service.

BEATRICE: 'Twere misery in me to give you cause, sir.

DE FLORES: I know so much, it were so, – misery
  In her most sharp condition.

60 BEATRICE: 'Tis resolved then;
  Look you, sir, here's three thousand golden florins:
  I have not meanly thought upon thy merit.

DE FLORES: What, salary? Now you move me.

BEATRICE: How, De Flores?

DE FLORES: Do you place me in the rank of verminous
    fellows,
  To destroy things for wages? Offer gold?
  The life-blood of man! – Is anything
  Valued too precious for my recompense?

BEATRICE: I understand thee not.

DE FLORES: I could ha' hired
  A journeyman in murder at this rate,

70 And mine own conscience might have [slept at ease,]
  And have had the work brought home.

BEATRICE [aside]:   I'm in a labyrinth;

44. *Capcase:* small travelling-case, wallet.

What will content him? I would fain be rid of him.
[*To* DE FLORES] I'll double the sum, sir.

DE FLORES: You take a course
To double my vexation, that's the good you do.

BEATRICE [*aside*]: Bless me! I am now in worse plight than
  I was;
I know not what will please him. [*To* DE FLORES] – For
  my fear's sake,
I prithee make away with all speed possible.
And if thou be'st so modest not to name
The sum that will content thee, paper blushes not;
Send thy demand in writing, it shall follow thee, –   80
But prithee take thy flight.

DE FLORES: You must fly too, then.

BEATRICE: I?

DE FLORES: I'll not stir a foot else.

BEATRICE: What's your meaning?

DE FLORES: Why, are not you as guilty, in, I'm sure,
As deep as I? And we should stick together.
Come, your fears counsel you but ill, my absence
Would draw suspect upon you instantly;
There were no rescue for you.

BEATRICE [*aside*]:   He speaks home.

DE FLORES: Nor is it fit we two, engaged so jointly,
Should part and live asunder.
    [*Tries to kiss her.*]

BEATRICE: How now, sir?   90
This shows not well.

DE FLORES: What makes your lip so strange?
This must not be betwixt us.

BEATRICE [*aside*]:   The man talks wildly.

DE FLORES: Come, kiss me with a zeal now.

BEATRICE [*aside*]:   Heaven! I doubt him.

DE FLORES: I will not stand so long to beg 'em shortly.

BEATRICE: Take heed, De Flores, of forgetfulness,
  'Twill soon betray us.

DE FLORES: Take you heed first;

Faith, y'are grown much forgetful, y'are to blame in't.

BEATRICE [aside]: He's bold, and I'm blamed for't!

DE FLORES: I have eased you
Of your trouble, – think on't, – I'm in pain,
100   And must be eased of you; 'tis a charity;
Justice invites your blood to understand me.

BEATRICE: I dare not.

DE FLORES: Quickly!

BEATRICE: Oh I never shall!
Speak it yet further off, that I may lose
What has been spoken, and no sound remain on't.
I would not hear so much offence again
For such another deed.

DE FLORES: Soft, lady, soft, –
The last is not yet paid for. Oh, this act
Has put me into spirit, I was as greedy on't
As the parched earth of moisture, when the clouds weep.
110   Did you not mark, I wrought myself into't,
Nay, sued and kneeled for't: why was all that pains
       took?
You see I have thrown contempt upon your gold,
Not that I want it [not], for I do piteously;
In order I will come unto't, and make use on't,
But 'twas not held so precious to begin with;
For I place wealth after the heels of pleasure,
And were I not resolved in my belief
That thy virginity were perfect in thee,
I should but take my recompense with grudging,
120   As if I had but half my hopes I agreed for.

BEATRICE: Why, 'tis impossible thou canst be so wicked,
Or shelter such a cunning cruelty,
To make his death the murderer of my honour?
Thy language is so bold and vicious,
I cannot see which way I can forgive it
With any modesty.

DE FLORES: Push, you forget yourself!
A woman dipped in blood, and talk of modesty?

BEATRICE: Oh misery of sin! Would I had been bound
  Perpetually unto my living hate
  In that Piracquo, than to hear these words.   130
  Think but upon the distance that creation
  Set 'twixt thy blood and mine, and keep thee there.
DE FLORES: Look but into your conscience, read me
    there,
  'Tis a true book, you'll find me there your equal:
  Push, fly not to your birth, but settle you
  In what the act has made you; y'are no more now.
  You must forget your parentage to me:
  Y'are the deed's creature; by that name
  You lost your first condition; and I challenge you,
  As peace and innocency has turned you out,   140
  And made you one with me.
BEATRICE: With thee, foul villain?
DE FLORES: Yes, my fair murd'ress; do you urge me?
  Though thou writ'st maid, thou whore in thy affection!
  'Twas changed from thy first love, and that's a kind
  Of whoredom in thy heart; and he's changed now,
  To bring thy second on, thy Alsemero,
  Whom – by all sweets that ever darkness tasted –
  If I enjoy thee not, thou ne'er enjoy'st;
  I'll blast the hopes and joys of marriage,
  I'll confess all, – my life I rate at nothing.   150
BEATRICE: De Flores!
DE FLORES: I shall rest from all lovers' plagues then;
  I live in pain now: that shooting eye
  Will burn my heart to cinders.
BEATRICE: Oh sir, hear me!
DE FLORES: She that in life and love refuses me,
  In death and shame my partner she shall be.
BEATRICE: Stay, hear me once for all; [*Kneeling*] I make
    thee master
  Of all the wealth I have in gold and jewels:
  Let me go poor unto my bed with honour,

137. *To:* in favour of.

And I am rich in all things.

160 DE FLORES: Let this silence thee:
The wealth of all Valencia shall not buy
My pleasure from me;
Can you weep fate from its determined purpose?
So soon may you weep me.

BEATRICE: Vengeance begins;
Murder I see is followed by more sins.
Was my creation in the womb so cursed,
It must engender with a viper first?

DE FLORES: Come, rise, and shroud your blushes in my
    bosom;
    [*Raises her.*]
Silence is one of pleasure's best receipts.

170   Thy peace is wrought for ever in this yielding.
'Las, how the turtle pants! Thou'lt love anon
What thou so fear'st and faint'st to venture on.
    Exeunt.

177. *Turtle:* turtle-dove.

ACT FOUR

*

[SCENE ONE]

(DUMB SHOW.)

Enter Gentlemen, VERMANDERO *meeting them with action of wonderment at the flight of* PIRACQUO. *Enter* ALSEMERO, *with* JASPERINO, *and Gallants;* VERMANDERO *points to him, the Gentlemen seeming to applaud the choice;* [Exeunt VERMANDERO], ALSEMERO, JASPERINO, *and Gentlemen;* BEATRICE *the bride following in great state, accompanied with* DIAPHANTA, ISABELLA *and other Gentlewomen:* DE FLORES *after all, smiling at the accident;* ALONZO's *ghost appears to* DE FLORES *in the midst of his smile, startles him, showing him the hand whose finger he had cut off. They pass over in great solemnity.*

Enter BEATRICE.

BEATRICE: This fellow has undone me endlessly,
Never was bride so fearfully distressed;
The more I think upon th'ensuing night,
And whom I am to cope with in embraces,
One that's ennobled both in blood and mind,
So clear in understanding, – that's my plague now, –
Before whose judgement will my fault appear
Like malefactors' crimes before tribunals;
There is no hiding on't, the more I dive
Into my own distress; how a wise man   10
Stands for a great calamity! There's no venturing
Into his bed, what course soe'er I light upon,
Without my shame, which may grow up to danger;
He cannot but in justice strangle me
As I lie by him, as a cheater use me;
'Tis a precious craft to play with a false die

S.D. *Accident:* incident.
11. *Stands for:* represents.

309

Before a cunning gamester. Here's his closet,
The key left in't, and he abroad i'th'park, –
Sure 'twas forgot, – I'll be so bold as look in't.
  [*Opens closet.*]
20 Bless me! A right physician's closet 'tis,
Set round with vials, every one her mark too.
Sure he does practise physic for his own use,
Which may be safely called your great man's wisdom.
What manuscript lies here? 'The Book of Experiment,
Called Secrets in Nature'; so 'tis, 'tis so;
'How to know whether a woman be with child or no'.
I hope I am not yet; if he should try though!
Let me see – folio forty-five. Here 'tis;
The leaf tucked down upon't, the place suspicious.
30 'If you would know whether a woman be with child or
not, give her two spoonfuls of the white water in glass
C –'
Where's that glass C? Oh yonder I see't now, –
'and if she be with child, she sleeps full twelve hours
after, if not, not.'
None of that water comes into my belly.
I'll know you from a hundred; I could break you now,
Or turn you into milk, and so beguile
The master of the mystery, but I'll look to you.
40 Ha! That which is next is ten times worse: –
'How to know whether a woman be a maid or not';
If that should be applied, what would become of me?
Belike he has a strong faith of my purity,
That never yet made proof; but this he calls
'A merry, slight but true experiment, the author An-
tonius Mizaldus. Give the party you suspect the quantity
of a spoonful of the water in the glass M, which upon
her that is a maid makes three several effects: 'twill make
her incontinently gape, then fall into a sudden sneezing,
50 last into a violent laughing; else dull, heavy and
lumpish.'

45. *Slight:* may mean 'sleight', i.e. trick or device.

Where had I been?
I fear it, yet 'tis seven hours to bedtime.
   Enter DIAPHANTA.
DIAPHANTA: Cuds madam, are you here?
BEATRICE [*aside*]:   Seeing that wench now,
  A trick comes in my mind; 'tis a nice piece
  Gold cannot purchase; [*To* DIAPHANTA] I come hither,
    wench,
  To look my lord.
DIAPHANTA [*aside*]: Would I had such a cause to look him
    too.
  [*To* BEATRICE] Why, he's i'th'park, madam.
BEATRICE: There let him be.
DIAPHANTA: Ay, madam, let him compass 60
  Whole parks and forests, as great rangers do;
  At roosting time a little lodge can hold 'em.
  Earth-conquering Alexander, that thought the world
  Too narrow for him, in the end had but his pit-hole.
BEATRICE: I fear thou art not modest, Diaphanta.
DIAPHANTA: Your thoughts are so unwilling to be
    known, madam;
  'Tis ever the bride's fashion towards bed-time,
  To set light by her joys, as if she ow'd 'em not.
BEATRICE: Her joys? Her fears, thou would'st say.
DIAPHANTA: Fear of what?
BEATRICE: Art thou a maid, and talk'st so to a maid?   70
  You leave a blushing business behind,
  Beshrew your heart for't!
DIAPHANTA: Do you mean good sooth, madam?
BEATRICE: Well, if I'd thought upon the fear at first,
  Man should have been unknown.
DIAPHANTA: Is't possible?
BEATRICE: I will give a thousand ducats to that woman

54. *Cuds:* corruption of 'God's'.
55. *Nice piece:* scrupulous girl.
64. *Pit-hole:* grave (here with obvious bawdy innuendo).
68. *Ow'd:* owned.

Would try what my fear were, and tell me true
Tomorrow, when she gets from't: as she likes,
I might perhaps be drawn to't.

DIAPHANTA: Are you in earnest?

BEATRICE: Do you get the woman, then challenge me,
80 And see if I'll fly from't; but I must tell you
This by the way, she must be a true maid,
Else there's no trial, my fears are not hers else.

DIAPHANTA: Nay, she that I would put into your hands, madam,
Shall be a maid.

BEATRICE: You know I should be shamed else,
Because she lies for me.

DIAPHANTA: 'Tis a strange humour:
But are you serious still? Would you resign
Your first night's pleasure, and give money too?

BEATRICE: As willingly as live; [*Aside*] alas, the gold
Is but a by-bet to wedge in the honour.

90 DIAPHANTA: I do not know how the world goes abroad
For faith or honesty, there's both required in this. –
Madam, what say you to me, and stray no further?
I've a good mind, in troth, to earn your money.

BEATRICE: Y'are too quick, I fear, to be a maid.

DIAPHANTA: How? Not a maid? Nay, then you urge me, madam;
Your honourable self is not a truer
With all your fears upon you –

BEATRICE [*aside*]:   Bad enough then.

DIAPHANTA: Than I with all my lightsome joys about me.

BEATRICE: I'm glad to hear't then; you dare put your honesty
Upon an easy trial?

100 DIAPHANTA: Easy? – Anything.

BEATRICE: I'll come to you straight.
      [*Goes to closet.*]

81. *Maid:* i.e. virgin.
89. *By-bet ... in:* side-bet to protect.   99. *Honesty:* chastity.

DIAPHANTA [*aside*]: She will not search me, will she
Like the forewoman of a female jury?

BEATRICE: Glass M: ay, this is it; – look, Diaphanta,
You take no worse than I do.
[*Drinks.*]

DIAPHANTA: And in so doing,
I will not question what 'tis, but take it.
[*Drinks.*]

BEATRICE [*aside*]: Now, if the experiment be true, 'twill praise itself
And give me noble ease: – begins already;
[DIAPHANTA *gapes.*]
There's the first symptom; and what haste it makes
To fall into the second, there by this time!
[DIAPHANTA *sneezes.*]
Most admirable secret! On the contrary, 110
It stirs not me a whit, which most concerns it.

DIAPHANTA: Ha, ha, ha!

BEATRICE [*aside*]: Just in all things and in order
As if 'twere circumscribed; one accident
Gives way unto another.

DIAPHANTA: Ha, ha, ha!

BEATRICE: How now, wench?

DIAPHANTA: Ha, ha, ha! I am so – so light at heart, ha, ha, ha, – so pleasurable!
But one swig more, sweet madam.

BEATRICE: Ay, tomorrow;
We shall have time to sit by't.

DIAPHANTA: Now I'm sad again.

BEATRICE [*aside*]: It lays itself so gently too! [*To* DIA-
PHANTA] Come, wench,
Most honest Diaphanta I dare call thee now. 120

DIAPHANTA: Pray tell me, madam, what trick call you this?

BEATRICE: I'll tell thee all hereafter; we must study
The carriage of this business.

DIAPHANTA: I shall carry't well,
Because I love the burthen.
BEATRICE: About midnight
You must not fail to steal forth gently,
That I may use the place.
DIAPHANTA: Oh fear not, madam,
I shall be cool by that time; – the bride's place!
And with a thousand ducats! I'm for a justice now,
I bring a portion with me; I scorn small fools.
   Exeunt.

[SCENE TWO]

Enter VERMANDERO *and* SERVANT.

VERMANDERO: I tell thee, knave, mine honour is in
   question,
A thing till now free from suspicion,
Nor ever was there cause; who of my gentlemen
Are absent? Tell me, and truly, how many and who.
SERVANT: Antonio, sir, and Franciscus.
VERMANDERO: When did they leave the castle?
SERVANT: Some ten days since, sir, the one intending to
Briamata, th'other for Valencia.
VERMANDERO: The time accuses 'em; a charge of murder
10   Is brought within my castle gate, Piracquo's murder;
I dare not answer faithfully their absence:
A strict command of apprehension
Shall pursue 'em suddenly, and either wipe
The stain off clear or openly discover it.
Provide me wingéd warrants for the purpose.
   Exit SERVANT.
See, I am set on again.
   Enter TOMAZO.
TOMAZO: I claim a brother of you.

12. *Apprehension*: arrest.

VERMANDERO: Y'are too hot,
 Seek him not here.
TOMAZO: Yes, 'mongst your dearest bloods,
 If my peace find no fairer satisfaction;
 This is the place must yield account for him,   20
 For here I left him, and the hasty tie
 Of this snatched marriage gives strong testimony
 Of his most certain ruin.
VERMANDERO: Certain falsehood!
 This is the place indeed; his breach of faith
 Has too much marred both my abuséd love,
 The honourable love I reserved for him,
 And mocked my daughter's joy. The prepared morning
 Blushed at his infidelity; he left
 Contempt and scorn to throw upon those friends
 Whose belief hurt 'em: oh 'twas most ignoble   30
 To take his flight so unexpectedly,
 And throw such public wrongs on those that loved him.
TOMAZO: Then this is all your answer?
VERMANDERO: 'Tis too fair
 For one of his alliance; and I warn you
 That this place no more see you.
     Exit.
     Enter DE FLORES.
TOMAZO: The best is,
 There is more ground to meet a man's revenge on.
 Honest De Flores!
DE FLORES: That's my name indeed.
 Saw you the bride? Good sweet sir, which way took she?
TOMAZO: I have blest mine eyes from seeing such a false
     one.
DE FLORES [*aside*]: I'd fain get off, this man's not for my
     company,   40
 I smell his brother's blood when I come near him.
TOMAZO: Come hither, kind and true one; I remember
 My brother loved thee well.

     34. *Alliance:* family relationship.

315

DE FLORES: Oh purely, dear sir,
   [*Aside*] – Methinks I am now again a-killing on him,
   He brings it so fresh to me.
TOMAZO: Thou canst guess, sirrah,
   – One honest friend has an instinct of jealousy, –
   At some foul guilty person?
DE FLORES: 'Las sir, I am so charitable, I think none
   Worse than myself. – You did not see the bride then?
50 TOMAZO: I prithee name her not. Is she not wicked?
DE FLORES: No, no, a pretty, easy, round-packed sinner,
   As your most ladies are, else you might think
   I flattered her; but sir, at no hand wicked,
   Till th'are so old their sins and vices meet,
   And they salute witches. I am called I think, sir:
   [*Aside*] – His company ev'n o'erlays my conscience.
    Exit.
TOMAZO. That De Flores has a wondrous honest heart;
   He'll bring it out in time, I'm assured on't.
   – Oh, here's the glorious master of the day's joy.
60 'Twill not be long till he and I do reckon.
   Enter ALSEMERO.
   Sir.
ALSEMERO: You are most welcome.
TOMAZO: You may call that word back,
   I do not think I am, nor wish to be.
ALSEMERO: 'Tis strange you found the way to this house
   then.
TOMAZO: Would I'd ne'er known the cause! I'm none of
   those, sir,
   That come to give you joy, and swill your wine;
   'Tis a more precious liquor that must 'lay
   The fiery thirst I bring.
ALSEMERO: Your words and you
   Appear to me great strangers.
TOMAZO: Time and our swords

   46. *Jealousy:* suspicion.
   51. *Round-packed:* meaning uncertain; probably 'well-fleshed'.

May make us more acquainted; this the business:
I should have a brother in your place;   70
How treachery and malice have disposed of him,
I'm bound to inquire of him which holds his right,
Which never could come fairly.

ALSEMERO: You must look
To answer for that word, sir.

TOMAZO: Fear you not,
I'll have it ready drawn at our next meeting.
Keep your day solemn. Farewell, I disturb it not;
I'll bear the smart with patience for a time.
   Exit.

ALSEMERO: 'Tis somewhat ominous, this: a quarrel
   entered
Upon this day; my innocence relieves me,
   Enter JASPERINO.
I should be wondrous sad else. – Jasperino,   80
I have news to tell thee, strange news.

JASPERINO: I ha' some too,
I think as strange as yours; would I might keep
Mine, so my faith and friendship might be kept in't!
Faith, sir, dispense a little with my zeal,
And let it cool in this.

ALSEMERO: This puts me on,
And blames thee for thy slowness.

JASPERINO: All may prove nothing;
Only a friendly fear that leapt from me, sir.

ALSEMERO: No question it may prove nothing; let's partake it, though.

JASPERINO: 'Twas Diaphanta's chance, – for to that
   wench
I pretend honest love, and she deserves it, –   90
To leave me in a back part of the house,
A place we chose for private conference;
She was no sooner gone, but instantly
I heard your bride's voice in the next room to me;

90. *Pretend:* offer.

317

And lending more attention, found De Flores
Louder than she.

ALSEMERO: De Flores? Thou art out now.

JASPERINO: You'll tell me more anon.

ALSEMERO: Still I'll prevent thee;
The very sight of him is poison to her.

JASPERINO: That made me stagger too, but Diaphanta
At her return confirmed it.

100 ALSEMERO: Diaphanta!

JASPERINO: Then fell we both to listen, and words passed
Like those that challenge interest in a woman.

ALSEMERO: Peace, quench thy zeal, tis dangerous to thy
bosom!

JASPERINO: Then truth is full of peril.

ALSEMERO: Such truths are.
— Oh, were she the sole glory of the earth,
Had eyes that could shoot fire into kings' breasts,
And touched, she sleeps not here! Yet I have time,
Though night be near, to be resolved hereof;
And prithee do not weigh me by my passions.

JASPERINO: I never weighed friend so.

110 ALSEMERO: Done charitably.
That key will lead thee to a pretty secret,
    [Gives key.]
By a Chaldean taught me, and I've made
My study upon some; bring from my closet
A glass inscribed there with the letter M,
And question not my purpose.

JASPERINO: It shall be done, sir.
    Exit.

ALSEMERO: How can this hang together? Not an hour
since,
Her woman came pleading her lady's fears,
Delivered her for the most timorous virgin
That ever shrunk at man's name, and so modest,

120 She charged her weep out her request to me,

---

97. *Prevent:* forestall.   107. *Touched:* tainted, corrupted.

That she might come obscurely to my bosom.
    Enter BEATRICE.
BEATRICE [*aside*]: All things go well; my woman's pre-
    paring yonder
For her sweet voyage, which grieves me to lose;
Necessity compels it; I lose all else.
ALSEMERO [*aside*]: Push, Modesty's shrine is set in yonder
    forehead. –
I cannot be too sure though. [*To her*] – My Joanna!
BEATRICE: Sir, I was bold to weep a message to you, –
Pardon my modest fears.
ALSEMERO [*aside*]:   The dove's not meeker,
She's abused, questionless.
    Enter JASPERINO [*with glass*].
                   – Oh, are you come, sir?
BEATRICE [*aside*]: The glass, upon my life! I see the letter. 130
JASPERINO: Sir, this is M.
ALSEMERO: 'Tis it.
BEATRICE [*aside*]:   I am suspected.
ALSEMERO: How fitly our bride comes to partake with us!
BEATRICE: What is't, my lord?
ALSEMERO: No hurt.
BEATRICE: Sir, pardon me,
I seldom taste of any composition.
ALSEMERO: But this, upon my warrant, you shall venture
    on.
BEATRICE: I fear 'twill make me ill.
ALSEMERO: Heaven forbid that.
BEATRICE [*aside*]: I'm put now to my cunning; th'effects I
    know
If I can now but feign 'em handsomely.
    [*Drinks.*]
ALSEMERO [*to* JASPERINO]: It has that secret virtue, it
    ne'er missed, sir,
Upon a virgin.
JASPERINO: Treble qualitied?   140

    121. *She:* i.e. Beatrice. *Obscurely:* in darkness.

[BEATRICE *gapes, then sneezes.*]

ALSEMERO: By all that's virtuous, it takes there, proceeds!

JASPERINO: This is the strangest trick to know a maid by.

BEATRICE: Ha, ha, ha!
You have given me joy of heart to drink, my lord.

ALSEMERO: No, thou hast given me such joy of heart
That never can be blasted.

BEATRICE: What's the matter, sir?

ALSEMERO [*to* JASPERINO]: See, now 'tis settled in a
  melancholy, –
Keep both the time and method; – my Joanna!
Chaste as the breath of heaven, or morning's womb,

150   That brings the day forth; thus my love encloses thee.
  [*Embraces her.*] *Exeunt.*

[SCENE THREE]

Enter ISABELLA *and* LOLLIO.

ISABELLA: Oh heaven! Is this the waiting moon?
Does love turn fool, run mad, and all at once?
Sirrah, here's a madman, a-kin to the fool too,
A lunatic lover.

LOLLIO: No, no, not he I brought the letter from?

ISABELLA: Compare his inside with his out, and tell me.
  [*Gives him letter.*]

LOLLIO: The out's mad, I'm sure of that, I had a taste on't.
  [*Reads.*] 'To the bright Andromeda, chief chambermaid
  to the Knight of the Sun, at the sign of Scorpio, in the

10   middle region, sent by the bellows-mender of Aeolus.
  Pay the post.' This is stark madness.

ISABELLA: Now mark the inside. [*Takes letter and reads.*]
'Sweet lady, having now cast off this counterfeit cover
of a madman, I appear to your best judgement a true and
faithful lover of your beauty.'

LOLLIO: He is mad still.

ISABELLA: 'If any fault you find, chide those perfections

in you which have made me imperfect; 'tis the same sun
that causeth to grow, and enforceth to wither, —'

LOLLIO: Oh rogue!   20

ISABELLA: '– Shapes and transshapes, destroys and builds
again; I come in winter to you, dismantled of my proper
ornaments: by the sweet splendour of your cheerful
smiles, I spring and live a lover.'

LOLLIO: Mad rascal still!

ISABELLA: 'Tread him not under foot, that shall appear an
honour to your bounties. I remain – mad till I speak with
you, from whom I expect my cure. Yours all, or one
beside himself, FRANCISCUS.'

LOLLIO: You are like to have a fine time on't; my master   30
and I may give over our professions, I do not think but
you can cure fools and madmen faster than we, with
little pains too.

ISABELLA: Very likely.

LOLLIO: One thing I must tell you, mistress: you perceive
that I am privy to your skill; if I find you minister once
and set up the trade, I put in for my thirds, – I shall be
mad or fool else.

ISABELLA: The first place is thine, believe it, Lollio;
If I do fall –   40

LOLLIO: I fall upon you.

ISABELLA: So.

LOLLIO: Well, I stand to my venture.

ISABELLA: But thy counsel now, how shall I deal with
'em?

LOLLIO: Why, do you mean to deal with 'em?

ISABELLA: Nay, the fair understanding, how to use 'em.

LOLLIO: Abuse 'em! That's the way to mad the fool and
make a fool of the madman, and then you use 'em kindly.

ISABELLA: 'Tis easy, I'll practise; do thou observe it.
The key of thy wardrobe.   50

LOLLIO: There – fit yourself for 'em, and I'll fit 'em both
for you.

    [*Gives her key.*]

ISABELLA: Take thou no further notice than the outside.

Exit.

LOLLIO: Not an inch; I'll put you to the inside.

Enter ALIBIUS.

ALIBIUS: Lollio, art there? Will all be perfect, think'st
thou?
Tomorrow night, as if to close up the solemnity,
Vermandero expects us.

LOLLIO: I mistrust the madmen most; the fools will do
well enough; I have taken pains with them.

60 ALIBIUS: Tush, they cannot miss; the more absurdity,
The more commends it, – so no rough behaviours
Affright the ladies; they are nice things, thou know'st.

LOLLIO: You need not fear, sir; so long as we are there
with our commanding pizzles, they'll be as tame as the
ladies themselves.

ALIBIUS: I will see them once more rehearse before
they go.

LOLLIO: I was about it, sir; look you to the madmen's
morris, and let me alone with the other; there is one or
two that I mistrust their fooling; I'll instruct them, and
70 then they shall rehearse the whole measure.

ALIBIUS: Do so; I'll see the music prepared. But Lollio,
By the way, how does my wife brook her restraint?
Does she not grudge at it?

LOLLIO: So, so. She takes some pleasure in the house, she
would abroad else; you must allow her a little more
length, she's kept too short.

ALIBIUS: She shall along to Vermandero's with us;
That will serve her for a month's liberty.

LOLLIO: What's that on your face, sir?

80 ALIBIUS: Where, Lollio? I see nothing.

LOLLIO: Cry you mercy sir, 'tis your nose; it showed like
the trunk of a young elephant.

ALIBIUS: Away, rascal! I'll prepare the music, Lollio.

64. *Pizzle:* bull's penis, used as whip. (With bawdy innuéndo.)

Exit ALIBIUS.

LOLLIO: Do, sir, and I'll dance the whilst; Tony, where
art thou, Tony?

Enter ANTONIO.

ANTONIO: Here, cousin, – where art thou?

LOLLIO: Come, Tony, the footmanship I taught you.

ANTONIO: I had rather ride, cousin.

LOLLIO: Ay, a whip take you; but I'll keep you out. Vault
in; look you, Tony, – fa, la la, la la.   90
   [*Dances.*]

ANTONIO: Fa, la la, la la.
   [*Dances.*]

LOLLIO: There, an honour.

ANTONIO: Is this an honour, coz?
   [*Bows.*]

LOLLIO: Yes, an it please your worship.

ANTONIO: Does honour bend in the hams, coz?

LOLLIO: Marry does it, as low as worship, squireship, nay,
yeomanry itself sometimes, from whence it first stiffened.
There, rise, a caper.

ANTONIO: Caper after an honour, coz?

LOLLIO: Very proper, for honour is but a caper, rise[s] as   100
fast and high, has a knee or two, and falls to th'ground
again. You can remember your figure, Tony?
   Exit.

ANTONIO: Yes, cousin, when I see thy figure, I can
remember mine.

Enter ISABELLA [*like a madwoman*].

ISABELLA: Hey, how he treads the air! Shough, shough,
t'other way! He burns his wings else; here's wax enough
below, Icarus, more than will be cancelled these eighteen
moons;

He's down, he's down, what a terrible fall he had!

Stand up, thou son of Cretan Dedalus,   110

92. *Honour:* curtsy or bow in dancing.
103. *Figure:* (i) dance-pattern, (ii) appearance.
107. *Cancelled:* in the form of legal seals.

And let us tread the lower labyrinth;
I'll bring thee to the clue.

ANTONIO: Prithee, coz, let me alone.

ISABELLA: Art thou not drowned?
About thy head I saw a heap of clouds,
Wrapped like a Turkish turban; on thy back
A crook'd chameleon-coloured rainbow hung
Like a tiara down unto thy hams.
Let me suck out those billows in thy belly;
120 Hark, how they roar and rumble in the straits!
Bless thee from the pirates!

ANTONIO: Pox upon you, let me alone!

ISABELLA: Why shouldst thou mount so high as Mercury,
Unless thou hadst reversion of his place?
Stay in the moon with me, Endymion,
And we will rule these wild rebellious waves
That would have drowned my love.

ANTONIO: I'll kick thee if again thou touch me,
Thou wild, unshapen antic; I am no fool,
You bedlam!

130 ISABELLA: But you are, as sure as I am, mad.
Have I put on this habit of a frantic,
With love as full of fury to beguile
The nimble eye of watchful jealousy,
And am I thus rewarded?
[*Reveals herself.*]

ANTONIO: Ha! Dearest beauty!

ISABELLA: No, I have no beauty now,
Nor never had, but what was in my garments.
You a quick-sighted lover? Come not near me!
Keep your caparisons, y'are aptly clad;
I came a feigner, to return stark mad.
   Exit.
   Enter LOLLIO.

140 ANTONIO: Stay, or I shall change condition
And become as you are.

124. *Reversion*: legal succession.

LOLLIO: Why, Tony, whither now? Why, fool?

ANTONIO: Whose fool, usher of idiots? You coxcomb!
I have fooled too much.

LOLLIO: You were best be mad another while, then.

ANTONIO: So I am, stark mad! I have cause enough,
And I could throw the full effects on thee,
And beat thee like a fury!

LOLLIO: Do not, do not; I shall not forbear the gentleman
under the fool if you do; alas, I saw through your fox- 150
skin before now: come, I can give you comfort; my
mistress loves you, and there is as arrant a madman
i'th'house as you are a fool, your rival, whom she loves
not; if after the masque we can rid her of him, you
earn her love, she says, and the fool shall ride her.

ANTONIO: May I believe thee?

LOLLIO: Yes, or you may choose whether you will or no.

ANTONIO: She's eased of him; I have a good quarrel on't.

LOLLIO: Well, keep your old station yet, and be quiet.

ANTONIO: Tell her I will deserve her love. 160
[Exit.]

LOLLIO: And you are like to have your desire.
Enter FRANCISCUS.

FRANCISCUS [sings]: 'Down, down, down a-down a-down,
and then with a horse-trick,
To kick Latona's forehead, and break her bowstring.'

LOLLIO: This is t'other counterfeit; I'll put him out of his
humour. [Takes out letter and reads] 'Sweet lady, having
now cast this counterfeit cover of a madman, I appear to
your best judgement a true and faithful lover of your
beauty.' This is pretty well for a madman.

FRANCISCUS: Ha! What's that? 170

LOLLIO: 'Chide those perfections in you, which made me
imperfect.'

FRANCISCUS: I am discovered to the fool.

LOLLIO [aside]: I hope to discover the fool in you ere I have
done with you. – 'Yours all, or one beside himself,
Franciscus.' This madman will mend, sure.

FRANCISCUS: What? Do you read, sirrah?

LOLLIO: Your destiny, sir; you'll be hanged for this trick, and another that I know.

180 FRANCISCUS: Art thou of counsel with thy mistress?

LOLLIO: Next her apron strings.

FRANCISCUS: Give me thy hand.

LOLLIO: Stay, let me put yours in my pocket first; [*Puts away letter*] your hand is true, is it not? It will not pick? I partly fear it, because I think it does lie.

FRANCISCUS: Not in a syllable.

LOLLIO: So; if you love my mistress so well as you have handled the matter here, you are like to be cured of your madness.

190 FRANCISCUS: And none but she can cure it.

LOLLIO: Well, I'll give you over then, and she shall cast your water next.

FRANCISCUS: Take for thy pains past.
        [*Gives him money.*]

LOLLIO: I shall deserve more, sir, I hope; my mistress loves you, but must have some proof of your love to her.

FRANCISCUS: There I meet my wishes.

LOLLIO: That will not serve, – you must meet her enemy and yours.

FRANCISCUS: He's dead already.

200 LOLLIO: Will you tell me that, and I parted but now with him?

FRANCISCUS: Show me the man.

LOLLIO: Ay, that's a right course now, see him before you kill him in any case, and yet it needs not go so far neither; 'tis but a fool that haunts the house and my mistress in the shape of an idiot; bang but his fool's coat well-favouredly, and 'tis well.

FRANCISCUS: Soundly, soundly!

LOLLIO: Only reserve him till the masque be past; and if
210 you find him not now in the dance yourself, I'll show you. In! In! My master!

184. *Hand:* (i) hand, (ii) handwriting.

FRANCISCUS: He handles him like a feather. Hey!
    [*Exit dancing.*]
    Enter ALIBIUS.
ALIBIUS: Well said; in a readiness, Lollio?
LOLLIO: Yes sir.
ALIBIUS: Away then, and guide them in, Lollio;
  Entreat your mistress to see this sight.
    [*Exit* LOLLIO.]
  Hark, is there not one incurable fool
  That might be begged? I have friends.
LOLLIO [*within*]: I have him for you, one that shall deserve
  it too.   220
ALIBIUS: Good boy, Lollio.
    [*Enter* ISABELLA, *then* LOLLIO *with Madmen and Fools.*]
    The Madmen and Fools dance.
  'Tis perfect; well, fit but once these strains,
  We shall have coin and credit for our pains.
    Exeunt.

213. *Well said:* stock-phrase meaning 'well done' rather than 'well
spoken'.

ACT FIVE

*

[SCENE ONE]

Enter BEATRICE. *A Clock strikes one.*

BEATRICE: One struck, and yet she lies by't – oh my fears!
　This strumpet serves her own ends, 'tis apparent now,
　Devours the pleasure with a greedy appetite
　And never minds my honour or my peace,
　Makes havoc of my right; but she pays dearly for't:
　No trusting of her life with such a secret,
　That cannot rule her blood to keep her promise.
　Beside, I have some suspicion of her faith to me
　Because I was suspected of my lord,
10　And it must come from her. – Hark by my horrors!
　Another clock strikes two.

　　Strikes two.

　　Enter DE FLORES.

DE FLORES:　　　　　　Psst, where are you?
BEATRICE: De Flores?
DE FLORES:　　　　Ay; is she not come from him yet?
BEATRICE: As I am a living soul, not.
DE FLORES:　　　　　　　　Sure the devil
　Hath sowed his itch within her; who'd trust
　A waiting-woman?
BEATRICE:　　　　I must trust somebody.
DE FLORES: Push, they are termagants,
　Especially when they fall upon their masters,
　And have their ladies' first-fruits; th'are mad whelps,
　You cannot stave 'em off from game royal; then
20　You are so harsh and hardy, ask no counsel,
　And I could have helped you to an apothecary's
　　daughter,
　Would have fall'n off before eleven, and thank you
　　too.
BEATRICE: Oh me, not yet! This whore forgets herself.

328

DE FLORES: The rascal fares so well; look, y'are un-
    done,

  The day-star, by this hand! See Phosphorus plain yonder.

BEATRICE: Advise me now to fall upon some ruin,

  There is no counsel safe else.

DE FLORES: Peace, I ha't now,

  For we must force a rising, there's no remedy.

BEATRICE: How? Take heed of that.

DE FLORES: Tush, be you quiet,

  Or else give over all.

BEATRICE: Prithee, I ha'done then.   30

DE FLORES: This is my reach: I'll set some part a-fire

  Of Diaphanta's chamber.

BEATRICE: How? Fire, sir?

  That may endanger the whole house.

DE FLORES: You talk of danger when your fame's on
    fire.

BEATRICE: That's true, – do what thou wilt now.

DE FLORES: Push, I aim

  At a most rich success, strikes all dead sure;

  The chimney being a-fire, and some light parcels

  Of the least danger in her chamber only,

  If Diaphanta should be met by chance then,

  Far from her lodging, which is now suspicious,   40

  It would be thought her fears and affrights then

  Drove her to seek for succour; if not seen

  Or met at all, as that's the likeliest,

  For her own shame she'll hasten towards her lodging;

  I will be ready with a piece high-charged,

  As 'twere to cleanse the chimney: there 'tis proper now,

  But she shall be the mark.

BEATRICE: I'm forced to love thee now,

  'Cause thou provid'st so carefully for my honour.

---

25. *Phosphorus:* morning star.
26. *fall . . . ruin:* devise some disaster.
28. *Force a rising:* disturb the whole house.
45. *Piece high-charged:* loaded fowling-piece.

DE FLORES: 'Slid, it concerns the safety of us both,
Our pleasure and continuance.

50 BEATRICE: One word now, prithee, –
How for the servants?

DE FLORES: I'll dispatch them,
Some one way, some another in the hurry,
For buckets, hooks, ladders; fear not you;
The deed shall find its time, – and I've thought since
Upon a safe conveyance for the body too.
How this fire purifies wit! Watch you your minute.

BEATRICE: Fear keeps my soul upon't, I cannot stray
from't.

Enter ALONZO's *Ghost.*

DE FLORES: Ha! What art thou that tak'st away the light
'Twixt that star and me? I dread thee not;

60   'Twas but a mist of conscience. – All's clear again.
Exit.

BEATRICE: Who's that, De Flores? Bless me! It slides by,
[*Exit Ghost.*]
Some ill thing haunts the house; 't has left behind it
A shivering sweat upon me: I'm afraid now.
This night hath been so tedious, – oh, this strumpet!
Had she a thousand lives, he should not leave her
Till he had destroyed the last. – List, oh my terrors!
Three struck by Saint Sebastian's!

Struck three o'clock.

[VOICES] *within*: Fire, fire, fire!

BEATRICE: Already? How rare is that man's speed!

70   How heartily he serves me! His face loathes one,
But look upon his care, who would not love him?
The east is not more beauteous than his service.

[VOICES] *within*: Fire, fire, fire!

Enter DE FLORES; *Servants pass over, ring a bell.*

DE FLORES: Away, dispatch! Hooks, buckets, ladders;
that's well said, –
The fire-bell rings, the chimney works, – my charge;

49. *'Slid*: corruption of 'God's blood'.

    The piece is ready.
     Exit.
BEATRICE: Here's a man worth loving! –
    Enter DIAPHANTA.
    Oh, y'are a jewel!
DIAPHANTA: Pardon frailty, madam,
    In troth I was so well, I ev'n forgot myself.
BEATRICE: Y'have made trim work.
DIAPHANTA: What?
BEATRICE: Hie quickly to your chamber, –
    Your reward follows you.
DIAPHANTA: I never made   80
    So sweet a bargain.
     Exit.
    Enter ALSEMERO.
ALSEMERO: Oh my dear Joanna,
    Alas, art thou risen too? I was coming,
    My absolute treasure.
BEATRICE: When I missed you,
    I could not choose but follow.
ALSEMERO: Th'art all sweetness!
    The fire is not so dangerous.
BEATRICE: Think you so, sir?
ALSEMERO: I prithee tremble not: believe me, 'tis not.
    Enter VERMANDERO, JASPERINO.
VERMANDERO: Oh bless my house and me!
ALSEMERO: My lord your father.
    Enter DE FLORES *with a piece.*
VERMANDERO: Knave, whither goes that piece?
DE FLORES: To scour the chimney.
    Exit.
VERMANDERO: Oh well said, well said;
    That fellow's good on all occasions.   90
BEATRICE: A wondrous necessary man, my lord.
VERMANDERO: He hath a ready wit, he's worth 'em all,
    sir;
    Dog at a house a-fire; I ha' seen him singed ere now.

The piece goes off.
Ha, there he goes.

BEATRICE [*aside*]: 'Tis done.

ALSEMERO: Come, sweet, to bed now;
Alas, thou wilt get cold.

BEATRICE: Alas, the fear keeps that out;
My heart will find no quiet till I hear
How Diaphanta, my poor woman, fares;
It is her chamber sir, her lodging chamber.

VERMANDERO: How should the fire come there?

100 BEATRICE: As good a soul as ever lady countenanced,
But in her chamber negligent and heavy;
She 'scaped a mine twice.

VERMANDERO: Twice?

BEATRICE: Strangely twice, sir.

VERMANDERO: Those sleepy sluts are dangerous in a
house,
And they be ne'er so good.

Enter DE FLORES.

DE FLORES: Oh poor virginity!
Thou hast paid dearly for't.

VERMANDERO: Bless us! What's that?

DE FLORES: A thing you all knew once, – Diaphanta's
burnt.

BEATRICE: My woman, oh my woman!

DE FLORES: Now the flames
Are greedy of her, – burnt, burnt, burnt to death, sir.

BEATRICE: Oh my presaging soul!

ALSEMERO: Not a tear more!

110 I charge you by the last embrace I gave you
In bed before this raised us.

BEATRICE: Now you tie me;
Were it my sister, now she gets no more.

Enter SERVANT.

VERMANDERO: How now?

SERVANT: All danger's past, you may now take your

102. *'Scaped ... twice:* had two narrow escapes.

rests, my lords; the fire is thoroughly quenched; ah,
poor gentlewoman, how soon was she stifled!

BEATRICE: De Flores, what is left of her inter,
And we as mourners all will follow her:
I will entreat that honour to my servant,
Ev'n of my lord himself.

ALSEMERO: Command it, sweetness.   120

BEATRICE: Which of you spied the fire first?

DE FLORES: 'Twas I, madam.

BEATRICE: And took such pains in't too? A double
    goodness!
'Twere well he were rewarded.

VERMANDERO: He shall be.
De Flores, call upon me.

ALSEMERO: And upon me, sir.
    Exeunt [all but DE FLORES].

DE FLORES: Rewarded? Precious, here's a trick beyond
    me!
I see in all bouts, both of sport and wit,
Always a woman strives for the last hit.
    Exit.

[SCENE TWO]

Enter TOMAZO.

TOMAZO: I cannot taste the benefits of life
With the same relish I was wont to do.
Man I grow weary of, and hold his fellowship
A treacherous bloody friendship; and because
I am ignorant in whom my wrath should settle,
I must think all men villains, and the next
I meet (whoe'er he be) the murderer
Of my most worthy brother. – Ha! What's he?
    Enter DE FLORES, *passes over the stage.*
Oh, the fellow that some call honest De Flores;

10 But methinks honesty was hard bestead
   To come there for a lodging, – as if a queen
   Should make her palace of a pest-house,
   I find a contrariety in nature
   Betwixt that face and me: the least occasion
   Would give me game upon him; yet he's so foul,
   One would scarce touch [him] with a sword he loved
   And made account of; so most deadly venomous,
   He would go near to poison any weapon
   That should draw blood on him; one must resolve
20 Never to use that sword again in fight
   In way of honest manhood, that strikes him;
   Some river must devour't, 'twere not fit
   That any man should find it. – What, again?

     Enter DE FLORES.

   He walks o'purpose by, sure, to choke me up,
   To infect my blood.

DE FLORES: My worthy noble lord.

TOMAZO: Dost offer to come near and breathe upon me?
   [*Strikes him.*]

DE FLORES: A blow!
   [*Draws sword.*]

TOMAZO: Yea, are you so prepared?
   I'll rather like a soldier die by th'sword,
   Than like a politician by thy poison.
   [*Draws.*]

30 DE FLORES: Hold, my lord, as you are honourable.

TOMAZO: All slaves that kill by poison are still cowards.

DE FLORES [*aside*]: I cannot strike, I see his brother's
     wounds
   Fresh bleeding in his eye, as in a crystal.
   [*To him*] – I will not question this, I know y'are noble;
   I take my injury with thanks given, sir,
   Like a wise lawyer; and as a favour,
   Will wear it for the worthy hand that gave it.

       10. *Hard bestead:* hard put to it.
       12. *Pest-house:* plague hospital.

[*Aside*] – Why this from him, that yesterday appeared
So strangely loving to me?
Oh but instinct is of a subtler strain,   40
Guilt must not walk so near his lodge again;
He came near me now.
    Exit.

TOMAZO: All league with mankind I renounce for ever,
Till I find this murderer; not so much
As common courtesy but I'll lock up:
For in the state of ignorance I live in,
A brother may salute his brother's murderer,
And wish good speed to the villain in a greeting.
    Enter VERMANDERO, ALIBIUS, *and* ISABELLA.

VERMANDERO: Noble Piracquo!

TOMAZO: Pray keep on your way, sir,
I've nothing to say to you.

VERMANDERO: Comforts bless you, sir.   50

TOMAZO: I have forsworn compliment, in troth I have, sir;
As you are merely man, I have not left
A good wish for you, nor any here.

VERMANDERO: Unless you be so far in love with grief,
You will not part from't upon any terms,
We bring that news will make a welcome for us.

TOMAZO: What news can that be?

VERMANDERO: Throw no scornful smile
Upon the zeal I bring you, 'tis worth more, sir.
Two of the chiefest men I kept about me
I hide not from the law, or your just vengeance.   60

TOMAZO: Ha!

VERMANDERO: To give your peace more ample satisfaction,
Thank these discoverers.

TOMAZO: If you bring that calm,
Name but the manner I shall ask forgiveness in
For that contemptuous smile upon you:
I'll perfect it with reverence that belongs
Unto a sacred altar.

[*Kneels.*]

VERMANDERO: Good sir, rise;
  Why, now you overdo as much o'this hand
  As you fell short o't'other. Speak, Alibius.

70 ALIBIUS: 'Twas my wife's fortune – as she is most lucky
  At a discovery – to find out lately
  Within our hospital of fools and madmen,
  Two counterfeits slipped into these disguises,
  Their names, Franciscus and Antonio.

VERMANDERO: Both mine, sir, and I ask no favour
  for 'em.

ALIBIUS: Now that which draws suspicion to their habits,
  The time of their disguisings agrees justly
  With the day of the murder.

TOMAZO: Oh blest revelation!

VERMANDERO: Nay more, nay more, sir – I'll not spare
  mine own

80 In way of justice – they both feigned a journey
  To Briamata, and so wrought out their leaves;
  My love was so abused in't.

TOMAZO: Time's too precious
  To run in waste now; you have brought a peace
  The riches of five kingdoms could not purchase.
  Be my most happy conduct, I thirst for 'em;
  Like subtle lightning will I wind about 'em,
  And melt their marrow in 'em.
    Exeunt.

[SCENE THREE]

Enter ALSEMERO *and* JASPERINO.

JASPERINO: Your confidence, I'm sure, is now of proof.
  The prospect from the garden has showed
  Enough for deep suspicion.

ALSEMERO: The black mask
  That so continually was worn upon't

Condemns the face for ugly ere't be seen –
Her despite to him, and so seeming bottomless.
JASPERINO: Touch it home then: 'tis not a shallow probe
Can search this ulcer soundly, I fear you'll find it
Full of corruption. 'Tis fit I leave you;
She meets you opportunely from that walk;   10
She took the back door at his parting with her.
   Exit JASPERINO.
ALSEMERO: Did my fate wait for this unhappy stroke
At my first sight of woman? – She's here.
   Enter BEATRICE.
BEATRICE: Alsemero!
ALSEMERO: How do you?
BEATRICE: How do I?
Alas! How do you? You look not well.
ALSEMERO: You read me well enough, I am not well.
BEATRICE: Not well, sir? Is't in my power to better you?
ALSEMERO: Yes.
BEATRICE: Nay, then y'are cured again.
ALSEMERO: Pray resolve me one question, lady.
BEATRICE: If I can.
ALSEMERO: None can so sure. Are you honest?   20
BEATRICE: Ha, ha, ha! That's a broad question, my lord.
ALSEMERO: But that's not a modest answer, my lady, –
Do you laugh? My doubts are strong upon me.
BEATRICE: 'Tis innocence that smiles, and no rough brow
Can take away the dimple in her cheek.
Say I should strain a tear to fill the vault,
Which would you give the better faith to?
ALSEMERO: 'Twere but hypocrisy of a sadder colour,
But the same stuff; neither your smiles nor tears
Shall move or flatter me from my belief: 30
You are a whore!
BEATRICE: What a horrid sound it hath!
It blasts a beauty to deformity;
Upon what face soever that breath falls,

        26. *Vault:* arch of sky.

It strikes it ugly: oh, you have ruined
What you can ne'er repair again.

ALSEMERO: I'll all demolish and seek out truth within
you,
If there be any left; let your sweet tongue
Prevent your heart's rifling; there I'll ransack
And tear out my suspicion.

BEATRICE: You may, sir,
40 'Tis an easy passage; yet, if you please,
Show me the ground whereon you lost your love;
My spotless virtue may but tread on that
Before I perish.

ALSEMERO: Unanswerable!
A ground you cannot stand on: you fall down
Beneath all grace and goodness, when you set
Your ticklish heel on't; there was a visor
O'er that cunning face, and that became you;
Now impudence in triumph rides upon't. –
How comes this tender reconcilement else
50 'Twixt you and your despite, your rancorous loathing,
De Flores? He that your eye was sore at sight of,
He's now become your arm's supporter, your
Lip's saint!

BEATRICE: Is there the cause?

ALSEMERO: Worse, – your lust's devil,
Your adultery!

BEATRICE: Would any but yourself say that,
'Twould turn him to a villain.

ALSEMERO: 'Twas witnessed
By the counsel of your bosom, Diaphanta.

BEATRICE: Is your witness dead then?

ALSEMERO: 'Tis to be feared
It was the wages of her knowledge; poor soul,
She lived not long after the discovery.

60 BEATRICE: Then hear a story of not much less horror
Than this your false suspicion is beguiled with:

46. *Ticklish*: fickle, lascivious.

To your bed's scandal, I stand up innocence,
Which even the guilt of one black other deed
Will stand for proof of: your love has made me
A cruel murd'ress.

ALSEMERO: Ha!

BEATRICE: A bloody one; –
I have kissed poison for't, stroked a serpent;
That thing of hate, worthy in my esteem
Of no better employment, and him most worthy
To be so employed, I caused to murder
That innocent Piracquo, having no
Better means than that worst, to assure
Yourself to me.

ALSEMERO: Oh, the place itself e'er since
Has crying been for vengeance, the temple
Where blood and beauty first unlawfully
Fired their devotion, and quenched the right one;
'Twas in my fears at first, 'twill have it now, –
Oh, thou art all deformed!

BEATRICE: Forget not, sir,
It for your sake was done; shall greater dangers
Make the less welcome?

ALSEMERO: Oh thou shouldst have gone
A thousand leagues about to have avoided
This dangerous bridge of blood. Here we are lost.

BEATRICE: Remember I am true unto your bed.

ALSEMERO: The bed itself's a charnel, the sheets shrouds
For murdered carcases; it must ask pause
What I must do in this, – meantime you shall
Be my prisoner only: enter my closet;
   Exit BEATRICE.
I'll be your keeper yet. Oh, in what part
Of this sad story shall I first begin?
   Enter DE FLORES.
                  Ha!
This same fellow has put me in. – De Flores!

89. *Put me in*: given me my cue.

DE FLORES: Noble Alsemero?

90 ALSEMERO: I can tell you
News, sir; my wife has her commended to you.

DE FLORES: That's news indeed, my lord; I think she would

Commend me to the gallows if she could,

She ever loved me so well, – I thank her.

ALSEMERO: What's this blood upon your band, De Flores?

DE FLORES: Blood? No, sure, 'twas washed since.

ALSEMERO: Since when, man?

DE FLORES: Since t'other day I got a knock

In a sword and dagger school; I think 'tis out.

ALSEMERO: Yes, 'tis almost out, but 'tis perceived, though.

100 I had forgot my message; this it is:

What price goes murder?

DE FLORES: How, sir?

ALSEMERO: I ask you, sir;

My wife's behindhand with you, she tells me,

For a brave bloody blow you gave for her sake

Upon Piracquo.

DE FLORES: Upon? 'Twas quite through him, sure;

Has she confessed it?

ALSEMERO: As sure as death to both of you,

And much more than that.

DE FLORES: It could not be much more;

'Twas but one thing, and that – she's a whore.

ALSEMERO: I[t] could not choose but follow; – oh cunning devils!

How should blind men know you from fair-faced saints?

110 BEATRICE *within*: He lies, the villain does belie me!

DE FLORES: Let me go to her, sir.

ALSEMERO: Nay, you shall to her.

Peace, crying crocodile, your sounds are heard!

Take your prey to you, – get you in to her, sir.

---

95. *Band:* neck-band, collar.
102. *Behindhand with:* indebted to.

Exit DE FLORES.

I'll be your pander now; rehearse again
Your scene of lust, that you may be perfect
When you shall come to act it to the black audience
Where howls and gnashings shall be music to you.
Clip your adult'ress freely, 'tis the pilot
Will guide you to the Mare Mortuum
Where you shall sink to fathoms bottomless.   120

Enter VERMANDERO, ALIBIUS, ISABELLA, TO-
MAZO, FRANCISCUS *and* ANTONIO.

VERMANDERO: Oh, Alsemero, I have a wonder for you.
ALSEMERO: No sir, 'tis I, I have a wonder for you.
VERMANDERO: I have suspicion near as proof itself
For Piracquo's murder.
ALSEMERO: Sir, I have proof
Beyond suspicion for Piracquo's murder.
VERMANDERO: Beseech you hear me, these two have been
disguised
E'er since the deed was done.
ALSEMERO: I have two other
That were more close disguised than your two could be,
E'er since the deed was done.
VERMANDERO: You'll hear me! These mine own ser-
vants –   130
ALSEMERO: Hear me! Those nearer than your servants,
That shall acquit them and prove them guiltless.
FRANCISCUS: That may be done with easy truth, sir.
TOMAZO: How is my cause bandied through your delays!
'Tis urgent in blood, and calls for haste;
Give me a brother alive or dead; –
Alive, a wife with him; if dead, for both
A recompense, for murder and adultery.
BEATRICE *within*: Oh, oh, oh!
ALSEMERO: Hark, 'tis coming to you.
DE FLORES *within*: Nay, I'll along for company.
BEATRICE *within*:   Oh, oh!   140

118. *Clip:* embrace.   119. *Mare Mortuum:* Dead Sea.

VERMANDERO: What horrid sounds are these?

ALSEMERO: Come forth, you twins of mischief!

Enter DE FLORES *bringing in* BEATRICE [*wounded*].

DE FLORES: Here we are; if you have any more
    To say to us, speak quickly, I shall not
    Give you the hearing else; I am so stout yet,
    And so, I think, that broken rib of mankind.

VERMANDERO: An host of enemies entered my citadel
    Could not amaze like this. Joanna, Beatrice-Joanna!

BEATRICE: Oh come not near me, sir, I shall defile you;
150   I am that of your blood was taken from you
    For your better health; look no more upon't,
    But cast it to the ground regardlessly, –
    Let the common sewer take it from distinction.
    Beneath the stars, upon yon meteor
    Ever hung my fate, 'mongst things corruptible;
    I ne'er could pluck it from him; my loathing
    Was prophet to the rest, but ne'er believed, –
    Mine honour fell with him, and now my life.
    Alsemero, I am a stranger to your bed,
160   Your bed was cozened on the nuptial night,
    For which your false bride died.

ALSEMERO: Diaphanta!

DE FLORES: Yes, and the while I coupled with your mate
    At barley-brake; now we are left in hell.

VERMANDERO: We are all there, it circumscribes [us] here.

DE FLORES: I loved this woman in spite of her heart;
    Her love I earned out of Piracquo's murder.

TOMAZO: Ha! My brother's murderer!

DE FLORES: Yes, and her honour's prize
    Was my reward; I thank life for nothing
    But that pleasure, it was so sweet to me
170   That I have drunk up all, left none behind
    For any man to pledge me.

VERMANDERO: Horrid villain!
    Keep life in him for further tortures.

163. *Barley-brake:* See III, iii, 171.

DE FLORES: No!
  I can prevent you; here's my penknife still.
  It is but one thread more, [*Stabs himself.*] – and now 'tis
    cut.
  Make haste, Joanna, by that token to thee:
  Canst not forget, so lately put in mind,
  I would not go to leave thee far behind.
    Dies.
BEATRICE: Forgive me, Alsemero, all forgive:
  'Tis time to die, when 'tis a shame to live.
    Dies.
VERMANDERO: Oh, my name is entered now in that
    record
  Where till this fatal hour 'twas never read.
ALSEMERO: Let it be blotted out, let your heart lose it,
  And it can never look you in the face,
  Nor tell a tale behind the back of life
  To your dishonour. Justice hath so right
  The guilty hit, that innocence is quit
  By proclamation, and may joy again.
  Sir, you are sensible of what truth hath done,
  'Tis the best comfort that your grief can find.
TOMAZO: Sir, I am satisfied, my injuries
  Lie dead before me; I can exact no more,
  Unless my soul were loose, and could o'ertake
  Those black fugitives that are fled from thence,
  To take a second vengeance; but there are wraths
  Deeper than mine, 'tis to be feared, about 'em.
ALSEMERO: What an opacous body had that moon
  That last changed on us! Here's beauty changed
  To ugly whoredom; here, servant obedience
  To a master sin, imperious murder:
  I, a supposed husband, changed embraces
  With wantonness, but that was paid before.
  Your change is come too, from an ignorant wrath
  To knowing friendship. Are there any more on's?
ANTONIO: Yes, sir; I was changed too, from a little ass as I

was, to a great fool as I am, and had like to ha' been
changed to the gallows, but that you know my innocence
always excuses me.

FRANCISCUS: I was changed from a little wit to be stark
mad,
Almost for the same purpose.

ISABELLA [*to* ALIBIUS]:   Your change is still behind,
210   But deserve best your transformation:
You are a jealous coxcomb, keep schools of folly,
And teach your scholars how to break your own head.

ALIBIUS: I see all apparent, wife, and will change now
Into a better husband, and never keep
Scholars that shall be wiser than myself.

ALSEMERO: Sir, you have yet a son's duty living,
Please you accept it; let that your sorrow
As it goes from your eye, go from your heart:
Man and his sorrow at the grave must part.

EPILOGUE

ALSEMERO: All we can do to comfort one another,
To stay a brother's sorrow for a brother,
To dry a child from the kind father's eyes,
Is to no purpose, it rather multiplies:
– Your only smiles have power to cause re-live
The dead again, or in their rooms to give
Brother a new brother, father a child:
If these appear, all griefs are reconciled.
    Exeunt omnes.

> 206. *Innocence:* (i) guiltlessness, (ii) idiocy.
> 209. *Still behind:* still to come.

ADDITIONAL NOTES

The references are to line numbers.
S.D. = Stage direction. Q = quarto reading

THE REVENGER'S TRAGEDY
Act One

SCENE ONE

39–40. *Vengeance . . . Tragedy:* Vengeance is tenant to Tragedy and offers Murder as quit-rent.

105–6. *Only excuse excepted . . . easy in belief:* their only weakness is the credulity of their sex.

119. *Unnatural:* Q 'unnaturally'.

SCENE TWO

4. *Thrown ink . . . state:* dishonoured us. The forehead, dishonoured or disgraced in cuckoldry, is one of the play's leading images.

24. *Call him . . . in law:* ignore the law and treat him as your son.

81. *Pox:* Q 'pax'.

108. *That wound:* i.e. the cuckold's horns.

130–42. I follow Harrier in printing as blank verse this and some other passages which Q prints as prose. The sense is that the man's height enabled him to peep over half-shut windows, so that men requested him to alight. When he rode, he knocked his hat against shop signs and barbers' basins.

143. *Beggar:* cf. the proverb 'Set a beggar on horseback and he'll ride a gallop'; with sexual innuendo.

184. *Rose:* Q 'rise'.

SCENE THREE

13. *That maid . . . time:* naked innocence, the Veritas of classical antiquity.

31–4. As prose in Q.

74. *Wide:* Collins's emendation. Q 'loud'.

81. *Disease o' th' mother:* the feminine weakness of loquacity (with quibble on mother = hysteria).

142. *To wind up . . . fellow:* perhaps the metaphor is that of a windlass (as G. B. Harrison suggests). 'Good fellow' was a cant phrase for a criminal.

187. *Blood:* Collins's emendation. Q 'good'.

SCENE FOUR

17. *Melius ... vivere:* better to die virtuous than to live in dishonour.

23. *Curae ... stupent:* light cares are uttered, greater ones are dumb (Seneca, *Hippolytus*, 1 607). A favourite of Jacobean dramatists.

38. *Heard:* Q 'hard'.

Act Two

SCENE ONE

17–19. As prose in Q.

85–6. As prose in Q.

132. *Madam:* 'mad-man'.

204. *To keep on their own hats:* Castiza's followers, unlike other social inferiors, need not uncover their heads in the presence of their betters, but could leave their hats on horn racks at home. (With the usual punning reference to cuckoldry.)

228–35. As prose in Q.

258. *Like a lord's ... in't:* a reference to the decay of traditional hospitality in the late sixteenth century.

SCENE TWO

2–6. As prose in Q.

48–9. As prose in Q.

64–8. As prose in Q.

78–83. Vindice's words as prose in Q. Also lines 84–7.

80–83. *Why, I would desire ... upon the rushes:* a satirical allusion to the system of granting monopolies.

97–8. *Oh lessen not ... honour her:* an allusion to Exodus XX, 12.

103. *Beneficial perjury:* the doctrine that to lie in good causes is morally justifiable.

SCENE THREE

34. *Words:* Q 'word'.

46. *Is ... socket?:* is the eye of the day (the sun) displaced?

70–72. As prose in Q.

125. *Rise:* Harrier's emendation; Q 'Which, rise'.

Act Three

SCENE ONE

15. *Blest:* Q 'Blast'.

SCENE THREE

22. *Die black:* in Nashe's *Jack Wilton*, a blasphemer's corpse turns black. (Noted by G. B. Harrison. See Nashe's *Works*, ed. McKerrow, Volume II, p. 326.)

SCENE FOUR

17–22. As prose in Q.

64. *Duns:* Duns Scotus, the subtle medieval philosopher.

66–8. As prose in Q.

79. *Without . . . sign:* bleeding had to be done under a favourable sign of the Zodiac.

SCENE FIVE

132–7. As prose in Q.

SCENE SIX

45. *Woo:* Q 'woe'.

90. *'T shall:* Q 'shalt'.

Act Four

SCENE ONE

29. *Razed:* Q 'rac'd'.

78. S.D. *The Nobles Enter:* printed as part of Lussurioso's speech in Q.

SCENE TWO

43 ff. Vindice in this role assumes a rustic accent and gestures.

67–70. Q ascribes these lines to Hippolito.

106. *Damned in colours:* a play on words – 'by a trick' or 'in a picture'.

146. *Fine:* Q 'five'.

154. *Coward:* Q 'a coward'.

156. *This* (Dodsley); 'Their' Q.

227–30. As prose in Q.

SCENE FOUR

3. *Parent:* Q 'parents'.

9. *Cut not . . . mother?:* see note on II, ii, 97–8 above.

45. *Wet . . . red:* An earlier state of Q reads: 'We will make you blush and change to red'.

96. *Forehead:* throughout the play, 'forehead' embodies the themes of honour, loyalty, and impudence, apart from obvious references to cuckoldry.

132. *Held:* Q. Most editors follow Collins' emendation, 'child'.
149. *Indeed ... honest:* the sense is: 'I did not speak truth when I pretended to assent to your proposal', with a quibble on 'honest' as (i) truth-telling, (ii) chaste.
157. *Be:* Collins's emendation; Q 'Buy'.

Act Five

SCENE ONE

61. *Sa, sa, sa:* expression used in fencing. (French 'Ça'.)
173. *Have at:* Harrier's emendation; Q 'have'.
180–83. As prose in Q.

SCENE THREE

15. *A blazing star:* a sign of ill omen to rulers. Cf. *Julius Caesar* II, ii, 'the heavens themselves blaze forth the death of princes'.
23. *Wear:* Q 'were'.
28. *Most near:* Symond's emendation; Q 'most it'.
57. Q assigns this line to Spurio. I accept Harrier's conjecture that the compositor misread 'Super' for 'Spur'.
110. *To:* Q 'two'.
119. *Murd'rers:* Q 'Murders'.
127. *He was a witch:* i.e. he could prophesy.

THE WHITE DEVIL

To the Reader

3. *Nos ... nihil:* 'we know these things are nothing' (Martial).
5. *Open:* referring to the unroofed courtyards of public theatres.
13–14. *Nec ... molestas:* 'you [my book] shall not fear the snouts of the malicious, nor provide wrapping for mackerel' (Martial).
16–17. *Non ... dixi:* 'you cannot say more against my trifles than I myself have said' (Martial).
23. *O dura ... ilia:* 'O strong stomachs of harvesters' (a line from Horace, where it refers to the peasants' fondness for garlic).
27. *Haec ... relinques:* 'what you leave will feed the pigs today' (Horace).
50. *Non ... mori:* 'these monuments know not how to die' (Martial).

The title: 'White Devil' was a common phrase, signifying evil attractively disguised, or simply hypocrisy. (Cf. *The Revenger's Tragedy* II, v, 146.)

Act One

SCENE ONE

24. *Phoenix:* the rarest of birds, since each unique creature rose up from the ashes of its predecessor.

26. *Meteor:* the sun was supposed to draw forth impurities in the form of vaporous exhalations (one of the many seventeenth-century meanings of 'meteor').

SCENE TWO

28-9. *Gilder . . . liver:* in gilding, mercury was used and then eliminated as an injurious vapour. The liver was the supposed seat of the passions.

31-3. The sense is that Camillo would be as ready to stake his non-existent virility as any Irish gambler.

35. *All his back . . . breeches:* a weak back was an alleged sign of impotence.

53. *Travailing:* the usual quibble on 'work' and 'journey'.

58. *Lose your count:* an obscene pun.

60-61. *Flaw:* with a quibble on 'squall' continuing the metaphor of two ships which 'lay together' (begun in 'travailing' and 'voyage'). The obscene pun on 'count' is continued in 'made up'.

70. *Your Aristotle:* your philosophical learning.

71. *Ephemerides:* astronomical almanacs.

78. *Horn-shavings:* horns were supposed to grow on cuckolds' foreheads.

89. *Where my nightcap wrings me:* Camillo refers to his cuckold's horns, Flamineo to Camillo's ass's ears.

97. *These politic enclosures . . . mutton:* a reference to the enclosure of common land for sheep-grazing.

119. *Ida:* a range of mountains near Troy, connected with Paris's youth as a shepherd. *Corinth:* a town renowned for its marble and its prostitutes. The two place-references in this line have an ironic undertone.

138. *Calves' brains . . . sage:* quibble on 'sage' as (i) the herb, (ii) wise.

145. *Covered:* with a sexual innuendo. Also at line 152.

155. *Philosopher's stone:* sought for by alchemists and reputed to turn base metals into gold.

182–4. *Your silkworm . . . the better:* there was some interest in silkworms at this time. King James kept them and tried unsuccessfully to encourage his subjects to do so.

226–33. There is sexual innuendo in the use of 'jewel'.

238 etc. Q italicizes 'yew' to point the pun ('you').

241. *Chequered with cross-sticks:* meaning uncertain. Perhaps supports for the coffin laid across an open grave (Harrison), or criss-crossed osiers protecting a grave (Lucas).

236–52. Vittoria's dream does not allow of a very precise interpretation. The general sense seems to be this: Camillo and Isabella accuse her of attempting to uproot the well-grown yew (Brachiano's well-established marriage) and plant instead a withered blackthorn (i.e. the ruin of Brachiano's good name and Isabella's 'widowhood'). 'The sacred yew' is Brachiano himself.

280. *Thessaly:* in ancient Greece; famous for witches and poisonous herbs.

295. *Times:* quibble on 'particular period' and 'state of affairs'.

298. *Blood:* quibble on 'bloodshed' and 'sensual appetite or passion'.

328–30. *For want of means . . . seven years:* poor undergraduates often maintained themselves by acting as servants for tutors.

330. *Conspiring with a beard:* meaning uncertain. Probably, merely the lapse of time (as opposed to the gaining of knowledge).

Act Two

SCENE ONE

S.D. *Attendants:* Q reads 'Little Jacques the Moor', but as Brown points out, he is a 'ghost' character with nothing to do or say, like 'Christophero' and 'Guid-antonio' of II, ii. The dramatist either intended to write in lines for such characters but did not, or deleted what he had written.

3. *Dove-house:* ironic, as doves were proverbially loving.

5. *Polecats:* ferret-like, foul-smelling animals. A common term of abuse.

15. *The precious unicorn's born:* unicorns' horns were regarded as very precious and as a charm against poison. Isabella describes an alleged test to determine the genuine article.

ADDITIONAL NOTES

28. *That:* Lucas's emendation.

39–40. *Flower . . . crowns:* a double quibble. Flower = jewel (thus appropriate to crowns). Crowns = garlands of flowers.

81. *Forehead . . . And:* Q 'forehead defiance, and'.

98. *Here comes a champion:* Giovanni enters wearing armour. (See line 7 above.)

114. *One of Homer's frogs:* a reference to *The Battle of Frogs and Mice*, a burlesque epic attributed to Homer and translated by W. Fowldes in 1603.

166. *I am to learn . . . Italian means:* Italians were proverbially jealous.

188–9. *Scorn . . . Polack:* according to a contemporary account the Poles were careless of taking life, and shaved all their hair, except for a long forelock.

268. *Manet . . . repostum:* 'it abides deep buried in my heart' (Virgil, *Aeneid* I, 26).

296. *To Candy:* Candy was a name for Crete, whose inhabitants were supposed to live on serpents and poisonous foods (with a possible quibble on candied = preserved, mummified).

298–300. *One that should . . . execution:* he escaped whipping for lechery by getting himself imprisoned for debt; but another rogue, pretending to be the creditor, collected the whole of the supposed debt.

305–6. *More ventages . . . lamprey:* in the seventeenth century, the cornet was a simple oboe-type wind instrument, like a penny whistle in appearance. The lamprey has seven openings ('ventages') on each side to convey water to the gills.

313. *Bloodshot:* Q 'bloodshed' (an obsolete adjectival form).

315. *Abhominable:* the spelling suggests the false etymology, *ab homine* (cf. *Love's Labour's Lost* V, i, 26–7).

332. *Inopem . . . fecit:* 'abundance has left me destitute' (Ovid). The application here seems to be: in the richness of his wife's beauty, Camillo is poor (because of her unfaithfulness).

334. *Plenty . . . horns:* the sense is: being cuckolded, Camillo has no sexual satisfaction.

338. *Keep . . . doors:* Camillo quibbles on 'given out' as 'published' and 'sent forth'.

358. *Fireworks:* Phoebus's fire and sexual ardour.

393–5. *There's naught . . . deathless shame:* only real ignominy will cure Brachiano's infatuation.

ADDITIONAL NOTES

8. *Nigromancer:* the spelling suggests the link with 'black art' (Latin *niger* = black. Cf. IV, i, 33).

19. *Fast and loose:* a cheating game involving a length of string which appeared to be knotted ('fast') but was really 'loose'.

A Dumb Show. Originally a means of presenting the dramatic action allegorically, the dumb show, apart from its intrinsic fascination, effectively 'telescopes' time and concentrates the action.

Act Three

SCENE ONE

15. *Tickler:* Brown suggests a quibble: (i) chastiser, (ii) exciter.

53. *On:* Lucas; Q 'or'.

55-6. *Alas, the poorest . . . strikes:* the sense is that the displeasure of great men, however apparently trivial, is in fact disastrous.

69. *Tilter:* Flamineo is probably exploiting the bawdy interpretations of this word in his replies.

SCENE TWO

10. *Domine . . . corruptissimam:* 'O Lord, turn your eyes on this plague, the most corrupted of women'. In his pompous language and affected knowledge, this lawyer is so different from the one in the previous scene that they may be different characters. Or, as Brown suggests, there may have been an error from copy ('Lawyer' instead of 'Courtier').

72. *Thou art . . . scarlet:* scarlet is the colour of legal robes as well as cardinals' vestments.

87. *Worse than . . . paid:* several contemporary writers commented on the high taxes on practically everything in the Low Countries.

100. *Guilty . . . coin:* possible quibble on 'gilt'!

117. *I'th'rushes:* rushes were used for strewing floors.

138. *Like Perseus:* in Jonson's *Masque of Queens* (1609) Perseus represents 'heroic and masculine virtue'.

169. *Sword:* figuratively 'instrument of justice'.

182. *Nemo . . . lacessit:* 'no one injures me with impunity'.

202. *Casta . . . rogavit:* 'she is chaste whom no man has solicited' (Ovid).

204. *Dog-days:* excessively hot period when the Dog-star

emerged from the light of the sun (usually the forty days from
11 August). They were generally supposed to be the most
unwholesome and lust-provoking time of the year.

218–19. *If the devil . . . picture:* a direct reference to the play's title
(cf. also 2 Corinthians XI, 14).

231. *Long:* Lucas; Q 'loving'.

SCENE THREE

7. *Pedlars in Poland:* seventeenth-century Poland was apparently
full of Irish and Scots pedlars. The Lithuanian for 'pedlar' is
'szatas' – Scot (Sampson).

9. *Piles:* an obvious pun.

23. *Yon:* Q 'you'.

30. *Those weights . . . death with:* up till 1772, those who refused
to plead, on charges other than treason, were tortured with
heavy weights; if the victim died without confessing guilt, his
goods could not be confiscated.

40. *First blood shed:* Cain's murder of Abel (Genesis IV, 3–8).

52. *Wolner:* a famous Elizabethan glutton who could eat practically anything. (See Moffet's *Health's Improvement,* 1655.)

82. *Genteel:* Dodsley; Q 'gentile'.

Act Four

SCENE ONE

2. *Loose . . . hair:* virgin brides wore their hair thus.

33. *Black book:* originally, black-bound official volumes; later,
lists of rogues (with a quibble on 'black' art).

51. *Taking up commodities:* a common swindle of the time, when
goods were lent at an inflated value and payment in cash de-
manded at their valuation.

   Politic bankrupts: another swindle, whereby those who
borrowed heavily declared themselves bankrupt and hid until
their creditors struck a bargain.

52–5. *For fellows . . . children:* force their wives' lovers to buy
goods at inflated prices.

57–8. *Usurers . . . scriveners:* apparently scriveners received a
'cut' from usurers for recommending clients.

71. *Tribute of wolves . . . England:* King Edgar (great-grandson of
Alfred) ordered the Welsh to pay 300 wolves as annual
tribute to rid the land of them.

138. *Flectere . . . movebo:* 'if I cannot prevail on the powers above,

I will move hell' (*Aeneid* VII, 312). The river Acheron signified hell.

SCENE TWO

45–6. *Where's this changeable stuff ... water:* Flamineo puns on 'water' and 'changeable' = 'shot' as in 'watered silk'.

53–4. *I tell you ... kept whole:* in Russia defaulting debtors were said to be cudgelled on the shins.

59. *I do look ... sallet:* expect to be poisoned.

80. *I'll give ... bells:* bells were tied to a hawk's legs to frighten prey.

81. *Hawk:* quibble on 'sharper, swindler'.

86. *Devil in crystal:* an allusion to the play's title, as well as to the current belief that evil spirits could be enclosed or revealed in crystals.

108–9. *Like those ... foxes 'bout them:* foxes were handled as a cure for those suffering from paralysis. Ben Jonson tried it.

118–20. *I had a limb ... on crutches:* cf. Christ's words in Mark IX, 45.

165–6. *Be not like ... blowing:* a widespread but mistaken notion about ferrets.

220–33. *The crocodile:* a common anecdote of bogus natural history.

SCENE THREE

9–14. *Knight of Rhodes,* etc.: for details of these orders, see W. Segar's *Book of Honour and Arms* (1590) and *Honour, Military and Civil* (1602).

36. *Conclavist:* Q 'A Car'[dinal] (Brown's conjecture). A Conclavist was a servant attending on Cardinals in conclave.

39. *Admiration:* the correct term was 'adoration'.

44–7. *Denuntio nobis ...:* 'I announce to you tidings of great joy. The Most Reverend Cardinal Lorenzo de Monticelso has been elected to the Apostolic See and has chosen the title of Paul.' ALL: 'Long live the Holy Father Paul IV!'

60–61. *Concedimus vobis ...:* 'We grant you the Apostolic blessing and remission of sins.'

140. *Your ... intelligence:* it was usual for statesmen to hire residents abroad to provide foreign news.

ADDITIONAL NOTES

Act Five

SCENE ONE

70. *The pommel . . . saddle:* in 1598, Edward Squire was hanged, following an unsuccessful bid to murder Queen Elizabeth I by putting poison on the pommel of her saddle.

74. *Hazard:* openings in inner wall of tennis-court; to strike a ball into a hazard = to win a stroke. (Here with a quibble on 'jeopardy'.)

112. *Patent to beg:* beggars without a J.P.'s licence could be whipped as vagabonds.

140. *Miserable:* (i) compassionate, (ii) miserly. The pun is tripled two lines later (Brown).

163. *Cools:* Flamineo takes 'cools' (which Zanche intended as 'subsides') to mean 'allays'.

168. *Satin:* pun on 'Satan'.

171–2. *A little painting . . . loathe me:* another's finery makes you desert me.

180. *Tumbling: double entendre.*

189. *Clapped . . . heels:* put in irons or stocks.

190. *Strike . . . court:* violence in the court was severely punished.

192. *Bedstaff:* a slat supporting bedding or staff used for beating up the bed in making it. Here (i) a man who would 'warm' the maid's bed, (ii) a stick for Cornelia to beat them with.

195–6. *Do you think . . . good fruit:* 'A spaniel, a woman, and a walnut-tree, The more they're beaten, the better still they be'. A proverb (quoted by Lucas).

209–11. *Like the two slaughtered sons . . . two ways:* the enmity between the two brothers, Eteocles and Polynices, was so great that the flames from their common funeral pyre drew apart.

212. *Geese:* prostitutes, readily found during the course of a royal progress (Brown). (Lucas suggests gestes – stopping places on a progress.)

220–21. *Spring at Michaelmas:* St Martin's summer (29 September).

SCENE TWO

79. *You . . . lodging:* see IV, ii, 50.

SCENE THREE

19. *Screech-owls:* owls portended death.

54. *Within . . . verge:* within twelve miles of the court.

86. *You have conveyed . . . territories:* a serious offence.

94. *Quails:* quails were a delicacy. There is a quibble on 'loose women'.

134. *Attende . . .:* 'Listen, Lord Brachiano.'

139–50. *Domine Brachiane . . .:* 'Lord Brachiano, you were used to be protected in battle by your shield; now you shall oppose this shield against your infernal enemy.'

'Once you prevailed in battle with your spear; now this holy spear you shall wield against the enemy of souls.'

'Listen, Lord Brachiano, if you now approve what has been done between us, turn your head to the right.'

'Rest assured, Lord Brachiano, consider how many good deeds you have done; and remember finally that should there be any peril my soul is pledged for yours.'

'If you now also approve what has been done between us, turn your head to the left.'

When the dying could not speak, priests would ask them for signs of faith.

161–2. *That would have broke . . . poisoned:* a contemporary rumour alleged that the Earl of Leicester had done this to his wife.

182. *Pest-house:* a pest-house was erected in London in 1594 for plague victims.

188. *Why we should wish . . . city:* an allusion to a scheme for a river from Ware to Islington, begun in 1609, completed in 1613.

203–4. *You see the feat . . . ice:* the adroitness of the Machiavellian points the fact that honesty at court is always perilous. (Or, possibly, that honesty as the court understands it is a precarious achievement.)

238. *Irish mantle:* blanket usually worn as sole covering by Irish peasants till the seventeenth century.

266. *That sun-burnt proverb:* see Jeremiah XIII, 23.

273–4. *Like the partridge . . . laurel:* according to Pliny, partridges purged themselves with laurel. (With a quibble on laurel as symbol of fame.)

SCENE FOUR

26. *Anacharsis:* an error for Anaxarchus, who was pounded to death by order of Nicocreon for speaking disrespectfully of the latter before Alexander.

ADDITIONAL NOTES

42. *Castle Angelo:* the Castel Sant'Angelo at Rome; the real-life Vittoria was imprisoned there for a time.

47-8. *Flaming firebrand:* perhaps Flamineo puns on his own name (Lucas).

66 ff. Cf. Ophelia (*Hamlet* IV, v).

70. *'Twill keep ... lightning:* another of Pliny's stories.

83 ff. Cornelia's lines are a compendium of contemporary superstition.

103-104. *But keep ... again:* wolves were believed to dig up the corpses of murdered men.

111. *Now the wares ... shop:* a proverb.

123. S.D. *Lily flowers:* lilies were emblems of vice.

143. *Beyond melancholy:* more than mere hallucination.

SCENE SIX

S.D. *A book:* a common theatrical 'prop' to indicate melancholy.

15. *Patent to beg by:* see note to V, i, 112.

43. *Fool that:* Wheeler's emendation; Q 'Fool'.

67. *Like mandrakes ... shrieking:* mandrakes were alleged to grow under gallows and to shriek when uprooted.

97-8. *Two of these ... your own:* two pistols are aimed at Flamineo, the other two are aimed at themselves by the survivors. (There were two pairs.)

109-15. *O Lucian ...:* Lucian's comic purgatory is in the *Menippos*.

114-15. *Pepin ... apples:* there is a quibble on 'pippin'.

130. *Styx:* one of the rivers of the nether world.

146. *Holy-bread:* normally, leavened bread provided for Eucharist. Here 'sodden sheep's liver' (Cotgrave's *Dictionary*, 1611).

148-9. *Drive a stake ... body:* traditional method of restraining ghosts of suicides.

152. *Doubled ... reaches:* been equal to all your scheming.

163. *Artillery yard:* weekly military exercises for citizens were revived in 1610 in the Artillery gardens, Bishopsgate.

167. *Hypermnestra:* one of the fifty daughters of Danaus compelled to marry the fifty sons of their uncle, Aegyptus. Danaus, warned by an oracle of impending death at the hands of his nephews, ordered his daughters to murder their husbands on the nuptial night; all obeyed except Hypermnestra, who spared her husband Lynceus.

172. *Matachin:* masked sword-dance. Basically, a masque consisted of the entry of masked and costumed dancers who invited the assembled company to dance with them. (See the closing scene of *The Revenger's Tragedy*.)

186. *Pillar:* probably one of the two permanent pillars supporting the 'heavens' above the Elizabethan stage.

232. '*Tis good . . . sickness:* yet another story from Pliny.

245. *Woeman:* the spelling brings out a popular etymology – 'man's woe'.

269. *Lions . . . Tower:* there was a small zoo in the Tower of London.

Epilogue. *Haec . . . placui:* 'these things will be our reward, if I have pleased'.

9. *Master Perkins:* Richard Perkins, a famous 'straight' actor of the day, who probably played the part of Flamineo.

THE CHANGELING

Dramatis Personae

ALIBIUS = 'in another place'. This character is offstage much of the time.

Act One

SCENE ONE

8. *The place blest:* Eden. Through marriage, paradise is regained. (Ironic, in view of what ensues.)

17. *Buy . . . witches:* it was a current belief that witches sold winds to men. (Cf. *Macbeth* I, iii).

78–83. *Yesterday . . . band royal:* a bill approved by both houses of Parliament ('eyes' and 'judgement') needs the sovereign's signature to become law.

84. *There's one above me:* her father above her, and God above the sovereign.

114. *Or:* most editors emend to 'of', but Q's reading seems to make good sense.

176–8. *He was wont . . . truth:* since Vermandero's 'best love' is Beatrice, he speaks truth if he means that she bids Alsemero welcome.

180. *Iulan down:* (three syllables). In Virgil's *Aeneid*(I, 267) the young hero Iulus Ascanius may have derived his first name from the Greek word 'ioulos', the first growth of a beard.

185. *Saint Jacques:* St James the Greater, patron Saint of Spain.

190. *The late league:* the Treaty of the Hague, 9 April 1609, provided for a twelve-year truce between Spain and the Netherlands.

SCENE TWO

24–5. *The old trees . . . plants:* the suggestion presumably is that Alibius's cuckolds horns would 'raise' him above his wife; the point would probably be clearer on the stage, where the actor playing Lollio would accompany his words with the appropriate gestures.

27–31. *I would wear my ring . . .:* for the real point of these lines, see the story of Hans Carvel in Rabelais' *Gargantua and Pantagruel* (Book III, Chapter 28).

52–3. *The daily visitants . . . patients:* Bethlehem Hospital, a lunatic asylum ('Bedlam'), was a regular place of entertainment for Londoners.

100. *Tony:* the later seventeenth-century use of the term 'Tony' to mean a fool may derive from the character of Antonio in this play.

105–6. *He can laugh . . . beast:* Aristotle mentions laughter as a distinctively human attribute.

117. *First sight:* a parody-echo of the main plot, cf. I, i, 66.

129–30. *The wit of constable:* the constable, as Shakespeare's Dogberry and Dull attest, was a figure of fun on the Elizabethan stage, especially noted for his stupidity.

144. *State:* i.e. madhouse-keeper. This may also be a sly attempt by Lollio to 'touch' Pedro again, in which case the latter's exit-line acquires a certain piquancy.

159. *How many . . . band?:* Tailors were reputedly dishonest, hence the point of Antonio's answer at line 155.

184. *Push-pin:* references to this game in other plays of the period invariably contain a sexual innuendo.

194–200. *Cousin, stand there . . .:* Antonio, Alibius, and Lollio stand in a row, in that order.

204. *We three:* alluding to the inscription on a picture of two fools, implying that the spectator is the third. (Cf. *Twelfth Night* II, iii, 16–17.)

213. *Her permasant:* the Welsh were proverbially addicted to cheese.

Act Two

SCENE ONE

20–21. *His blessing . . . his name:* his blessing is conditional on my maintaining his good name (by marrying well).

58. *Standing toad-pool:* a reference to the repulsive appearance of De Flores' skin.

60–76. *My lord your father . . .:* De Flores makes a vain effort to spin out his meeting by using formal language.

80. *Garden-bull:* allusion to Paris Garden, Southwark, home of bear- and bull-baiting.

108. *No bringing on you:* no convincing you. (Harrier suggests: 'no making a convincing actor in a love-scene out of you'.)

138. *In his passions:* this phrase is omitted as difficult to explain by most editors. 'His' refers to 'passions rightfully belonging to him' (the lover), since he is their source; thus the meaning would appear to be: 'Though the lover cannot actually beget children, he shares in them, because the passions aroused in the woman during the act of procreation are due to her lover, not her husband.'

138–40. *How dangerous . . . sufferings:* if she is restrained, her shameful and dangerous behaviour would be painful to contemplate.

153. *How much . . . lovingly:* how grateful we should be to heaven for parting without a quarrel.

SCENE TWO

4–5. *I dare not . . . deal with:* too much praise of Alsemero may make Beatrice suspicious of Diaphanta.

17. *Hateful one:* i.e. Alonzo, who would wish this kiss to be poisoned.

33. *You're:* Q 'your'.

42. *Marred . . . scorn:* spoiled the use of (De Flores) by scorning him.

82. *Faugh:* Q 'Vauh'.

98–9. *I would but wish . . . mounts to:* the verbal ambiguity discussed in the Introduction is already evident in these lines.

149. *Dog-face:* i.e. De Flores.

Act Three

SCENE ONE

10. S.D. *Exeunt . . .:* a common stage-direction, denoting change of scene.

SCENE TWO

14. *Dwell:* Bawcutt suggests a sinister pun: (i) pause, linger, (ii) inhabit (as De Flores plans to put his corpse there).

SCENE THREE

38. *Shooting a bolt:* a quibbling allusion to the proverb: 'A fool's bolt is soon shot.'

43–5. *Anacreon . . . the cup:* seventeenth-century writers were familiar with the story that Anacreon choked to death on a grape-stone while drinking wine.

45. *Spider . . . cup:* spiders were supposed to be poisonous (cf. *A Winter's Tale* II, i, 39–45).

58. *Danger:* a possible quibble: (i) peril, (ii) dominion (i.e. the limits you may not cross).

59. *Diomed:* not the Greek hero but a Thracian king who fed his horses with human flesh.

61. *Bucephalus:* the celebrated horse of Alexander the Great, which only he could ride.

66. *Esculapius:* Greek god of healing and medicine.

68. *Tiresias:* Theban soothsayer who changed into a woman and back again. According to Ovid (*Metamorphoses*, Book III), Juno blinded him for revealing that the sexual act gave more pleasure to women than men.

84. *Luna . . . big-bellied:* the moon is at the full.

85. *Hecate:* evil aspect of moon-goddess.

87. *Dog . . . bush:* the dog and bush belong to the man in the moon.

89. *Lycanthropi:* persons suffering from a derangement in which they imagine themselves to be wolves.

111. *Cousin:* Bawcutt suggests that Isabella's indignant repudiation of the relationship may be due to the fact that in Elizabethan drama it is common for an unfaithful woman to gain access to her lover by pretending to be his cousin.

119. *Left-handed Orlando:* after the crazed hero of Ariosto's Italian epic, *Orlando Furioso*. The epithet 'left-handed' may

mean 'awkwardly' (since Lollio will 'play' a madman among real madmen).

140. *He:* Q 'she'.

171. *Catch . . . in hell:* An allusion to the popular game of 'barley-brake', in which a couple occupying a central space ('hell') tried to catch others as they ran through it from both ends. Those caught replaced the original pair, and the game went on till every couple had been in 'hell'.

178. *Speak . . . clothes:* speaking seriously does not suit you.

179–81. *Shall I alone . . . apple:* one of Hercules' twelve labours was to obtain the golden apples guarded by the Hesperides, daughters of the giant Atlas.

185. *Lipsius:* famous scholar and jurist. Here mainly for quibble on 'lip'.

 Ars Amandi: art of love; an allusion to Ovid.

188. *Do you smile:* old form of imperative; cf. line 191 and IV, i, 79.

196. *Cuckoo, cuckoo!:* announcing Alibius's imminent cuckoldry.

241. *Lacedemonian:* probably someone who speaks tersely. There may, as Sampson suggests, be a tortuous quibble on 'laced-mutton' a cant term for a prostitute.

254. *Bounden:* Isabella presumably emphasizes this word to express her resentment of the restraints imposed on her by Alibius.

SCENE FOUR

14. *And if . . . offends me:* Bawcutt suggests a New Testament echo (Matthew XVIII, 9; Mark IX, 47). Beatrice is, of course, thinking of Alonzo.

70. *Slept at ease:* Dilke's addition. Not in Q.

113. *It not:* Q 'it' (Dilke's addition).

Act Four

SCENE ONE

S.D. *Dumb Show:* dumb shows as essential parts of the plot are fairly common in Jacobean drama.

5. *that's:* Q 'both' (Bawcutt's emendation).

25. *Secrets in Nature:* the title of a treatise by the French scholar Antonius Mizaldus. But virginity tests are mentioned in another work by him. They were fairly common and probably derive from Pliny.

ADDITIONAL NOTES

128–9. *I'm for ... small fools:* i.e. 'I'm for a big fool, a justice'
(Spencer).

SCENE TWO

8. *Briamata:* in the original source of the plot, a country house.
54. *Sins and vices:* most editors, following Dyce's conjecture,
assume an error of transcription and emend to 'chins and
noses'. As it stands, Q makes good sense, though the emendation would strengthen the gloss of 'well-fleshed' for 'round-
packed'.
60. *'Twill:* Dilke; Q 'I will'.
84–5. *Dispense ... this:* let me be less zealous than usual in your
service, so that I may keep this news to myself.
88. *though:* Q 'thou'.

SCENE THREE

8–11. *To the bright Andromeda ... the post:* this is gibberish, but
there may be some shadowy sense struggling to get out.
Perseus rescued Andromeda from the dragon; thus Franciscus
will presumably rescue Isabella from the dragon Alibius.
The Knight of the Sun is the hero of a popular romance often
contemptuously alluded to by Jacobean dramatists. Scorpio
was the sign governing the sexual parts (hence 'middle
region' has a bawdy innuendo).
37. *Thirds:* the other two thirds being shared by Alibius and
Isabella's lover.
45. *Why:* Q 'We'.
46. *The fair understanding:* (take my words in) the best sense.
81–2. *'Tis your nose ... elephant:* the joke about the nose is
obscure. Three possibilities have been suggested: (i) a varia-
tion on the cuckold's horns (Bawcutt); (ii) Alibius is being led
by the nose (Spencer); (iii) a compliment to Alibius's virility
(Harrier: this last seems rather far-fetched).
88. *Ride:* often used in Jacobean drama and poetry with sexual
innuendo, as here.
105. *He:* Q 'she'.
111–12. *Let us tread ... clue:* an allusion to the thread given to
Theseus by Ariadne so that he could find his way out of the
labyrinth.
120. *straits:* Dyce; Q 'streets'.
125. *Endymion:* a beautiful youth with whom the moon fell in love.

166 ff. *Sweet lady . . .*: some editors emend Franciscus's letter to correspond exactly with line 12 ff. above, but some allowance can surely be made for Lollio's imperfect reading.

177. *What? Do you read, sirrah?*: most editors emend to 'What do you read, sirrah?' but Franciscus could simply be expressing surprise that Lollio can read. The latter's reply would still make sense.

217–18. *One incurable fool . . . begged:* to 'beg a fool' was to acquire control of his estate by seeking appointment as his guardian.

Act Five

SCENE ONE

25. *Phosphorus:* Q 'Bosphorus' – compositor or transcriber's misreading.

93. *A-fire:* Harrier; Q 'of fire'.

SCENE TWO

15. *Give me game:* probably 'make fighting him a pleasure' (Harrier).

SCENE THREE

3. *Black mask:* usually glossed as 'De Flores' ugliness' but this hardly makes sense – De Flores' ugliness cannot 'condemn' his face, and if 'the face' refers to Beatrice, it makes even less sense. Probably 'black mask' refers to Beatrice's hypocrisy.

138. *Adultery:* Tomazo possibly regards Beatrice as Alonzo's wife, so that her marriage to Alsemero is a kind of adultery.

146. *Rib of mankind:* an allusion to Genesis II, 21–3.

154–5. *Beneath the stars . . . corruptible:* in Elizabethan cosmology, the stars were pure, eternal and immutable, while the meteors were transient and impure.

175. *That token:* the wound De Flores has just given himself.

193. *Black fugitives:* the damned souls of Beatrice and De Flores.

212. *Teach . . . head:* another reference to the eternal joke of the cuckold's horns.